Public Archaeology for the
Twenty-First Century

CARL & SALLY GABLE FUND
for Southern Colonial American History

Public Archaeology for the Twenty-First Century

EDITED BY JAMES F. BROOKS WITH JEREMY M. MOSS

THE UNIVERSITY OF GEORGIA PRESS
ATHENS

Published in part with generous support from the Carl and Sally Gable
Fund for Southern Colonial American History

© 2025 by the University of Georgia Press
Athens, Georgia 30602
www.ugapress.org
All rights reserved
Designed by Melissa Buchanan
Set in Minion Pro

Most University of Georgia Press titles are
available from popular e-book vendors.

Printed digitally

Library of Congress Cataloging-in-Publication Data
Names: Brooks, James, 1955– editor. | Moss, Jeremy M., editor.
Title: Public archaeology for the twenty-first century /
edited by James F. Brooks with Jeremy M. Moss.
Description: Athens : The University of Georgia Press, [2025] |
Collection of essays by Tori Mason and 26 others. | Includes
bibliographical references and index.
Identifiers: LCCN 2024059221 | ISBN 9780820373515 (hardback) |
ISBN 9780820373522 (paperback) | ISBN 9780820373539 (epub) |
ISBN 9780820373546 (pdf)
Subjects: LCSH: Community archaeology—United States. | Cultural
property—Protection—United States.
Classification: LCC CC77.C66 P829 2025 |
DDC 363.6/90973—dc23/eng/20250220
LC record available at https://lccn.loc.gov/2024059221

Contents

List of Illustrations   vii

Introduction | James F. Brooks   1

CHAPTER 1. Mound Key: Past and Future in Public Archaeology | An Interview with Dr. Victor D. Thompson   10

CHAPTER 2. Community Archaeology on a Heritage at Risk Site: Pockoy Island Shell Rings on Botany Bay Plantation Heritage Preserve, Charleston County, South Carolina | Meg Gaillard   25

CHAPTER 3. Silent Stories: The Archaeology of Unrecorded Lives at Colonial Michilimackinac | Kathlyn Guttman   37

CHAPTER 4. How One Archaeological Project Unearthed Both the Living and the Dead | Tori Mason and Kate Sproul   49

CHAPTER 5. The Impact of Publicly Funded Archaeology: A Case Study in Prince George's County, Maryland | Stephanie T. Sperling and Kristin M. Montaperto   61

CHAPTER 6. Public Archaeology over the Long Haul: Education at the Fairfield Plantation Site, Virginia | David Brown, Jessica Taylor, Ashley McCuistion, and Thane Harpole   76

CHAPTER 7. Putting the Washington Home Back on the Land and the Obstacles to Re-creating a Colonial Virginia Landscape | Philip Levy and David Muraca   91

CHAPTER 8. The Future of Collection Stewardship and Exhibition in Small-Town Museums: A Case Study from Southeastern Utah | Tara Beresh   109

vi CONTENTS

CHAPTER 9. From Santa Barbara to Gila River: Multisited Histories and Collaborative Archaeology | Koji Lau-Ozawa   119

CHAPTER 10. Teaching Middle School Students about Migration Using Archaeological Inquiry: An Evaluation of the Investigating Migration Curriculum Project | Elizabeth C. Reetz, Katherine Hodge, Jeanne M. Moe, and Erika Malo   137

CHAPTER 11. Water Heritage of the Mountain West: Integrating Public Archaeology with Multidisciplinary Approaches to Water Research | Molly Boeka Cannon and Anna S. Cohen   151

CHAPTER 12. An Asset of the People: A History of Urgency, Management, and Interpretation at the Tonto Upper Cliff Dwelling | Matthew C. Guebard, Sharlot Hart, Jade Robison, and Iraida Rodriguez   166

Epilogue. Why Words, Shared Authority, and Seeking Community Benefit Matter in Public and Collaborative Archaeology | Jeremy M. Moss   182

Contributors   195

Index   199

Illustrations

Figures

0.1. Mission San José de Tumacácori   2

0.2. Map of sites covered in the November 2022 special issue of the *Public Historian* and in this volume   9

1.1. Map of southern Florida   11

1.2. Lidar digital elevation model of Mound Key   13

2.1. Excavation trench at the Pockoy Island Shell Ring Complex (aerial)   26

2.2. Excavation trench at the Pockoy Island Shell Ring Complex   26

2.3. Erosion of Pockoy Island   27

2.4. Volunteers receive identification badges at the Pockoy Island Shell Ring Complex   29

2.5. Volunteers at the Pockoy Island Shell Ring Complex   31

2.6. Third-grade volunteers at the Pockoy Island Shell Ring Complex   31

2.7. Tour group at the Pockoy Island Shell Ring Complex   33

3.1. Michel Chartier de Lotbinière's Map of Fort Michilimackinac   43

3.2. Archaeology master map of Fort Michilimackinac   43

4.1. Staff working on the Grassmere cemetery site   51

4.2. Map of Nashville Zoo cemetery interments   51

4.3. Carroll Van West at the dedication of the Nashville Zoo cemetery   54

4.4. Frank Morton   57

4.5. Frank and Albert Morton   57

4.6. Maude Morton Webb   58

viii ILLUSTRATIONS

4.7. Morton descendants in front of the Morton Family Exhibit 59

4.8. Morton descendants cutting the ribbon for the Morton Family Exhibit 59

5.1. Frederick Douglass reenactor at the Northampton Slave Quarters and Archaeological Park 64

5.2. Artifact processing at Mount Calvert Historical and Archaeological Park 65

5.3. Kayakers touring the Jug Bay Complex archaeological sites 66

5.4. Archaeology office staff teaching virtual summer camp 70

5.5. Echoes of the Enslaved 2021 72

6.1. Fairfield archaeology site 77

6.2. Excavation units near the Fairfield manor house 78

6.3. Fairfield manor house 79

6.4. Anna Rhodes teaching a young volunteer 86

7.1. Rebuild of the Washington home 92

7.2. Memorial House at the George Washington Birthplace National Monument 95

7.3. Reconstructed work yard behind the Peyton Randolph House 100

7.4. River-facing front of the Ferry Farm house 101

7.5. Concrete foundation of the Ferry Farm house 103

7.6. Hall of the rebuilt Washington home 104

8.1. Interpretive text for a pre-Hispanic artifact 114

8.2. Ancient load basket discovered in Moab 117

9.1. Map of the Nihonmachi neighborhood of Santa Barbara 125

9.2. Asakura Hotel 126

9.3. Map of the Butte subcamp of the Gila River Incarceration Camp 129

9.4. Block 57 of the Butte subcamp 129

9.5. Feature 63 at Gila River, a small concrete pond 130

9.6. Hotelware dishes manufactured by the Homer Laughlin Company 130

9.7. Proportions of holloware and flatware at Gila River 131

ILLUSTRATIONS ix

10.1. Student questionnaire   141

10.2. Average rubric score per question   142

11.1. Impact of outreach initiatives for the Water Heritage
Anthropological Project   153

11.2. Excerpts from the Water AnthroPak   156

11.3. Molly Boeka Cannon and Native student mentee discuss
water heritage   158

12.1. Map of the Upper Cliff Dwelling   167

12.2. Room 5/40(2) at the Upper Cliff Dwelling   169

12.3. East wall of Room 5/40(2) before reconstruction   172

12.4. Stabilizing brace for the east wall of Room 5/40(2)   177

12.5. Iraida Rodriguez conducting ground-penetrating radar
survey   177

12.6. East wall of Room 5/40(2) following deconstruction   177

13.1. Map of Pecos National Historical Park   185

13.2. Pecos Pueblo drawing   186

13.3. Tribal members from Jemez Pueblo in front of Spanish
colonial remains   186

13.4. Trail wayside exhibit, Pecos National Historical Park   187

13.5. Remains of Pecos Pueblo   187

13.6. Model of Pecos Pueblo   188

13.7. Re-created Pueblo Room, Pecos National Historical Park   188

Tables

3.1. Documentary Personal Use/Adornment Objects Found
in Trade Rosters   45

3.2. Personal Adornment Artifacts Found in Table 3.1,
British Contexts   46

3.3. Personal Adornment Artifacts Not Found in Table 3.1, British
Contexts   46

10.1. Difference between Scores for the Treatment Group and Control
Group   143

Public Archaeology for the
Twenty-First Century

Introduction

JAMES F. BROOKS

Jeremy M. Moss and I first met more than a decade ago at Tumacácori National Historical Park, some fifty miles south of Tucson on I-19, in the Rio Santa Cruz Valley. As chair of the Western National Parks Association Board of Directors, I and my fellow trustees had bused down from our headquarters in Oro Valley to tour one of the seventy-six national park units that our organization supported. Jeremy was our National Park Service guide for the day.

One goal of our National Park Service historic sites is to offer an experience to visitors that enlivens the past while speaking to the present. Tumacácori presents such an opportunity. Its story reaches from the precolonial era of the Indigenous O'odham, Yaqui, and Apache peoples of the Santa Cruz Valley who developed a rich array of cultural adaptations to life in the Sonoran Desert through Spanish colonization and the establishment of the mission in 1691 and of Presidio San Ignacio de Tubac in 1751. Tumacácori's time as a portion of Mexican Sonora, short-lived yet enduring in regional culture, preceded the U.S. conquest of 1847–48. The twentieth century saw explosive post–World War II growth made possible by the hydroindustrial West. And in our present, the transnational inequalities and insecurities that make the international border—just twenty miles south—an unstable zone of promise and peril.

Jeremy led our group of thirty through the mission church, convento, and faint remnants of "dormitories" wherein lived the Akimel O'odhams (Akimel O'othams), then called Pima, who were Native converts. His specialization in historic preservation, especially that of adobe architecture, allowed us to see both the construction and the constructed history of the site: every alteration in the interests of preservation introduces inventions that are themselves agents of transformation. His anthropological sensibilities afforded us a longer view of the Akimel O'odhams who occupied the region for millennia, as descendants of the widespread Hohokam civilization of the Salt, Gila,

FIGURE 0.1.
Artist's rendering of Mission San José de Tumacácori, ca. 1800. Art by James R. Mann, National Park Service.

and Santa Cruz River valleys, as well as of their enduring presence today.

My day job at the time was president of the School for Advanced Research in Santa Fe, an anthropological institute founded in 1907 to support the study and interpretation of both ancient and contemporary peoples at first regionally and for decades now globally. Many of my duties were similar to what Jeremy offered us that day: rendering specialized professional insights so that they can receive appreciation and support from an interested public. Especially effective were our professionally led archaeological fieldtrips and publications, ranging in focus from nearby sites like Bandelier National Monument and Pecos National Historical Park to more off-the-grid excursions to the Hembrillo Battlefield in the San Andreas Mountains or to the archaeological footprints of ancient communities that gathered on the Hopi Mesas. These shared experiences later brought Jeremy onto the board of editors of the *Public Historian*, the editorship of which I took up in 2015, and his role as guest editor for the journal's November 2022 special issue on public archaeology. Our call for proposals for that issue resulted in more than thirty fine submissions that deserved to see print, more than the journal alone could accommodate. I therefore assumed the role of editing this companion volume. The pieces featured in the *Public Historian* were curated with that subscribing readership in mind (public historians, historic preservationists, archivists, museum and tribal archaeologists, archivists), while the essays gathered herein were not only targeted at those constituencies but also intended to have a broader reach that encompassed avocational archaeologists (so essential to funding and staffing fieldwork projects today), historic and archaeological site educators, teachers, and university instructors.

The thirteen chapters in this volume range across several millennia as well as the North American continent, from Florida's Gulf Coast to the canyonlands of Utah and to California. The authors wrestle with key tensions in the field of public archaeology (and history): What do we mean by *public*? Should we strive to be "public facing" (educating site visitors) or "public participating" (sharing interpretive authority with descendant peoples)? Does *public* imply simplifications in scholarly rigor, or does it require even more rigorous attention to our methods of analysis and interpretation to render our stories sensible for those beyond our professional circles? Public tax dollars often underwrite the archaeology we undertake, with grants from the National Science Foundation or the National Endowment for the Humanities, organizations that increasingly require a public-facing aspect. Must public archaeology have an applied component that puts fieldwork and findings "to work in the world," to borrow a catchphrase from our colleagues at the National Council for Public History? As diverse as these chapters are, however, they share some common elements: as Jeremy wrote in the *Public Historian*, in the "broadest sense the articles are concerned with the relationship between archaeological practice, the presentation of archaeology and history, and the public. A common thread is the involvement, consideration, or concern with the public and collaboration with descendant communities or groups that have direct connections to the heritage resources studied."[1] Readers will find all of these threads in this book.

The volume opens with my conversation with Victor D. Thompson, my colleague at the University of Georgia and leading scholar of southeastern coastal archaeology, about his recent high-profile discoveries at Mound Key, south of Florida. Once the capital, according to sixteenth-century Spanish accounts, of the Calusa Kingdom, this anthropogenic (human-made) island of some 126 (current) acres was inhabited as early as the 400s CE and may have hosted a population as large as four thousand people at time of first contact with Europeans in 1656. Sustained by a remarkable system of canals and "water courts" for cultivating the saltwater fish that sustained the Calusa people, Mound Key was a world city of its time, with political influence that reached well around the coast of southern Florida. But it is also among the most fragile, imperiled by its all-too-easy accessibility, rising seas, and intensifying tropical storms.

Meg Gaillard extends the coastal archaeology focus to the eastern seaboard in chapter 2 with her treatment of the ancient shell rings of Pockoy Island, South Carolina. The state Department of Natural Resources has a three-decade engagement with volunteers who assist with excavation, artifact processing, and disaster-recovery work. Growth in the construction sector has lent a particular urgency to these efforts, as has environmental degradation associated with rising sea levels. At Pockoy Island, the vulnerability of the recently discovered shell ring complex has provoked a surge of community engagement. The island, experiencing startling erosion rates, harbors these enigmatic constructions that are sure to be lost within a decade. The shell ring complex (38CH2533) is a late archaic archaeological site some forty-three hundred years old and is now the focus of intense excavation and recovery efforts. Beyond the immediate heritage-at-risk actions, "these cultural sites also present opportunities for local community engagement, education, and heritage tourism to take place simultaneously." The chapter offers fine-grained details regarding volunteer management, site protection, and archaeological analysis that may "save" (at least in archives and collections) an extraordinary resource.

In chapter 3, Kathlyn Guttman takes us west into the colonial Great Lakes region with her chapter on how public archaeology can recover details of the "unrecorded lives" that once made colonial Michilimackinac a key outpost in the fur trade. Turning archaeological tools to the work of recovery allows interpreters to break the silences associated with subaltern peoples. Material culture, food butchering marks, and use-wear patterns all reveal actors in the fur trade too long overlooked: cooks, "Panis" (a catchword for any number of war captives) slaves, and mysteries such as rosary beads in the home of a Jewish trader. Public archaeology can help visitors feel the textures and even quirkiness of colonial life.

Chapter 4 turns to the Nashville Zoo, where Tori Mason and Kate Sproul take us into the intricacies of working with descendant communities. The 1989 construction of a new wildlife park within the bounds of the zoo at the site of Grassmere, a five-generation family farm, led to the discovery of an unmarked cemetery containing the graves of twenty enslaved African Americans. These graves dated back to 1810, and some of the laborers built the first house at Grassmere, owned by Michael and Elizabeth Dunn.

The zoo had acquired the property in 1973, and when the effort to develop the area uncovered evidence of the cemetery, Mason and Sproul took the opportunity to extend the zoo's mission to encompass public archaeology, using the material and textual remains to tell a story of unfree labor in early Nashville. The zoo decided to exhume the graves and relocate the remains to the Grassmere family cemetery, where the laborers' enslavers were interred, cautiously publicizing those plans.

As the burials were removed and prepared for reinternment, several were found to be well preserved enough to undertake limited DNA testing as well as bioarcheological analysis by researchers at Middle Tennessee State University. These analyses, combined with census and other research, produced information about places of birth as well as the names of some of the enslaved laborers, whose descendants could then be traced. Descendants of those who lived at Grassmere, including Grace Hilliard and Joyce Hilliard, are participating in the reconstruction of the story of a Black family in post–Civil War Nashville and have helped to create a family interpretive exhibit.

Stephanie T. Sperling and Kristin M. Montaperto show us another landscape of slavery in chapter 5. Prince George's County, Maryland, has twenty-eight thousand acres of public land that holds scores of archaeological sites and hundreds of aboveground historic resources. Public excavations, volunteerism, and partnerships with local schools have long been central to the Prince George's County Archaeology Office, and recent years have seen a specific focus on projects that engage major themes like settler colonization and slavery. The office has also assumed stewardship of the historically Black Cherry Hill Cemetery, and officials are negotiating the challenge of its interpretation as the demographics of the surrounding neighborhood change. The office also has responsibility for the Northampton Plantation Slave Quarters and Archaeological Park. The long-running Mount Calvert public excavation project has garnered extensive public participation, which has produced enormous benefits (massive numbers of artifacts) but also has increased the demands on staff (sorting and analysis of these objects). Other innovations by the Archaeology Office include Public Lab Days and kayak tours to the Jug Bay Complex, where the last of the Mattaponi and Patuxent Indigenous peoples resided during the eighteenth century. The office also participated in an overnight campout sponsored by Outdoor Afro that explored the legacies of slavery in archaeological contexts and the present.

For chapter 6, David Brown, Jessica Taylor, Ashley McCuistion, and Thane Harpole cross the Potomac into Virginia to the Fairfield Plantation site, which has served for more than twenty years as a location of public programming to emphasize Indigenous culture, colonization, slavery, and African American life after emancipation. These topics are integral to eastern Virginia's history, and many of them lie at the root of contemporary inequities in the region. The modest-to-the-eye site harbors material evidence of human occupation from the archaic era through the emergence of the Tidewater plantation complex in the seventeenth century and into the post-1865 era of Black tenant farming.

Partnering with local schools and the College of William and Mary, the Fairfield Foundation supports internships for fieldwork and laboratory experience as well as opportunities for local schoolteachers to share the experience. This chapter demonstrates the power of the stories that archaeology can recover, highlighting the voices of the interns themselves, an important qualitative aspect to consider in assessment efforts.

The chapter on Fairfield Plantation pairs nicely with chapter 7, Philip Levy and David Muraca's treatment of how public archaeology has allowed the recovery and re-representation of Ferry Farm, George Washington's boyhood home, which has vanished from the landscape yet is preserved beneath surface soils. The construction of a massive Walmart triggered intervention and the site's reinvention as a full-scale rebuild, controversial in public interpretation. Addressing in historical perspective archaeological and historic preservation's long-term resistance to historical reconstructions (often derided as forgeries), the authors argue that technical and interpretive advances in recent decades mean that now is the time for "preservationists of all stripes to embrace rebuilding." Levy and Muraca draw a line from the disastrous 1931 presentation of Washington's birthplace to the development of professional, historically sensitive architectural reconstructions at historic St. Mary's City and Colonial Williamsburg, demonstrating that the Ferry Farm project has created a space that can "show—among other things—how intertwined the lives of the enslaved and their enslavers were by placing visitors within the spaces of colonial-era daily life." Rebuilding may provide an additional level of appreciation for the public and can therefore increase support for historic preservation.

In chapter 8, Tara Beresh brings us to the canyonlands of Utah to share the struggles experienced by many small-town museums, like the Moab Museum, where she serves as curatorial and collections manager. Unlike the historic homes of the plantation class or the dwellings of the enslaved whose lives sustained that wealth, the archaeology of the Desert Southwest is subtle to the eye and fragile to the touch. Beresh offers a frank assessment of the preservation and presentation challenges for a museum with a very modest budget in a high-visitation region. Trained in preservation archaeology, committed to consultation with descendant communities, and dedicated to sharing with the visiting public, Beresh walks us through a case of tribal consultation that brought important new insights and appropriate representation for a single object, a "cone-shaped basket constructed of yucca fiber and split willow" found by hikers more than thirty years ago. The museum's consultations with Ute and Hopi cultural specialists helped Beresh to determine an appropriate storage and presentation regime that situates the basket as a living object of cultural patrimony rather than as a relic of the past.

Farther west, Koji Lau-Ozawa's chapter 9 explores two sites that shaped his family's history: the Santa Barbara, California, Nihonmachi (Japantown) neighborhood, which two centuries earlier housed the Presidio Santa Barbara, now entirely reconstructed; and the Gila River Relocation Center in Arizona. A descendant of Japanese Americans forcibly dispossessed from Santa Barbara in 1941 and a Stanford-trained archaeologist, he conducted excavations and oral histories with descendants and the Akimel O'odham and Pipaash (Pee Posh) peoples who had the prison imposed on them. In an archaeology of the present, he is developing interpretive narratives with both the Santa Barbara Trust for Historic Preservation, which owns the Nihonmachi site, and the Gila River nations.

Chapter 10 offers a fascinating discussion of that most feared of all terms in public-facing scholarship, assessment. Elizabeth C. Reetz (director of strategic initiatives in Iowa's Office of the State Archaeologist), Katherine Hodge, Jeanne Moe, and Erika Malo walk us through their evaluations of Investigating Migration, a prizewinning curriculum for grades 6–9 developed by the Bureau of Land Management's Project Archaeology that investigates the topic through archaeological inquiry, primary sources, and geographical information systems. Tested in four schools in Montana and Wyoming, this project focused on the Overland Trail and introduced the students to an impressive array of skills but nevertheless fell short of its goals for students' grasp of interpretive takeaways, offering a reminder that bells and whistles may delight the ear, but the tune carries the message over time.

In chapter 11, Molly Boeka Cannon and Anna S. Cohen illustrate how bringing a "deep time" perspective can facilitate students' engagement with a defining aspect of the American West, aridity. The Water Heritage Anthropological Project emphasizes a long view on creative responses to unpredictable precipitation across the Mountain West. Working across and beyond traditional public engagement in classrooms and lecture halls to engage present and future water users in understanding the long traditions of creative water management strategies evident in the archaeological, historical, and ethnographic record, the project employs digital technology to provide novel resources. During the 2020–21 COVID-19 pandemic, the project found creative methods for reaching traditional audiences: for example, the Utah State University Museum of Anthropology inspired the authors to create a water-focused version in the museum's AnthroPaks series of take-home kits for students.

Chapter 12 features Matthew C. Guebard, Sharlot Hart, Jade Robison, and Iraida Rodriguez's exploration of the preservation challenges that lie hidden in plain sight at the thirteenth-century community now called Tonto National Monument in Arizona. Where standard practice for masonry and adobe architectural preservation previously involved reconstruction of dwellings and public

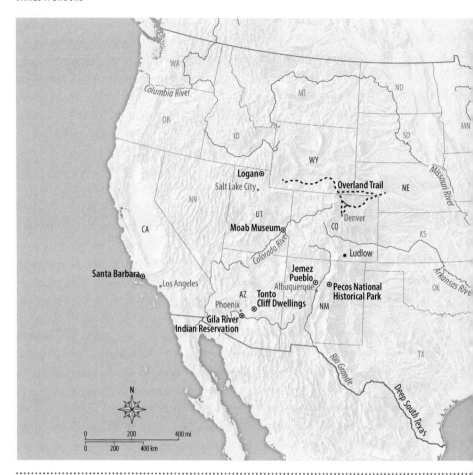

architecture in ways that often misrepresented the original fabric and techniques, National Park Service protocols now focus on "teaching the transformation" in these ancient communities. Working collaboratively with members of descendant peoples, new interpretive approaches allow a natural process of transformation to be perceived as an essential element of architecture whether in the thirteenth century or the twenty-first.

Finally, Jeremy M. Moss's epilogue brings to life the interpretive power of his consultations with Puebloan peoples who descend from a now-depopulated but not disavowed Towa community, Pecos National Historical Park, located on a pass that connects the Rio Grande Valley to the Great Plains. He illustrates the process and outcomes that the park has enjoyed while refining the public-facing aspects of the museum exhibits and interpretive trails at the former center of the Plains/Pueblo exchange economy—the most impressive of the dozens of Indigenous towns Spanish intruders encountered in the sixteenth century. The exhibits feature Towa terms and cultural interpretation from the

FIGURE 0.2.
Map of North America showing sites covered in the November 2022 special issue of the *Public Historian* (indicated by squares) and in this volume (bullets).

descendants of the twenty-one occupants who relocated with Jemez Pueblo relatives in 1838, enabling visitors to understand that the ancient town is not a ruin but rather a still-vital cultural lodestone.

As Moss suggested in the introduction to the special issue of the *Public Historian*, the field of public archaeology grows stronger as it increases its breadth, both in spatial terms and in the professional and cultural locations that participants bring to their work. This map showing the locations of all the sites covered in that special issue and this volume not only situates readers but also suggests just how much we have yet to research and share about public archaeology in the twenty-first century.

Notes

1. Jeremy M. Moss, "Public Archaeology in the Twenty-First Century: Strength in Breadth," *Public Historian* 44, no. 4 (2022): 9.

Mound Key

Past and Future in Public Archaeology

AN INTERVIEW WITH DR. VICTOR D. THOMPSON

JAMES F. BROOKS: I'm with Victor Thompson at the Laboratory of Archaeology at the University of Georgia, May 27, 2022. We're talking today about Mound Key, perhaps one of the most stunning North American archaeological stories of the last decade. Thompson is a specialist in southeastern coastal archaeology and has recently published startling new findings about Mound Key—a human-made island off the Gulf Coast of Florida. A top-ranked researcher, Thompson is also dedicated to educating the public about archaeology and our duty to preserve the resources that hold stories about our past.

Thank you for taking the time to chat, Victor. I want to begin by asking how you came to be involved with Mound Key. It seems that it's kind of been one of the better-kept secrets of southeastern archaeology, but in the last few years you and your colleagues have learned some extraordinary things there.

VICTOR D. THOMPSON: Yes. I've always been fascinated with the Calusa, which is the name of the sixteenth-century Indigenous group that occupied Mound Key and the greater Caloosahatchee area, centered in the modern Fort Myers and the Charlotte Harbor area of southwestern Florida. Really ever since I was an undergrad, I've been drawn to the history of the Calusas. I saw a documentary on them when I was an undergrad. That film centered on Dr. Bill Marquardt of the Florida Museum of Natural History [and his work] at the Calusa settlement of Pineland. In recent years, I've had the opportunity to go there and even work with Bill at this other fantastic Calusa settlement. And those early exposures really piqued my interest, but then I went off and did research in different areas. It wasn't until almost fifteen years ago [that] I started in earnest working and doing archaeology in Florida. Then, around 2010 or 2011, I connected with Bill Marquardt because he had invited me to do some work at Pineland. And I became more and more interested in Mound Key because there was so little work done there. And I started thinking about a bigger project to look at

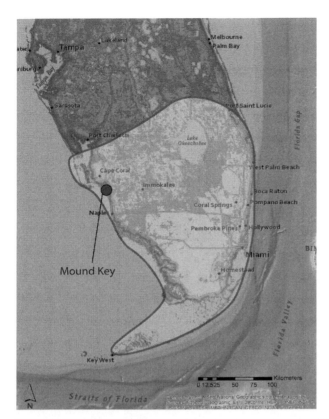

FIGURE 1.1.
Map of southern Florida showing the location of the capital, Mound Key, and the extent of the influence of the Calusa polity.

Mound Key and invited Bill to collaborate with me, and from there we assembled a big research team of specialists and people who had done work in the region. That was really the genesis of the project.

JB: This involves you focusing primarily on the historic era? The publications I've read attend to the post-Spanish context, which is a fascinating story indeed. Yet while doing my homework for today's conversation, I understand there's human occupation on Mound Key as early as the fourth century AD.

VT: Mound Key is one of the most amazing sites I've had the opportunity to work. I mean, I think the reason why I'm so drawn to this cultural site is that there are so many different stories to tell that are situated in one geographic location. For example, there's a climate story in terms of how the Calusa were able to manage a large population sustainability in the faces of global-climate and sea-level shifts. There's a story of colonialism, resistance, and resilience on the part of Calusa regarding how they interacted with the Spaniards when they arrived on the Calusas' shores. There's another story about how a large dense population was able to thrive in the surrounding estuaries in terms of creating food surpluses and managing the surpluses in complex ways—that is, managing all the sorts of social problems that come with having large numbers of people living together. There are all these different stories to tell, and they are very much anthropological stories that can be told from the perspective of Mound Key and the Calusa. In many ways, how the Calusa met and solved these challenges parallels that of other societies, but also the Calusa as a group had a unique history. That's really this thing that draws me into Mound Key.

JB: Mound Key seems unusual as well in that conventional archaeological theory tells us that you're not supposed to have complex, socially stratified chiefdoms without agriculture. And yet here we have an extraordinarily complex chiefdom.

VT: Yes, the work about Mound Key and the Calusa in general that had been written before tends to emphasize that they are fisher-gatherer-hunters or hunter-gatherer-fishers or however you want to phrase it. But even this nomenclature falls short. It is probably more appropriate to think about them as a fishing society, much like you would see at medieval fishing villages, with aquaculture and even perhaps coastal port cities. There are many more dimensions to this than simply just talking about them regarding their economic base.

JB: How would the peoples of Mound Key compare to the complex hierarchical societies of the Pacific Northwest, also largely oriented toward maritime resources?

VT: When one looks at the literature of so-called complex hunter-gatherers, the northwest coast of course is right up there, and these groups of people are fascinating and have unique histories in terms of the various ways they organized and solved problems. The difference between the northwest coast and the Calusa is the geographic extent of the influence of some of their respective polities. On the one hand, the polities along the northwest coast were more limited in their geographic scope and organized a bit differently than what we see in southwest Florida. The Calusa polity, on the other hand, at least by the sixteenth century, had a reach that extended hundreds of kilometers, from just south of Tampa Bay all the way to the Florida Keys. So there is some difference between the two groups in terms of the geographic footprint. And there's probably some similarities in terms of social structure and things like that with the northwest coast but also differences as well. A comparison between the two would be a very interesting story.

JB: One difference might be that the Calusa are a single language family across all South Florida, as compared to the isolated language pockets of the polities in the Pacific Northwest?

VT: Probably there is some linguistic diversity [among the Calusas], but not as much as the Northwest, which is one of the most linguistically diverse areas. And so probably in a comparative sense, much less in South Florida. That's not to say there isn't linguistic diversity in South Florida. It's just we don't know as much about it. Certainly, we know that some of the Calusas were multilingual in the 1600s: there is documentation of them being able to speak the languages of northern Florida groups, for example.

JB: Given the long occupation at Mound Key, which had human presence as far back as the fourth century, what would be the temporal range of this kind of explosive complexity?

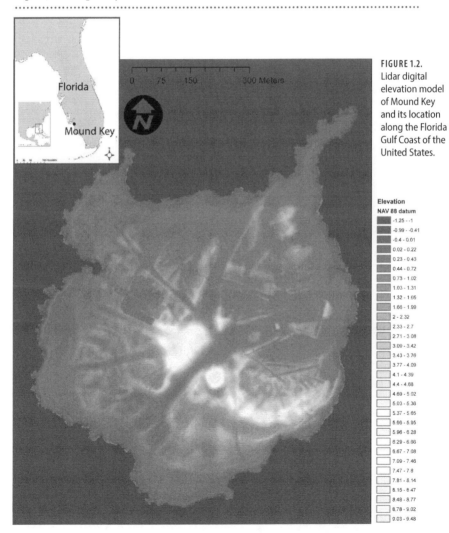

FIGURE 1.2. Lidar digital elevation model of Mound Key and its location along the Florida Gulf Coast of the United States.

VT: It's hard to say in terms of the radiocarbon dates, right, so there are fifth-century dates. Because those are early dates and are kind of hard to situate in their archaeological context, it is hard to say what they mean. And so, one way you could look at it is that it represents occupation. There is an alternative hypothesis that they went and mined out some fifth-century midden from some other site to begin the construction of the anthropogenic island that is Mound Key. I'm not saying they did this, but one must consider alternate ideas to test. Okay. How do you test that? I mean, I can't: at this point at least, I've not thought of a way to test it. What is clear is that by around AD 900 or around 1000, you get massive construction efforts to sculpt the Mound Key landscape.

JB: That's when things really start—

VT: The two largest mounds [at Mound Key] certainly reach their approximate apex by around AD 1000.

JB: So the main mounds have been maintained for centuries before we see Spanish colonizers describe them? And even then, those Spanish descriptions are mind-blowing.

VT: At least for those two mounds. And, in fact, the big house that Pedro Menéndez de Avilés walks into in 1566 is already reconstructed. There's a previous version of that structure built around AD 1000. That structure goes through at least three major building phases—one at around 1000, another around the 1300s, and then the final one sometime just before the arrival of the Spaniards.

JB: Are these remodels in a continuous occupation, or are there punctuated occupations with gaps between?

VT: Well, this is where I differ with some of my colleagues—where they see possible gaps in the record. I do not think there is a gap in occupation at Mound Key. I do think there are punctuated building episodes, like boom-and-bust cycles of construction of different features on the landscape, but I don't think Mound Key was ever abandoned—certainly not in its last five hundred years of occupation.

JB: So by way of comparison, the Mound Key polity endures at least twice as long as the United States so far (250 years). Given that long occupancy, one of the questions that the puzzles me is that of freshwater supply? Is there fresh water on Mound Key? It's hard to build a civilization without drinking water.

VT: It is. And if you go there today, you'd be hard-pressed to find fresh water. However, one of the things about the Florida aquifer is that we've had significant drawdown due to a wide variety of factors—most notably due to industry and development. And so that freshwater lens that would normally be present and bubbling up through springs is no longer the case in many areas. You still get those some of those springs on the Gulf Coast, but it was probably nothing compared to what it was in the past—even in the recent past.

JB: Yet no fresh water on the key now?

VT: Not that I'm aware of. But surely there were springs, including in the bay itself. Spaniards would often sail into an embayment and find the springs to replenish water stores. They could see the clear water bubbling out of the springs.

JB: True. You see in the documents that Menéndez puts in for water right on the coast—that's a historical example of how groundwater resources and ocean levels affected by climate change can have unexpected consequences.

VT: Yeah, there were springs all along these coastlines. In fact, a portion of the Gulf Coast of Florida just north of the Calusa region is referred to as the springs coast.

JB: Yet when the first human set foot on Mound Key, may we truly call it an anthropogenic island? There must have been someplace to put the first human foot.

VT: The short answer is I don't know.

JB: There's no bedrock bed, coral bed anything?

VT: In our earlier survey work at Mound Key, we cored most of the island, and there was nothing that looked like a natural terrestrial surface. So once you push through the shell deposits associated with Calusa habitation and construction, what you typically find are very loose sands and small shellfish like what you typically see if you did a core out in the bay today. So it's open-bay conditions once you get below those shell deposits. Could there have been a small sandspit? Could there have been a small little mangrove island? That's possible. Perhaps we just didn't recover it in the cores. I mean, after all, Mound Key is about 51 hectares, which is around 126 acres. So it is expansive and our cores are small, and it is possible that we missed something.

The point is that the vast majority of Mound Key is human constructed. It's hard to put a percentage on it, but 95 percent would be a good guess.

JB: And I'm sure people speculate on why all the work to build an island when you have a resource-abundant coast? What would inspire someone? What is the travel time in the ancient world by canoe between the coast and the island?

VT: Oh, let's see. From Lovers Key it is about 1.5 miles and about 4 miles from some mainland areas. So maybe an hour by canoe; it just depends.

JB: And today one can kayak?

VT: You can easily kayak there in an hour or so from a few different places. The Calusa were probably much better at it and faster than modern kayakers—at least when you put me in a kayak, I'm slow. The other thing is the Calusa had what are more rightly called proper ships—that is, these vessels were much larger than your modern canoe or kayak, [according to] some of the historic descriptions we have and some of the archaeologically recovered dugouts. We have descriptions of them being double-hulled, with matting in between. So it's a vessel, and scores of people rode in them.

JB: I guess [Mound Key] wouldn't have provided any particular defensive advantage. Do you have any speculations on why would people invest that much human energy in building this extraordinary site when there appear to be plenty of other locations? Or are those places filled up on the coast by that point?

VT: I suppose there would be a certain defensive advantage to Mound Key. However, there are large villages on Estero Island that are contemporaneous with Mound Key, and they're big too. So why is Mound Key in the middle of the bay, and those weren't? Did they not need defending in the same way? [Having Mound Key in the bay] makes a certain statement when you come up to it by boat. I mean, if you can imagine a Spaniard seeing Mound Key as it was in the sixteenth century, it would have been impressive. When you go there today, it's all overgrown, and it is hard to get a sense of the scale because of the jungle of plants that covers the key. Not so in the past. It would be a gleaming white city in the middle of the bay with thousands of people coming and going. And, Mound 1 [at thirty feet tall] would have been the tallest structure around for miles.

JB: As a political statement, it would have been quite stunning.

VT: I like to think of it as the New York of the Calusa area, to put it in terms people can sort of relate to.

JB: Do we know that it maintained any kind of tributary relationships with the coast? Was it the powerhouse, the paramount chiefdom, as we hear applied to interior polities like Coosa or Cofitachequi? We know that there's conflict between Mound Key and Tocobaga on the north shore of Tampa Bay. Are those the two principal powers in the area?

VT: Yes, Spanish documents note that Mound Key received tribute from all over a good portion of peninsular Florida—all the way to the Florida Keys at its tip. So I'd say it is easily over two hundred kilometers to go along the coast from Fort Myers to the upper keys today. Even driving across the state from Fort Myers to, let's say, Key Largo takes about three hours or more. In terms of tribute in the sixteenth century, the documents note some of the different kinds of tributes that come to Mound Key, such as Spanish shipwreck survivors, breads that were made from a root plant that comes from the interior Okeechobee basin, woven mats, and so forth. So you got food (also called staple items) and you have wealth goods coming in, which is kind of interesting, because you don't normally think of that for polities in this region. Much of the writing about tribute focuses on wealth items. In Mesoamerica, it is more common to talk about staple and wealth finance together.

JB: So by war canoe, you're probably talking [an] overnight [journey]. And Tocobaga maintains its own tributary clients in the north?

VT: Yeah, they were another powerful Native American polity in the Tampa Bay region. And, yes, they had their own tribute system.

JB: Is there any archaeology about Tocobaga?

VT: My colleague Dr. Tom Pluckhahn of the University of South Florida is leading some new work there, and UGA is collaborating. They just did some coring and a lot of geophysics and even some new excavations.

VT: Tocobaga, known as the Safety Harbor site, is a little different than Mound Key. Instead of being in the middle of a bay, Safety Harbor is situated on a point of land adjacent to Tampa Bay. And [it was] clearly a military equal of Calusa, since the king of the Calusa tries to recruit the Spanish to accompany him on a punishing raid.

JB: Your recent discovery of evidence for aquaculture at Mound Key is probably the biggest news of the last couple of years out of southeastern archaeology. Do you want to say a few words about that?

VT: There are fish impoundments—what we colloquially call water courts. The term goes back to Cushing, when he was working in the region in late 1800s. Frank Hamilton Cushing, most known for his work among the Zuni, thought that these structures could possibly be fish impoundments. He simply had no way of really testing this idea.

No one had really gone out and evaluated this empirically over the intervening years. There was a lot of speculation about them. And so that was one of our big objectives, both with grants from the National Geographic Society and the National Science Foundation—to dive deep into the science of testing of this idea. And yeah, we found this smoking gun—or smoking fish, as it were—looking at these very, very large impoundment areas. The ones at Mound Key would have been able to store massive amounts of fish. And then you could process all the stored fish for surplus by smoking them. This work helped to answer one of the big questions of Mound Key—that is, How was such a large population fed? And how were they fed particularly in the absence of refrigeration? This work was a multidisciplinary team that included soil scientists, geologists, people who were experts in paleobotany and zooarchaeology, radiocarbon dating, and the like that Bill Marquardt and I led. And these excavations revealed some fantastically preserved materials such as fish scales, net cordage, and other things you usually don't find in dry-land sites.

JB: At its maximum, what might you say about the sustaining power of this extraordinary case of aquaculture? What kind of a population might it nourish?

VT: Indeed! It is such an extraordinary example of this kind of technology in the region.

In terms of the population of Mound Key, it really depends on how you read the documents. Certainly, this site is very large, at about 51 hectares or 126 acres. I'm perfectly comfortable for a sixteenth-century population of two thousand, possibly more. It is not out of the question for the population to be four thousand. We do know that in 1697 there were at least one thousand people that lived in sixteen houses.

JB: And that was after a significant population contraction—

VT: Right! There are all sorts of reasons to think that Mound Key had a very large population.

JB: We know where the big house was, and we know where the Spanish fort was. But where would the residential areas be found?

VT: Well, that is the next big research question. Where indeed are all the Calusa houses? In other areas of Florida, you have evidence of stilt houses—in other words, houses out over water or wetland areas. In the Mound Key Lidar—that is, remote-sensing digital-elevation models—I think we have the outline of some of these possible stilt houses. That is one of the hypotheses I have for these features that you can see in the data. There are these sorts of long linear features in the lidar that are out over the wetland areas of the site. And so what I think is that there were houses out there and debris and shellfish accumulated around the edges and created the negative space low areas underneath the house that you see in the data.

JB: You see postholes?

VT: We may be able to see postholes if we do some larger-scale excavation. What I think would be the first way to evaluate it is to just look at from a sedimentological perspective of what's in the negative space versus what's around it. So that's the next big research effort that I think needs to happen.

JB: That's exciting. And that extends out beyond the visual footprint.

VT: Yeah. I do think there are houses on top of these mounds as well.

JB: Because of the work you've done there, we now understand just how extraordinary Mound Key is. Usually, when something extraordinary like this happens, there is a mass migration of avid archaeology buffs who want to see it. And what we're trying to do with this book is to help people understand the struggles that professional archaeologists encounter when you want to share what you've done. But sometimes that means putting at risk the very thing that you wish most to protect. What have been the processes for you developing an interpretive approach and plan for Mound Key?

VT: Well, Mound Key is currently in part managed by both the state and the city of Fort Myers Beach. Up until about 2019 or so, a portion of Mound Key was in private ownership, and it was recently sold to the city. For a while now, there has been an interpretive trail. It's really a single trail, [but] there's two landings—one that you could come up with via boat, and the other that you could come up by kayak.

JB: There's a dock to which boats can tie up?

VT: There is a dock, and formerly it was private, and I don't think the state and/or city allow access to the dock landing ingress currently. And that would be the easiest way to get onto the island. The trail is interesting, as it goes up Mound 1 and then down through the canal and over to Mound 2 to reach either side of the island. It is well worth going out there to walk it. I think it is about three-quarters of a mile from end to end.

VT: The trail itself has a few interpretive signs. I think one of the challenges is making the interpretations durable enough for that whole area to withstand the elements. So there's a couple of issues there. Fort Myers Beach is obviously a big tourist area—sportfishing and things like that. There are a lot of boats around the area, and people. Currently, no one is out [on Mound Key] full time like you would see at other archaeological parks that one can visit in mainland settings. That said, the state does a really good job of monitoring. In fact, I was there two or three days ago, and the state came out to check on us to make sure that we were not a group of looters.

JB: They see you out there, and somebody came out to check. That's encouraging, in terms of volunteer site stewardship, like the Archaeological Conservancy supports.

VT: We had a permit to be there and showed them the paperwork and told them who we were. They checked it and everything and allowed us to proceed with the work. So it was great to see that they were doing such a good job in making sure that the site is protected.

JB: There's no formal gate of entry on the coast? You don't have to get a ticket to go out there?

VT: Right. And so actually, they had some possible looting going on—nothing major, but even surface collecting is a problem and illegal. People think, "Oh what's the harm?" but it is a big problem, especially if everyone takes a little piece then it's thousands of artifacts out of context and there is nothing left.

And, you know, the fines are very stiff in Florida. For the state, there is a fine per artifact, no matter how small and what condition it's in.

JB: Regardless of the value of the artifact, if you take a tiny ceramic sherd, it's the equivalent of stealing any other artifact?

VT: Right, no matter how big the artifact is or even if it's an oyster shell, of which there are billons at the site.

The other issue is the vegetation on Mound Key. To some extent, the vegetation is very helpful in stabilizing the deposits from the elements. However, it also impedes the experience of visitors to the site in terms of being able to see the mounds. There have been several plans that I've seen about walkways and things like that through the mangroves—which of course are managed and protected as well. Also, you have other plants that either are rare or endangered that grow in these anthropogenic sediments—for example, I think there's a specific kind of hackberry, it's endangered, that grows on the island. So there are all these concerns with regard to the public experience, protection of the cultural resources, and protection of the biological resources at the site. All that needs to be taken into consideration in any kind of plans for public interpretation and visitation.

JB: Is there an interdisciplinary scientific team concerned with taking care of and monitoring the key itself? I assume biologists are concerned, and the whole aquaculture story right now invites a wide variety of scientific interest.

VT: Right now, Mound Key is monitored by the state, and the expertise that the state has in these areas is good. So the park rangers are trained biologists; they have training in archaeology and things like that. So I feel like they really do a good job with the resources and expertise they have in monitoring and managing the site.

JB: That's encouraging that you're seeing that broad range of professional interest.

VT: That said, there is funding and issues like that. Things could always be enhanced and better, of course.

JB: Are the guided tours led by archaeological interpreters?

VT: The Florida Public Archaeology Network, known as FPAN (https://hms.fpan.us), has done tours out there before. And Mound House, another large Calusa site that you can visit on Estero Island, has run tours. When we've been doing work out there, we always try to do public days and coordinate with FPAN. So Mound Key represents, I think, a significant kind of challenge with regard to public history and public archaeology just by the nature of where it is located in the middle of the bay.

JB: Is there any thought of using Mound Key as a model? You have a visitor center at Mound House (https://moundhouse.org/) with nine-tenths of the interpretation there. If you had unlimited funds and unlimited staff, what would you be your dream for Mound Key? How might we use that to imagine a public archaeology success?

VT: I think the logical way is to have a more of an interpretive visitor center focused on Mound Key that is accessible by car. That's one option. The other option is to enhance exhibits at Mound House, which again is on the Estero Island site. The town at Mound House was contemporaneous with Mound Key, and it also has a fantastic small museum.

It's very easy to get from Mound House to Mound Key, so there's a point of departure. Yeah. And in fact, like I said, they do the tours from there sometimes.

JB: To wrap things up, what are the things that you've done recently with your work in coastal archaeology? You've tried to alert the public to the dangers of sea-level rise. Could you talk about some of that in the big picture, as you've done a lot with the Georgia coast? Is Mound Key imperiled by this same phenomenon?

VT: From a larger perspective, there are two things that we need to think about. The first is the threats to the sites themselves. We talked about sea-level rise, but it's not just sea-level rise. It's storm frequency as well. We're heading into probably one of the worst Atlantic hurricane [seasons] according to the models. Again, this is all driven by global climate change. And it's not just the increase in the strength of the storms, but it's the recovery rates: if you have a large storm that hits, it may do a lot of damage. But if you have a smaller storm that comes right behind it in a short period of time, where things haven't had a chance to rebound, you can cause more damage. I experienced this when I lived along with Gulf Coast. So we are losing sites due to coastal erosion, to sea-level inundation, and things like that.

So the natural reaction to that is that we need to do more archaeology, and we need to monitor the endangered sites. Florida is doing a good job with this in terms of a citizen-science approach with a program they call the Heritage Monitoring Scouts in Florida, which is run by FPAN. They enlist people who are living in the area to sort of monitor these things, which is good. So there's that one dimension to it. The other dimension is what I think about when I put on my curator hat for a second, and that is all the collections that we have from sites from the coastal areas. These collections are for some the only window into that site that we'll ever have because the site has already eroded away. Thus, the artifacts and information from those sites must be properly curated and preserved in a way that they'll be accessible. In essence, like I said, they're the only snapshot we're going to have because they're gone. Thus, you have this dual dimension of where do you put resources, because even though we have a place for a museum or here at the laboratory of archaeology where we curate and do the best we can, some of the collections from these sites are from the 1970s and they're still in paper bags, and we still need to transition them to archival-quality housing. But until we do that, they're vulnerable.

The other thing that we need to consider is [making sure that] collections are not themselves stored in locations that are in storm-prone areas. There are collections that are in coastal areas that are not properly housed [and] that we need to move to safer facilities. There is the climate issue and then bigger, broader problems that we face. Thus, it not so simple as to just go out and excavate as much as we can before we lose the information. Key, too, is consultation and how different Indigenous Native American communities feel about their ancestral lands and cultural sites. This must be taken into consideration. It is a must-do.

JB: You move the site above the waterline and reproduce it, like the Tennessee Valley Authority did for Fort Loudoun.

VT: There are these big issues that don't have easy answers unless you have a lot a lot of money. And then the answer is easy at least in one dimension. If you have a lot of money, one can envision something on the scale of the Works Progress Administration from the New Deal. In the next fifty years, climate models in terms of storm frequency, in terms of sea-level rise, are not looking good, and we're going to lose a lot. So funds would help, but it still will be a lot of hard work that must be done in collaboration with descendant communities.

JB: And at the same time, those same phenomena are impacting contemporary living populations all along coastlines—groups who have their own agendas and who might resist seeing money spent to save prehistoric sites when their own residences are in peril. So from the standpoint of this book, focused on the notion of preservation archeology to make sure that this resource is here for generations forward, what would you wish readers to take away that will allow them to feel as if they're contributing?

VT: Well, I would say there's a couple of different things that people can do. First, if you live in a coastal area, again, get engaged with the public archaeology network—particularly if you live in Florida, but also if you're in Georgia, too. And I think there are other opportunities and such. So engage in citizen-science monitoring. However—and this is key—you need to learn to do it ethical way. That's one thing that you can do. The other thing you can do is to realize the importance of these cultural sites not just to the people living in the local areas but also to the descendant communities—including African American communities and Native American federally recognized tribes. These cultural sites are incredibly important and are still very much directly connected to different groups regardless of whether they live in Florida or in Oklahoma or wherever. The other thing I would say is that heritage laws are sometimes up for debate. And, also, there are resource allocations by state, local, and federal governments. People, I would say, need to pay attention to those kinds of things—they crop up in the news—and advocate for cultural heritage. I think we can all agree that history is important, no matter what your political persuasion. I think everyone can agree that this is important. The knowledge that we gain from experiencing these cultural sites is what connects us to the past.

JB: In your perfect world, how would you wish the public to be involved in protecting, preserving, and interpreting Mound Key?

VT: Like I said, the more engaged that you can become with your local heritage monitoring scouts and being an advocate for preservation are really the key things you can do. Beyond that, I would say that the biggest thing is that if you're reading this and you have children, take your children out and teach your kids that this kind of history exists. Get them on board early with the importance of cultural sites and heritage. Because if you're reading this, then I don't need to convince you that these things are important. Right? But what I do need you to do is to pass on that information and share your excitement with other people, especially young people, who aren't convinced yet.

JB: A perfect framing of our goals for this book.

Epilogue

On September 28, 2022, almost exactly four months after this interview took place, Hurricane Ian made landfall at Fort Myers Beach, passing directly over Mound Key. On September 25, with the storm approaching and sea levels rising, Thompson and others from the Florida Museum of Natural History visited the site to conduct rescue excavations at Mound House, but the storm surge completely engulfed these excavations. As of the fall of 2024, Thompson and colleagues from the Florida Museum of Natural History and Penn State University are continuing to assess the storm's impacts on Mound House, Mound Key, and Pineland. Supported by the National Science Foundation, this work is providing insight into the nature of the threats that major storms pose to such cultural heritage sites.

Community Archaeology on a Heritage at Risk Site

Pockoy Island Shell Rings on Botany Bay Plantation Heritage Preserve, Charleston County, South Carolina

MEG GAILLARD

For nearly three decades, the Cultural Heritage Trust Program of the South Carolina Department of Natural Resources (SCDNR) has provided public archaeology programs across the state, disseminating information about the state's cultural resources. Our programs include members of the public as vital members of our team, which works to preserve and protect these resources for current and future generations. Volunteers of all ages and experience levels have assisted with archaeological excavations, helped process artifacts at our lab at the Parker Annex Archaeology Center in Columbia, and helped us with disaster recovery work.[1] Educators have taken part in virtual and in-person Project Archaeology workshops. K–12 students have participated in hands-on Archaeology for Kids programs, and high school and university students have participated in the Archaeology Internship program.[2] While each of these programs provides a unique, stand-alone archaeology opportunity for the public, together they comprise a comprehensive archaeology experience. By gathering and disseminating information about the resources managed by the Cultural Heritage Trust Program, each public program also ties back to and supports the law that founded the trust nearly fifty years ago, and the law's language guides the development of trust's programming.[3]

The Pockoy Island Shell Ring Complex: Community Archaeology on a Heritage at Risk Site

Two of the most visible and sought-after community archaeology programs offered by our team are volunteer and guided tour opportunities on active archaeological excavations. For many people, the word *archaeology* brings to mind Indiana Jones–type images of adventure and discovery. The opportunity to participate in an archaeology program by assisting with or visiting an excavation can offer members of the community a very memorable experience while concurrently providing archaeologists with much-needed assistance.[4] In 1972, Charles

FIGURE 2.1.
During a May 2018 king tide event, tent coverings shade the excavation trench at the Pockoy Island Shell Ring Complex, Ring 1. Courtesy of Koelker & Associates.

FIGURE 2.2.
The excavation trench at the Pockoy Island Shell Ring Complex, Ring 1, May 2018. Courtesy of SCDNR.

R. McGimsey wrote that "public participation provides the potential for archeology's salvation. There is too much to do and too little time to do it in for the professionals to hope that they can accomplish everything themselves with their present or any foreseeable resources. There is only one place to look for the assistance that is essential to success—the public."[5] What was true fifty years ago in the face of development is even more true today with the added threat of climate-related impacts on cultural resources. In recent years, the effects of that threat have been most visible for our team at the Pockoy Island Shell Ring Com-

FIGURE 2.3. The location shown in figure 2.2 photographed in September 2020, illustrating Pockoy Island's high rate of erosion. Courtesy of SCDNR.

plex (38CH2533). This cultural site dates to forty-three hundred years ago (the Late Archaic period) and is located about an hour southwest of the historic city of Charleston on the SCDNR's Botany Bay Plantation Heritage Preserve/Wildlife Management Area (BBPHP/WMA) on Edisto Island. While the climate-related impacts on this property have been severe for many decades, the immediate threat to the recently discovered Pockoy Island Shell Ring Complex has heightened the level of interest in the property and elevated the amount of community engagement during excavation seasons at the site. This interest has benefited both ongoing research about the site and public archaeology opportunities.

Since July 2017, our team has organized hundreds of volunteers, students, and professional archaeologists in an intense excavation effort at Pockoy Island. For nearly seventy years, BBPHP/WMA has experienced one of the highest erosion rates in coastal South Carolina. Between 1851 and 2022, the shoreline of Pockoy Island has retreated about half a mile, and more retreat has been measured north and south of the island. As recently as 1972, Pockoy Island was an interior sea island surrounded by marsh, with Botany Bay Island on its seaward side.[6] Between 2016 and 2022, the site has eroded at an average rate of 12.19 meters per year, and triage-level archaeological investigations have sought to salvage portions of this site—the oldest known shell ring complex in South Carolina—before it is lost.[7]

What Are Shell Rings?

Native Americans built shell rings along the Atlantic and Gulf Coasts of the southeastern United States between three thousand and five thousand years ago. In the area known as the Georgia Bight, shell rings are circular or C-shaped and range between approximately forty and one hundred meters in diameter. The Pockoy Island Shell Ring Complex consists of two sixty- to seventy-meter rings that were constructed from shells such as oysters, whelks, arks, ribbed mussels, and periwinkles as well as pottery sherds, stones, and animal bones. The plazas encompassed by the rings were deliberately kept empty, free of shells. SCDNR protects and manages one-third of the twenty-four shell rings that have been recorded in the state.[8]

During recent decades, archaeological work on shell ring sites has provided new insights regarding seasonality and subsistence, shell and bone tool production and use, formative ceramic style and function, site formation processes, and occupational histories.[9]

Heritage at Risk in the Southeastern United States

The Pockoy Island Shell Ring Complex is among thousands of coastal archaeological sites threatened by erosion, sea-level rise, and other climate-related factors. Because of this threat, this site is considered an example of heritage at risk, a global term used to define cultural resources threatened by natural and human impacts. Heritage at risk sites like the Pockoy Island Shell Ring Complex present compelling challenges for archaeologists as well as opportunities for local community engagement, education, and heritage tourism.

A one-meter rise in sea level between now and the end of the twenty-first century will result in the loss of more than twenty thousand recorded archaeological sites in the southeastern United States.[10] Among those sites is the Pockoy Island Shell Ring Complex: current estimates indicate that it will erode away between 2043 and 2047.[11] Monitoring the impacts to and loss of cultural sites and conducting rapid archaeological investigations on some at-risk sites is critical.[12]

The Pockoy Island Shell Ring Complex was discovered in the winter of 2016 during a review of lidar imagery, and archaeological investigations of the site began in July 2017.[13] By 2021, six archaeological field seasons lasting between one and four weeks had taken place. Prior to our fourth field season in May 2019, our team spent months engaged in logistical planning so that we could expand and offer both volunteer opportunities and guided tours at the site. This effort resulted in a model for future excavations.

Planning for the Public

In April 2019, we issued a press release advertising the field season and opportunities for public involvement.[14] The press release included links for individuals to register for five-hour volunteer shifts and spaces on guided tours through Eventbrite, an online event management application. Multiple media outlets immediately picked up the press release, and information about the excavation and associated public opportunities was shared on the SCDNR social media platforms.[15]

Within twenty-four hours, all 168 volunteer slots (twelve per day for fourteen days) were filled and waiting lists were automatically created. The number of people on each day's waiting list varied from a handful on weekdays to approximately thirty on Saturdays and Sundays. Because BBPHP/WMA regularly attracts a high volume of visitors—we expected between three hundred and four hundred per day in May 2019—we planned to accommodate another four to six walk-up and waitlisted volunteers at all times. We wanted to avoid turning away anyone who wanted to help.

We also opened registration for thirty-minute guided tours beginning at 10 a.m., 1 p.m., and 2 p.m. each day. An SCDNR archae-

FIGURE 2.4. Volunteers of all ages receive identification badges at the check-in station from Alyssa Jones (SCDNR) and Helena Ferguson (South Carolina Archaeology Public Outreach Division). Courtesy of SCDNR.

ologist or one of twelve trained tour guides who regularly volunteered at BBPHP/ WMA led the tours. While we planned for thirty people in each tour group, we did not turn anyone away. Extra staff were always in place to accommodate the occasional waves of as many as ninety visitors to the site, whom we sorted into smaller tour groups.

Event Management and Public Archaeology

Advance registration through Eventbrite enabled our team to anticipate when we would have higher numbers of visitors and adjust staff assignments to ensure that excavation work could move forward as planned while providing members of the public with a meaningful experience.

Volunteers, tour guides, and staff received clip-on identification badges to help our team and visitors better identify each other. Tour participants did not receive badges but remained in their group with their guide throughout their time at the site. The identification badges also helped staff visually double-check that all volunteers on the site had checked in.

The check-in station at the entrance to the site was staffed by at least one SCDNR archaeologist at all times, ensuring that everyone who walked onto the site checked in and out. Past excavations at this and other SCDNR cultural sites had used paper visitor and volunteer logs, but during the May 2019 field season, our team began using the Eventbrite Organizer app installed on iPads. The app allowed us to monitor the number of community members on the site at any given time and calculate total community engagement daily, a much more efficient and cost-effective method for gathering these analytics. Our analysis showed that most volunteers stayed for an average of approximately three hours, information that has helped us plan future volunteer schedules.

Volunteers

Between May 6 and May 24, 2019, 406 individuals donated 1,341 hours of their time to help our team sift soil and carefully bag artifacts.

Our team used methods from teaching archaeology in the classroom setting to provide a quick orientation for volunteers. After checking in, each volunteer received a pair of work gloves, which were available in all sizes for children and adults. Volunteers were then guided to one of the shaker screens close to open units excavated by SCDNR archaeologists. Each screen had a double-sided artifact identification card that featured photographs and information regarding the most common artifacts found at the site. An SCDNR archaeologist reviewed the artifact identification card with each volunteer and then emptied a bucket of excavated soil into the screen to be sift. SCDNR archaeologists monitored volunteers at the screens, answered questions, and assisted when necessary. When volunteers finished sifting and bagging artifacts, an SCDNR archaeologist per-

COMMUNITY ARCHAEOLOGY 31

FIGURE 2.5.
A family of volunteers at one of the sifting screens. Courtesy of SCDNR.

FIGURE 2.6.
Third-grade volunteers sift artifacts and place them into the outstretched hand of an SCDNR archaeologist. Courtesy of SCDNR.

formed a final check of the screen for any remaining artifacts. At the end of their shifts, volunteers returned their badges and work gloves to be used by the next round of volunteers and checked out of the site.

Student Volunteers

While the most common volunteers were family groups, our team also worked alongside students. Like most archaeological sites, the Pockoy Island Shell Ring Complex offers an opportunity to provide students with place-based education. Field trips to cultural sites link what students learn in the classroom to a physical place and to real-world learning experiences.[16] Field trips also allow students to contribute to community archaeology projects in meaningful and memorable ways.

During the May 2019 field season, approximately fifty local third graders volunteered at the site for an hour during their field trip to BBPHP/WMA. The methodology used to teach these students was similar to that used with other volunteers. However, in addition to the standard volunteer orientation, SCDNR archaeologists working with the students made a point of including archaeology vocabulary and addressing South Carolina state teaching standards.

To focus the students' volunteer efforts, SCDNR archaeologists reviewed the artifact identification card with the students and then asked them to collect one specific artifact type—for example, whelks, which were one of the largest and most easily identifiable artifact types in the screen. The archaeologists then moved on to other artifacts—periwinkles, pottery sherds, and so on. Staff pointed out features of these artifacts as they were collected—for example, a hole in the side of a whelk that indicated its use as an adz. This targeted approach created a productive competition as students raced to find each type of artifact. This method prompted students to ask questions about what they were finding and to engage in critical thinking about the site as a whole.

Visitors and Guided Tours

Between May 6 and May 23, 2019, 1,393 people took part in guided tours of the Pockoy Island Shell Ring Complex. SCDNR archaeologists led about half of these tours, while volunteer tour guides led the remainder. Because these volunteer guides had previous volunteer experience at BBPHP/WMA, they were quite familiar with the property and knew what questions visitors commonly ask. This knowledge made them significant assets to our team and to visitors and allowed Cultural Heritage Trust staff to focus on the excavation and on assisting volunteers.

In preparation for leading the tours, each volunteer received a packet that included a tour guide badge, a detailed script with space for additional notes, background information about the site and the topic of heritage at risk, an archaeology vocabulary list, archaeology and coastal geology quick reference guides, a map of the site showing the shoreline of Pockoy Island and all excavation units, and 2016 lidar imagery of the two rings that make up the Pockoy Island Shell Ring Complex.

Shortly before the first day we were open to the public, the volunteer tour guides gathered for an informal two-hour training session at BBPHP/WMA. They collected their information packets, and an SCDNR archaeologist reviewed the material page by page. The volunteer tour guides thus had time to review the information on their own and clarify any details prior to the first day of tours. Throughout the field season, volunteer tour guides updated their scripts based on information provided by Cultural Heritage Trust staff regarding modifications to excavation plans and recent discoveries. These daily interactions

FIGURE 2.7. SCDNR archaeologist Meg Gaillard leads a tour group. Information panels can be seen in the foreground. Courtesy of SCDNR.

also enabled volunteer tour guides to obtain answers to any visitor questions not covered in the information packet or training.

The area near the check-in station featured six information panels and maps detailing the site's discovery, the results of previous archaeological investigations, and how volunteers were helping. These information panels were pulled directly from a museum exhibit about the Pockoy Island Shell Ring Complex installed at SCDNR's Parker Annex Archaeology Center in January 2019. Following each tour, the guide escorted visitors to another space where experimental archaeologist Scott Jones demonstrated techniques for making shell tools such as whelk adzes and other artifacts found at the site. When space was available, tour participants could also volunteer to sift artifacts, and many visitors enthusiastically did so.

Volunteer Lab Days and Intern Projects

At the end of each excavation season at the Pockoy Island Shell Ring Complex, artifacts were transported to the Parker Annex Archaeology Center for processing. Here, too, we invite the public to participate, with volunteer lab days and summer intern research projects.

Prior to the COVID-19 pandemic, volunteer lab days took place each Wednesday. Community members could register to spend an hour washing and sorting artifacts for further analysis. As in the field, we welcomed volunteers of all ages, and they worked alongside SCDNR archaeology staff. These days were especially popular with local homeschool networks and offered another opportunity for place-based education for students, some of whom had joined us in the field.

SCDNR archaeology interns also assisted in processing artifacts from the site. Many interns focused their efforts on washing, sorting, and conducting preliminary research. Summer interns from the South Carolina Governor's School for Science and Mathematics did additional research about the site, its rate of erosion, and the artifacts they were processing, producing written reports and presenting their findings during the school's annual colloquium.

Conclusion

When working on a heritage at risk site, where speed and accuracy are essential, having large groups of visitors and volunteers might seem daunting, especially since these occasions might constitute the first—and sometimes only—direct archaeological experience for these people. Fully engaging with the public under these conditions can be challenging, but it can also be equally rewarding. With proper planning and effective teaching tactics, we can provide a memorable community archaeology experience for visitors and volunteers of all ages on both heritage at risk sites and those sites not at risk. Community archaeology opportunities at excavations and in the lab offer visitors a chance to learn more about the work we do as archaeologists and can enhance understandings of community history. In addition, volunteers and students contribute to active scientific investigations, working shoulder to shoulder with professional archaeologists.

While the COVID-19 pandemic forced the cancellation of the 2020 field season and of volunteer lab days, the SCDNR archaeology team was able to complete two more field seasons in May and September 2021. Volunteers and visitors were not invited to the site during that time, and the cultural material excavated was processed in the lab with the assistance of archaeology interns.

Cultural Heritage Trust staffers' research on the Pockoy Island Shell Ring Complex would not have been possible without our dedicated volunteers in the field and in the lab. Community archaeology takes on a deeper meaning in the case of heritage at risk sites like the Pockoy Island Shell Ring Complex. Whether one person is volunteering for one hour or hundreds of people are volunteering for thousands of hours, community involvement can mean the difference between saving or losing cultural resources for current and future generations.

Notes

SCDNR would like to acknowledge and pay respect to the Indigenous inhabitants of the land that we work on. Since time immemorial, tribes inhabited, protected and preserved these lands until their forcible removal from their homelands. We respect their histories and the connections that they maintain to this area. The Pockoy Island Shell Ring Complex is located on the ancestral homelands of the Muscogee Nation, who still retain strong cultural ties to the region today.

1. Meg Gaillard, *The South Carolina Archaeological Archive Flood Recovery Project*, Society of Historical Archaeology Heritage at Risk Committee, September 3, 2021, https://sha.org/blog/2021/09/the-south-carolina-archaeological-archive-flood-recovery-project/.

2. Meg Gaillard, "The South Carolina Department of Natural Resources (SCDNR) Archaeology Internship Program," *Horizon & Tradition*, October 2021, https://www.southeasternarchaeology.org/wp-content/uploads/SEAC-Newsletter-Fall-2021final-2.pdf.

3. South Carolina Code of Laws Unannotated, Title 51—Parks, Recreation and Tourism, Chapter 17—Heritage Trust Program, Article 1—Heritage Trust Program, 2006.

4. Cornelius Holtorf, *Archaeology Is a Brand! The Meaning of Archaeology in Contemporary Popular Culture* (Walnut Creek, Calif.: Left Coast Press, 2007).

5. Charles R. McGimsey III, *Public Archaeology* (New York: Seminar Press, 1972), 37.

6. Meg Gaillard, Katie Luciano, Gary Sundin, Karen Smith, Kiersten Weber, Bess Kellett, "Pockoy Island, South Carolina: A Case Study for Collaborative Shoreline Change Research to Heritage at Risk, Coastal Geology, and Community Science Monitoring" (paper presented at the Society for Historical Archaeology Conference, Lisbon, Portugal, 2022).

7. SCDNR, *Shorelines of Botany Bay: A Map Gallery of Historical & Recent Imagery*, 2019, DOI: https://arcg.is/0KPCv1.

8. Karen Y. Smith, "South Carolina's 4,000-Year-Old Shell Rings," 2023 (document on file with the SCDNR Heritage Trust Program).

9. Rebecca Saunders, "Shell Rings of the Lower Atlantic Coast of the United States: Defining Function by Contrasting Details, with Reference to Ecuador, Columbia, and Japan," in *The Cultural Dynamics of Shell-Matrix Sites*, ed. M. Roksandi (Albuquerque: University of New Mexico Press, 2014), 41–56; Karen Y. Smith, Sean Taylor, Tariq Ghaffar, Meg Gaillard, and Tanner Arrington, "Pockoy Island Shell Ring 1 Management Summary," 2021 (document on file with the SCDNR Heritage Trust Program).

10. David G. Anderson, Thaddeus G. Bissett, Stephen J. Yerka, Joshua J. Wells, Eric C. Kansa, Sarah W. Kansa, Kelsey Noack Myers, R. Carl DeMuth, and Devin A. White, "Sea-Level Rise and Archaeological Site Destruction: An Example from the Southeastern United States Using DINAA," *PLoS ONE* 12, no. 11 (2017): e0188142, https://doi.org/10.1371/journal.pone.0188142.

11. Katie Luciano, email to author, November 19, 2021.

12. *North American Heritage at Risk (NAHAR): An Introduction and Plans for the Future*, accessed February 15, 2023, https://hcommons.org/app/uploads/sites/1002202 /2021/04/NAHAR-Overview.pdf.

13. Karen Y. Smith, Sean Taylor, Tariq Ghaffar, Meg Gaillard, and Tanner Arrington, "An Archaeological Survey of Pockoy Island, Botany Bay Plantation Heritage Preserve, Charleston County, South Carolina" (document on file with the SCDNR Heritage Trust Program).

14. Meg Gaillard, "Archaeological Excavation at Botany Bay Plantation Heritage Preserve Open to Public," *South Carolina Department of Natural Resources*, April 8, 2019, https://www.dnr.sc.gov/news/2019/apr/apr8_pockoyisland.php.

15. David Dickson, "A Moment of Science: Lowcountry Archaeology: A Race against Erosion," NBC News 2, May 13, 2019, https://www.counton2.com/weather/a-moment -of-science/lowcountry-archaeology-a-race-against-erosion/; Bo Peterson, "Desperate Dig for the Past under Way on Disappearing S.C. Island," *Charleston Post & Courier*, May 12, 2019, updated June 14, 2021, https://www.postandcourier.com/news/desperate -dig-for-the-past-under-way-on-disappearing-sc/article_8e73cca4-727f-11e9-a9ae -b73bd8b47b53.html; Tim Renaud, "You Can Join S.C. DNR's Archaeological Excavation at Botany Bay," NBC News 2, April 9, 2019, https://www.counton2.com/news/local-news /you-can-join-sc-dnrs-archaeological-excavation-at-botany-bay/.

16. David Sobel, *Place-Based Education: Connecting Classrooms and Communities*, 2nd ed. (Great Barrington, Mass.: Orion Society, 2013).

Silent Stories

The Archaeology of Unrecorded Lives at Colonial Michilimackinac

KATHLYN GUTTMAN

North American fur trade archaeology became popularized at the turn of the twentieth century, just as the lucrative fur-trade business was waning. One of the first subdisciplines of historical archaeology to gain widespread attention from archaeologists, historians, and the general public, fur trade archaeology has forever been entangled with romantic myths of the independent North American pioneer.[1] North American fur trade archaeologists have focused their excavation efforts on the forts and trading posts built and occupied by European American men, to the exclusion of the wide network of other camps, homes, and villages that were equally integral to the trade.[2] Fort Michilimackinac figures prominently in fur trade archaeology both as a historical nexus for the Great Lakes fur-trading industry and as one of the first sites excavated by trained archaeologists. For many years, the archaeological programs at sites such as Fort Michilimackinac sought primarily to gather information for reconstructing buildings as well as artifacts for exhibits. Instead of critically assessing the archaeological record and historical record against each other, many early archaeologists working at Fort Michilimackinac chose to fit the archaeology into the historical narrative that had already been constructed—a narrative that often dismisses or minimizes the lives of subaltern peoples.[3] Archaeological rigor in interpretation has improved significantly in the past six decades, but the narratives of the past continue to hold sway.

Fort Michilimackinac was constructed in 1715 on the southern edge of the Straits of Mackinac, located between Lake Huron and Lake Michigan in northern Michigan. The location, which had previously been home to a small Jesuit mission, was ideal for monitoring and directing Indigenous fur-trading traffic. Though the fort was a military outpost in name, it primarily functioned as a hub for the Great Lakes fur trade during its sixty-six-year occupation. It was home to many fur traders and the laborers they employed, known as voyageurs. Records indicate that the fort was also home to Indigenous people, especially Indigenous and Métis women who married traders or military men. After the French and Indian War, the British took control of Fort Michilimackinac in 1761. Two years later, a confederation of Native tribes briefly took over the fort during Pontiac's War. The British passed a law banning Indigenous people from full-time residence inside the fort's walls, although evidence that Métis persons continued to live inside the fort implies that the law was enforced selectively.[4] The British maintained control of Fort Michilimackinac until residents destroyed it in 1781 out of fear that approaching American troops would use it to stage an attack on the better-defended Mackinac Island.

Now dubbed Colonial Michilimackinac, select parts of the fort have been reconstructed by the State of Michigan as a living history museum that interprets the period of British occupation at the fort. Although part of the fort's palisade was reconstructed as early as the 1930s and some amateur excavations took place in the first half of the twentieth century, professional archaeology has been key to Colonial Michilimackinac's reconstruction since Michigan State University archaeologists conducted the first professional excavations in 1959.[5] Excavations have taken place every summer since, making Colonial Michilimackinac one of the longest active archaeological programs in North America.

Although the archaeology and interpretation at Fort Michilimackinac have for decades been sophisticated and ahead of their time in many ways, the history presented at the fort is subject to many of the pitfalls and stereotypes that commonly affect institutions interpreting colonized places and peoples. Although individuals at Colonial Michilimackinac are constantly striving to improve interpretation, it is nevertheless necessary to continually reevaluate the entrenched assumptions in both the academic and public presentations of the site's history and archaeology. The stories told by historians and archaeologists at Michilimackinac are most often the stories of white, literate, upper-class European American men. Others, especially Indigenous peoples and women, are excluded from the narrative. The costumed interpreters and museum staff who are tasked with conveying the fort's history to the public every summer obtain their information from these historians and archaeologists, leading to an interpretive program that is likewise exclusionary. Therefore, changing the public interpretation at Fort Michilimackinac must start with us.

This chapter focuses on reanalyzing artifact assemblages from Colonial Michilimackinac using methodologies that better elucidate the lived experiences of subaltern peoples who lived and worked in these spaces.[6] I selected these methodologies using the framework suggested by Haitian anthropologist Michel-Rolph Trouillot's concept of historical silencing.[7] The avenue of inquiry that provided the most interesting findings and the most promise for further use is a modified version of feminist archaeologists Margaret Conkey and Janet Spector's activity-differentiation framework.[8]

Michel-Rolph Trouillot and Silencing

Like most subdisciplines in historical archaeology, fur trade archaeology is hindered by the dearth of documentation produced by subaltern peoples. Instead, the written record of the fur trade predominantly reflects the preoccupations and activities of upper-class European American men. Archaeologist Stephen Silliman has utilized Trouillot's theory of silencing to discuss the erasure of Indigenous peoples from historical archaeology.[9] Through this theory, Trouillot illuminates the multilayered way in which history is created or denied. Silences can enter history at "four crucial moments": the "moment of fact creation" (the event itself), "the moment of fact assembly" (the creation of "archives," or records), "the moment of fact retrieval" (the combination of records to create a narrative), and "the moment of retrospective significance" (the reification of the narrative as history). All histories are "a particular bundle of silences" rather than a linear creation and curation of unchanging facts, as pop history and textbooks would have one believe.[10] Therefore, Trouillot's approach is useful for investigating the archaeology and history of subaltern peoples.

Silences in Trouillot's sense have been created in all four ways at Fort Michilimackinac over the past three hundred years. The first set of silences were created by the fort's residents when they selected what persons, events, and thoughts they would or would not record. Silences were created in the archaeological record at this time as well, although the residents did not know it. Archaeological silences at the source differ from historical silences but are also intentional: an archaeological assemblage is shaped by personal selections of what should or should not be discarded, taken, or left behind. Luckily, the selections (or lack thereof) that result in the archaeological record often create a site full of those illicit, broken, or minor objects that people purposefully or inadvertently silence by discarding or hiding.[11] An archaeological assemblage offers the opportunity to study things silenced in written sources.

The creation of archives and records at Fort Michilimackinac introduced more silences. Sizable documentary archives are available for study but like any archive are not all-encompassing. The librarians and historians who curated these archives were and are limited by time, space, and financial constraints and like all curators were subject to bias about what materials were significant enough to be saved. The excavation of Fort Michilimackinac created the archaeological equivalent of a documentary archive, with ceramics, food remains, and other artifacts constituting the primary documents. Like historians and librarians, archaeologists are limited by time, space, and funding. Archaeologists must be selective about what is collected when excavating; not even the painstakingly fine screening techniques used at Michilimackinac can recover every artifact. Excavation also creates its own written records, in which archaeologists document the features and stratigraphy destroyed by excavation. Again, not every detail of every artifact or feature can be recorded: to create any sense out of the archaeological record and to be efficient at their job, archaeologists must select what parts of the record they will and will not collect or pay attention to. Some artifacts and information will inevitably be missed.

When scholars analyze the documents, artifacts, and archives created at Fort Michilimackinac, they establish a narrative. The establishment of a narrative must include silences: every detail of every document or artifact cannot be included in the narrative. Historians' and curators' inherent biases guide the type of narrative created: those who actively seek to highlight the lives of Indigenous people at Fort Michilimackinac create narratives that include Indigenous people, while those who focus uncritically on the recorded residents of the fort will re-create the narratives of the literate European American men who penned the primary documents. The archaeological narrative at Fort Michilimackinac often suffers from a similar problem: previous archaeologists interpreted their findings through the lens of the recorded residents of the fort, excluding the agency of large swaths of the fort's population in the creation of the archaeological narrative.

Silences are finally enacted and reinforced in the synthesis of records and narratives as history. History in sensu Trouillot at Fort Michilimackinac is regularly reified through publications and news media; most frequently, however, the established history of the fort is reinforced in the public imagination by the written and living interpretations enacted at the historic site.

The historians, archaeologists, and other scholars who study Fort Michilimackinac must try to rectify those silences that flatten our interpretation of the past. The silences created by primary documents and archives are unchangeable: additional primary documents cannot be created, and sites cannot be reexcavated. Instead, those silences must be redressed at the narrative stage, reevaluating the available records, sources, and archives with a deliberate focus on parsing out what has or has not been silenced. This practice is needed not just for the benefit of archaeologists but also for the benefit of the public: uncritical acceptance of the received narrative and history is a disservice to those who have been silenced, both past and present.

To paraphrase Trouillot, the past is not singular and objective but multiple.[12] The facts that come together to form an "objective" or accepted history are simply one bundle of silences that have been chosen from among many. These histories are not stagnant in the popular imagination: rather, "they inform and are informed by contemporary worldviews" that affect people's lived experiences.[13] Archaeologists, along with the historians and interpreters with whom we work, are on the front line of the creation of narratives and histories. As such, we have an obligation to approach the archaeological record as holistically as possible.

The Activity-Differentiation Framework

I began my research with close study of primary documents and archaeological reports related to Fort Michilimackinac's House C and its residents, intending to follow the long tradition focusing on the ethnic and religious identity of the two recorded owners of the house, Solomon and Levy. However, I noticed time and again that archaeological reports briefly mentioned the ways in which unrecorded peoples could have contributed to the assemblage at House C. For example, feminist archaeologist Elizabeth May Scott mentions that the faunal assemblage at House C was more indicative of a French or Métis diet, and Jill Halchin mentions that evidence of manufacturing suggested employees lived or worked in the house.[14] In both cases, these observations did not change the interpretation of House C as a site occupied exclusively by upper-class European American men. The primary documentary evidence created a similar problem: unrecorded or underrecorded people who lived and worked in Michilimackinac's homes, such as the unnamed Panis (enslaved Indigenous) woman Solomon bought and sold before he moved into House C, might be mentioned in a single document or not at all.[15] As at many historical sites, archaeologists at Michilimackinac rely on primary documents to guide excavation and interpretation. This reliance created a body of early archaeological work that focused on shaping the archaeological record to fit the documentary record and the popular imagination. Despite the theoretical and interpretive progress of more recent decades, the narratives created by Michilimackinac's wealthy, literate occupants had already been reified.

I utilized four different analytical methodologies that either had not previously been used at Fort Michilimackinac or had not been used on this assemblage. The methods were selected to approach the archaeological assemblage creatively, in ways that would avoid fixing the meaning of artifacts, which Silliman argues results from many approaches to the archaeological record.[16] While the goal was to provide a discussion of new avenues of inquiry rather than a definitive answer to the question of who lived at each house, some of the methodologies produced results with surprising implications for our understanding of artifacts at Michilimackinac. This chapter discusses the method that produced the most interesting results and that has the most potential for further usage at Colonial Michilimackinac and beyond—the activity-differentiation framework.

I used a modified version of the activity-differentiation framework pioneered by Conkey and Spector to analyze the personal and adornment artifacts recovered from Houses C, D, and 7. Scott has proposed that further feminist-materialist analysis of the personal use and adornment–related artifacts from Michilimackinac should be undertaken using primary documents to determine which objects were used by people with certain gender, ethnic, and class identities.[17] Archaeologists often group artifacts into broad categories, and the category "trade goods" commonly used at Fort Michilimackinac encompasses a wide variety of artifacts, among them beads, religious paraphernalia, and gun parts.[18] This category is broad enough to contain artifacts that could be sorted in multiple other ways, and many publications on Fort Michilimackinac do not explain why certain artifacts are included in or excluded from the trade goods category.

Conkey and Spector define the activity-differentiation framework as a tool to study gendered activities or tasks in a way that is sensitive to the variability of gender across cultures.[19] The goal is to achieve a more emic (insider) understanding of gendered artifact associations rather than to uncritically apply gender stereotypes from the contemporary world. In Conkey and Spector's framework, the social, temporal, spatial, and material dimensions of any task must be considered as a whole, although the nature of the available information means that archaeologists utilizing the framework tend to focus on the spatial and material dimensions.

Evidence: Houses C, D, and 7

House C is perhaps the most published single house at Fort Michilimackinac because of its occupants: during the British period, it was home to Ezekiel Solomon, the first recorded Jewish resident in what is now Michigan. Solomon and his business partner, Gershon Levy, were Montreal-based German Jewish merchants who conducted enough business in Michilimackinac to purchase this house from the French Canadian Parant family. Because of Solomon's unique place in Michigan history, House C has attracted both popular and academic attention, which has been devoted solely to these recorded residents.

Since the 1970s, the archaeological program at Colonial Michilimackinac has focused on discretely excavating large features, such as houses and streets, an endeavor aided by multiple maps, some of them highly accurate, created during the fort's occupation. These maps make comparing artifact assemblages by house a simple process. House C, House D, and House 7 seem to represent three distinct types of recorded residents. House C was owned first by French Canadian fur traders and then purchased by Solomon and Levy, who were among the traders who arrived at the fort shortly after the 1761 British takeover. During the 1763 Native American attack on the fort, both Solomon

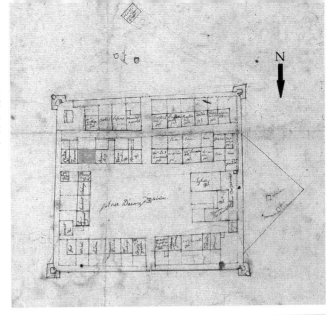

FIGURE 3.1. Michel Chartier de Lotbinière's map of Fort Michilimackinac, 1749. Courtesy of Mackinac State Historic Parks.

FIGURE 3.2. Archaeology master map of Fort Michilimackinac showing House C (shaded spot on right), House D (shaded spot in center), and House 7 (shaded spot on left). Courtesy of Mackinac State Historic Parks.

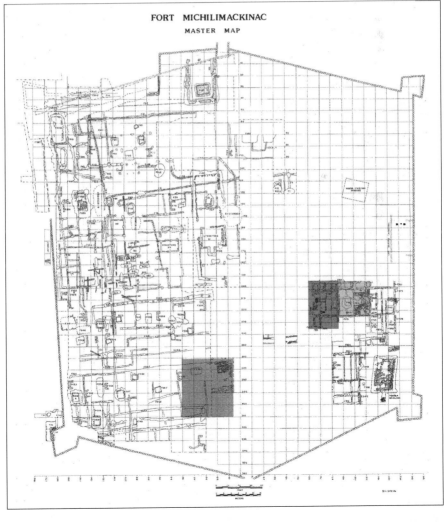

and chronicler Alexander Henry were captured. House D was the home of a British officer and likely of his Métis wife, whose name is unknown. House 7 was home to French fur traders during the British period. All three houses were excavated following the same methodologies that have been used at Colonial Michilimackinac since the 1980s.[20]

Similarities between House C and House 7 should indicate Solomon and Levy's presence as British-influenced traders; similarities between House C and House D (when accounting for the preponderance of British military artifacts in House D) could indicate the cultural influence of Métis, French Canadian, or Indigenous residents.

Findings

The activity-differentiation framework requires archaeologists to identify how tasks are divided by gender, ethnicity, occupation, and other social categories and then relate artifacts to each task. To achieve a better understanding of what personal adornment objects were traded, I reviewed multiple rosters from British and French traders at Michilimackinac, including Solomon.[21] Although participation in the trade was not strictly regulated by social category and many women and Métis people are known to have traded for furs, these specific rosters reflect the purchasing choices of European men. I posit that those categories of personal use and adornment artifacts excavated at Fort Michilimackinac that also appear in these records are more likely point to the trade activities of European men such as Solomon and Levy. I similarly posit that personal use and adornment objects that did not appear on the trade lists, especially those of Indigenous rather than European manufacture, were less likely to have been part of fur-trading activities. Instead, they may point toward the activities and personal choices of individuals other than the European American men who created these lists. Of course, this analysis is not exhaustive, and further analysis using other historical documents may provide different results.

I included all artifacts created for personal use or adornment except for seed beads, which are found in huge quantities at Fort Michilimackinac and would constitute a separate study. Table 3.1 lists all personal use and adornment items found in the rosters. Organic objects with no components likely to survive in Fort Michilimackinac's wet and sandy soil, such as blankets, were excluded. Even with these restrictions, the variety of personal goods bought and sold by European traders is extensive. Table 3.2 lists types and quantities of personal use and adornment artifacts excavated from the British-occupation layers of Houses C, D, and 7 that appear in these trade rosters. Table 3.3 lists personal use and adornment artifacts that do not appear in the rosters.

The variety of personal use and adornment artifacts excavated at the three

TABLE 3.1
Documentary Personal Use/Adornment Objects Found in Trade Rosters

beads
  blue beeds
  mock garnetts [beads]
  long blk beads
  small white beads
  long white beads
  [bunch] small round do
  small yellow beeds
  White wampum
  Wampum
  red bruised beads
Blue Romals [braided hide]
Bottles of Essence peperment
box combs
  horn Combs
  Bone Combs
Boxes or/Relliquaries
  steel tobacco boxes
Brass ring Dial
broaches
  Silver Broaches
  large Scolopt Broaches
  small do do
broad tincel'd laced
  Rich broad gold laced
  broad Tinsel Lace all yellow
Broad Council Bells
  narrow Beed Bells
Buttons
  Glom Buttons for Jillets
    [jacket] etc.
  Vest buttons 1/6
  Dos Inlaid do
  Gold coat button
Large horn Buttons
  solid enlaid coat buttons
Coats
  Boys Ditto Ditto
  Spotted Jacketts
  Double Rateen Jacketts
  Men's bound Duffil great

Dutch looking Glasses
  small Dutch glasses
  looking glasses in gilt
Earrings
  stone earrings
  Pr. Ear bobs
  silvre ear bobs
  Ear Wheels
false Silveer works
fiddle strings
Gimps [silk with wire]
hats
  boys hats
  Men's plain Hats
  Castor hats
  Capots de Molton
  Worsted Caps
Jewes harps
large arm bands
  smaller do
  large strong silver arm bands
    with The King's Arms en-
    graved on them . . .
  silver wrist bands such as were
    sent in the year 1779
  largest silver Arm Band
  pair silver wrist bands
  Plain yellow rings
  plain yellow bath Rings
  Brass rings
Shirt
  Men's 3/4 Irish shirts
  Ditto 7/8 Ditto
  Ditto 8/8 Ditto Ruffled
  small white shirts
  Cotton shirts
  Check Ditto
  Indian Shirts
  pr sleeves
  Boys shirt

silver hairplate the Best S.
Suits clothes
Tinsell, 18 Yds each very gaudy
  Tinsell do
large silver medals
  smaller Do
Metal Crosses
  small Crosses 8d
  large Crosses
  middling do
  large silver crosses
mittasses [leggings]
  Leather Breeches
playing cards
pair of Shoes
  pair of womans Shoes
  pair of Indian Shoes
  pair of shoe buckles
  pr of Mogizins
  pair mans fine Shoes
  pair mens strong shoes
paper cases
pair of Cotton Trowsers [*sic*]
pinchback buckles
  Common do
[pipes] short Indians
platillas [plaits] Royal
rings
  stone rings
  Ring Silver Basses
  white metal rings
  plain Bath do

houses is more limited than the extensive variety found in trade rosters, which is expected as a consequence of preservation issues. Only certain components of many goods can be found in the archaeological record: leather and cloth rarely survive in the site's wet beach sand matrix. The artifacts have also been grouped more generally by the excavators than would have been the case in extant documents.

The greatest number and variety of goods were found at House 7, which unsurprisingly, belonged to a trader. House D had the fewest artifacts found in the

TABLE 3.2
Personal Adornment Artifacts Found in Table 3.1, British Contexts

TRADE GOODS	HOUSE C	HOUSE D	HOUSE 7
Buttons (nonbone)	5	Not Present	19
Jewelry/jewelry fragments	6	4	18
Buckles/fragments (shoes, hats)	1	Not Present	10
Rings/fragments (Jesuit/brass)	1 (brass)	3	5
Brooches/fragments	1	Not Present	Not Present
Clothing fragments (hooks and eyes, metallic trim)	1 (hook and eye)	3	75 (hook and eye, trim, and sequins)
Native stone pipes/fragments	3	4	3

Source: Unpublished Colonial Michilimackinac excavation reports, 1983–2007 seasons, Mackinac State Historic Parks.

TABLE 3.3
Personal Adornment Artifacts Not Found in Table 3.1, British Contexts

NON-TRADE GOODS	HOUSE C	HOUSE D	HOUSE 7
Rosary beads/fragments	11	Not Present	19
Tinkling cones	15	5	18
Metal/stone beads	1 (metal)	1 (metal)	1 (lithic)
Buttons (bone)	Not Present	1	3

Source: Unpublished Colonial Michilimackinac excavation reports, 1983–2007 seasons, Mackinac State Historic Parks.

trade rosters, a finding that is consistent with the fact that its occupants were British officers rather than traders. The variety of artifacts found in the trade rosters at House C is similar to that found at House 7, but the number of artifacts is significantly lower. The same is true for the artifacts not found in the trade rosters at Houses C and 7.

The analysis shows that the majority of the personal adornment objects at House C were potential trade goods, consistent with the presence of Solomon and Levy. Multiple artifact types not listed in the trade rosters were found at all three houses, and some of these were artifacts of Indigenous manufacture, such as tinkling cones and metal or stone beads. Previous publications have often explained the presence of rosary beads at House C, occupied by Jewish men, by labeling the beads as trade goods.[22] However, rosaries were not found in any of the trade rosters, and Catholicism was practiced primarily by the fort's French Canadian and Métis residents. The rosary beads and the other categories of artifacts not found in the trade rosters will have to be considered more critically if they cannot be lumped into the category of trade goods. Instead of conforming artifacts to the lives of recorded individuals, these artifacts could provide avenues of inquiry that illuminate the lived experiences of silenced persons.

Conclusion

Utilizing the activity-differentiation framework on this assemblage has provided a new avenue for thinking critically about artifacts and their relationship to the people at Fort Michilimackinac. This analysis provides a starting point for thinking about ways in which archaeologists and historians can rectify the silences of history. Colonial Michilimackinac is a prime candidate for this exercise because of its status as a place where both historical fact and record were created and history was reified in the public eye. Creation, assembly, retrieval, and retrospective significance are all enacted on the same geography, creating a microcosm of Trouillot's concept of silences.

Silences are necessary for any museum or archaeological excavation to function coherently: interpreting every relevant story at Colonial Michilimackinac would create an unpleasant jumble of information that would not attract many visitors, and recording every single observation at an excavation would make for a never-ending field season. Nevertheless, silences regarding subaltern peoples, especially Indigenous and Métis people, have been as prevalent in the creation of history at Michilimackinac as they have been in history writ large. Academic studies such as this one provide a starting point for mending the silences that erase or cause harm, but academia has a small scope. Colonial Michilimackinac's interpretive program reaches thousands of people every year, and changes that broaden the site's established history would inform visitors about the diverse residents of the original fort and challenge common misconceptions about the nature of the fur trade.

The history currently presented in Michilimackinac's interpretive program is bounded by the comfort zone of Colonial Michilimackinac's primary visitors—white, middle-class midwestern families, often on vacation. Much of the programming resembles that at other U.S. historic sites: cooking demonstrations, military reenactments, and exhibits detailing the lives of European residents. Interpretation of Indigenous lives has increased in recent years, but these changes—panels of text in a merchant's house and a few minutes of footage of tribal members—remain background noise against interpretive "highlights" of the site. Rather than making changes to the core interpretive program, staff shimmied bits of Indigenous histories into the spaces in between.

I hesitate to call potential changes to Colonial Michilimackinac's programming decolonization, as the site's existence is predicated on the effects of colonization. However, rectifying the silences at Michilimackinac will require tactics similar to those used in decolonizing efforts, such as centering holistic interpretation that includes those who have previously been silenced. Creating new histories at Michilimackinac will not be an easy or comfortable process, but it is a necessary one.

Notes

1. Michael S. Nassaney, *The Archaeology of the North American Fur Trade* (Gainesville: University Press of Florida, 2015), 6–10.

2. Olga Klimko, "Fur Trade Archaeology in Western Canada: Who Is Digging up the Forts," in *The Archaeology of Contact in Settler Societies*, ed. Tim Murray (Cambridge: Cambridge University Press, 2004), 157–75.

3. A prime example of early archaeologists at Fort Michilimackinac reifying historical biases occurs in Moreau S. Maxwell and Lewis H. Binford, *Excavation at Fort Michilimackinac, Mackinac City, Michigan, 1959 Season* (East Lansing: Michigan State University Museum, 1961). The authors state that the French "appear to have been more careless than the British" (18), echoing contemporary writers' negative views of the French Canadians.

4. Alexander Henry, *Travels & Adventures: In Canada and the Indian Territories between the Years 1760 and 1776* (Carlisle, Mass.: Applewood Books, 2009).

5. For the earliest professional excavations at Fort Michilimackinac, see Maxwell, and Binford, *Excavation at Fort Michilimackinac.*

6. Kathlyn Guttman, "Invisible Residents: Archaeological Evidence and the Question of Indigenous Presence at House C of British Fort Michilimackinac, 1765–1781" (master's thesis, Cornell University, 2019), https://doi.org/10.7298/b1q4-1644.

7. Michel-Rolph Trouillot, *Silencing the Past: Power and the Production of History* (Boston: Beacon Press, 2015).

8. Margaret W. Conkey and Janet D. Spector, "Archaeology and the Study of Gender," *Advances in Archaeological Method and Theory* 7 (1984): 1–38.

9. Stephen Silliman, "Indigenous Traces in Colonial Spaces: Archaeologies of Ambiguity, Origin, and Practice," *Journal of Social Archaeology* 10, no. 1 (2010): 28–58.

10. Trouillot, *Silencing the Past.*

11. Nassaney, *Archaeology.*

12. Trouillot, *Silencing the Past*, 25–28.

13. Guttman, "Invisible Residents," 10–11.

14. Elizabeth May Scott, "'Such Diet as Befitted His Station as Clerk': The Archaeology of Subsistence and Cultural Diversity at Fort Michilimackinac, 1761–1781" (PhD diss., University of Minnesota, 1991), appendix 1; Jill Y. Halchin, *Excavations at Fort Michilimackinac, 1983–1985: House C of the Southeast Row House, the Solomon-Levy-Parant House* (Mackinac Island, Mich.: Mackinac Island State Park Commission, 1988), 217.

15. Keith R. Widder, *Beyond Pontiac's Shadow: Michilimackinac and the Anglo-Indian War of 1763* (East Lansing: Michigan State University Press, 2013), 154.

16. Silliman, "Indigenous Traces in Colonial Spaces," 41–43.

17. Scott, "Such Diet as Befitted His Station," 205.

18. See Halchin, *Excavations at Fort Michilimackinac.*, 160–69.

19. Conkey and Spector, "Archaeology and the Study of Gender," 25–26.

20. For detailed information on excavation methods and stratigraphy for all three houses, see Guttman, "Invisible Residents," 11–25.

21. For a full listing of the rosters included in this study, see Guttman, "Invisible Residents," appendix A.

22. See, for example, Halchin, *Excavations at Fort Michilimackinac*, 182–83.

How One Archaeological Project Unearthed Both the Living and the Dead

4

TORI MASON AND KATE SPROUL

"We'll just need to cut this fence to access the rest of the graves," the archaeologist told us, oblivious to the fact that that fence was a perimeter fence that was required to keep the zoo secure in accordance with the regulations of the Association of Zoos and Aquariums, which accredits Nashville Zoo. The archaeologists, who worked for Nashville's TRC Solutions (now known as TRC Companies), were professionals who were proficient in respectfully disinterring and moving bodies to a place where their rest would not be disturbed. These archaeologists always documented their work through photographs and carefully recorded notes. They knew and followed all the rules of their profession. But they knew nothing about the rule requiring a perimeter fence around the zoo—just one of the paradoxes that arose from Nashville Zoo's location on the site of Grassmere, a family farm that includes a house built in 1810 by people enslaved by Michael and Elizabeth Dunn and that contained the final resting places of some of those enslaved people.[1]

While most of the people working at Nashville Zoo focus on the animals, historic site manager Tori Mason and members of the interpretive team work to educate the public about the historic home and the people who lived there. Team members also focus on the associated outbuildings and the cemeteries that lay just beyond the cabin that housed enslaved families and then emancipated Black families from about 1810 to 1973.[2]

The fields where enslaved people and later tenant farmers tended crops and the pastures where they raised livestock are now home to exhibits of exotic animals, and many visitors cannot imagine Grassmere as the three-hundred-acre farm that it used to be. The sherds of pottery and ceramics and the pieces of farm equipment found around the property help us tell their story: the abandoned grain seeder at the back of the property shows where the edge of a field was, and sherds discovered during the construction of the kangaroo exhibit show where field hands had their middens, not too far from their cabins.

Joyce Hillman, a great-granddaughter of tenant farmer Frank Morton, recognized a Red Goose Shoe token found near the cabin where he used to live.[3] These discarded objects help to tell the story of how Black families lived at Grassmere.

Excavation of the Original Cemetery

In 1989, when Grassmere Wildlife Park was being established on the property at the request of the final owners, researchers from the Tennessee Division of Archaeology discovered an unmarked cemetery containing what appeared to be five graves close to the new parking lot. There were no markers in the cemetery indicating who was buried there, when they were buried, or what their ethnicity was. The location of the graves was noted, and that part of the site was not developed at the time. Grassmere Wildlife Park closed in 1995, and Nashville Zoo began managing the site two years later. The zoo initially developed around the cemetery, leaving it undisturbed. In 2013, however, an increase in zoo attendance meant that a new entry plaza would soon be required, leading to the need to relocate the cemetery. Zoo president and director Rick Schwartz reached out to the Tennessee state archaeologist, the Nashville Metropolitan Historical Commission, and the Tennessee Historical Commission to see how this relocation could be accomplished. A plan was created that would move the cemetery to a new location near the existing family cemetery behind the historic home, where it could finally be properly interpreted. As dictated by law, the zoo published its intention to move the cemetery in the local papers for a month to give any possible descendants the opportunity to come forward. No one claimed descent from the individuals buried in the cemetery, but this step would have been important even if it had not been legally required: it opened a dialogue with the public, showed people that Nashville Zoo was being transparent about what was being done, and allowed people to ask questions with the expectation that they would get honest answers.[4]

After the required time had elapsed, Nashville Zoo hired TRC Companies to move the cemetery. The firm had extensive experience respectfully and professionally exhuming, relocating, and reinterring human remains. Publicizing this step was also very important: visitors needed to know that the remains would be treated respectfully and properly reinterred.[5]

From February 27 through March 6, 2014, TRC carefully disinterred nineteen graves containing the remains of nine adults and eleven children or infants. The archaeologists noted, numbered, photographed, and mapped each grave site and recorded the numerous artifacts found in the grave shafts, which included nails and other hardware, buttons, beads, and pins. Each person had been buried in a wooden coffin, and at least seventeen of the coffins were hexagonal. Most of the people were buried wearing clothing; some of the infants may have

FIGURE 4.1.
TRC staff working on the Grassmere cemetery site at the entrance to the Nashville Zoo, March 2014. Courtesy of Nashville Zoo.

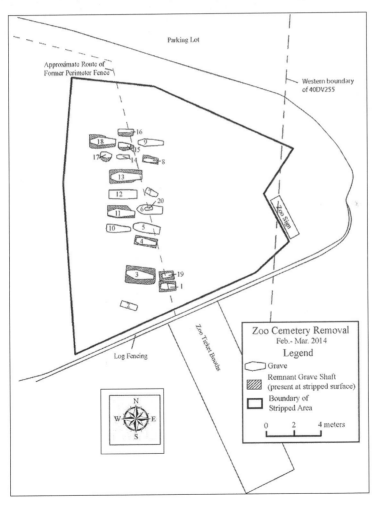

FIGURE 4.2.
Map of Nashville Zoo cemetery interments. Courtesy of TRC Companies.

been wrapped in shrouds that had beads sewn on them. Using the material remains as a guide, the archaeologists dated the burials to between 1830 and 1860.[6] These two findings indicate that the individuals received a good deal of respect when they were first buried, either by the enslaved community or their enslavers or both.

Although some of the remains had deteriorated as a result of the acidic soil, most of the adult remains were well preserved, surprising the archaeologists and presenting a unique and exciting opportunity for deeper research. Larry McKee from TRC asked Dr. Shannon Hodge, a bioarchaeologist and associate professor of anthropology at Middle Tennessee State University in Murfreesboro, to assist with the research. The possibility of DNA testing was proposed, and funding for three DNA tests was provided by Nashville Zoo, Historic Nashville Inc., and the Nashville Metropolitan Historical Commission Foundation. The test for Individual 1 was inconclusive. The test for Individual 2 showed definitive African ancestry. A mitochondrial DNA test showed that Individual 3's ancestors came from northern Africa or Western Europe. This individual was also the only one placed in a coffin that may have had a viewing window on top to enable mourners to see their loved one's face.

Hodge volunteered to do a thorough examination of the bones of the nine adults, determining that five of the adults were probably male and four were probably female. All of them had received adequate nutrition to grow normally and prevent dietary diseases. Seven individuals were younger than forty, while two were between thirty-five and fifty at the time of their deaths. She found that while the bones showed that the individuals had done hard physical labor, they had not done anything strenuous enough to damage the bones or pull the muscles away from the bones. Six of the adults had arthritis in their spines or knees. One set of adult remains contained the remains of an approximately twenty-two-week-old fetus.

A few of the individuals had healed injuries, showing that they had received some kind of medical care. One man died with a healed infection on one toe that could have been the result of a puncture wound or a bug bite. One woman had compression fractures of her lower spine, which Hodge noted might have been resulted if the woman fell off the back of a wagon and landed on her tailbone. Time would have been required to heal from these injuries.

One young male was more than six feet tall, but his growth plates had not yet closed, meaning that he was still a teenager. There were signs of gout in one of his toes, he had a slipped malformed hip joint, and he showed signs of a brain aneurysm. All of these symptoms are indicators of sickle cell disease, which affects people of African descent at a much higher rate than people of other ethnicities.

Dr. Tiffiny Tung, a bioarchaeologist and associate professor of anthropology at Vanderbilt University in Nashville, is analyzing the stable oxygen and carbon isotopes of some of the individuals buried in the cemetery. Water contains location-specific proportions of oxygen isotopes. As our teeth form during childhood, they take on the same proportion of isotopes as the water we drink. If the oxygen isotope number in a person's teeth matches the local water source, we know that they grew up in that area rather than in another location.[7]

Tung's research has determined that four individuals were probably born and raised at Grassmere; one probably spent their childhood somewhere other than Grassmere; and five were born elsewhere and then relocated to Grassmere. Despite their varying origins, these people appear to have created a community, leading the enslaved at Grassmere to bury loved ones together.[8]

Zoo staff and TRC archaeologists carefully shielded the exhumations from visitors, although social media and news outlets made guests aware of what was happening behind the barriers. We expected to receive some criticism of the decision to relocate the cemetery: many people feel it is disrespectful to exhume a body for any reason, and some believe it puts a soul in peril. We received only a small handful of emails and phone calls expressing concerns, and we responded directly to those concerns. We received several more negative responses on social media, and though we followed up with each of those commenters, we did not receive any replies. In responding to visitors, correspondence, and phone calls as well as in articles and presentations, we have been very careful to stress that TRC is an experienced archaeological company with a long track record of respectfully exhuming bodies and relocating cemeteries. We emphasized that any artifacts found with an individual were reburied with that individual, including all of the dirt in each burial shaft. We also mentioned that the people were reinterred in the same configuration as at the original location. While we do not know the family connections between the deceased, we respect the fact that they were buried in specific relation to each other for a reason. We honored that choice when they were reinterred.

We do not know the names of any of the people who were exhumed, but we know the names of some of the people enslaved at Grassmere: Viney; Robertson; Andrew; Ann; Henry; Milly; William; Tanny; Charles; Augustus; Mariah and her children, Louisa, Rhoda, and Stephen; Ben; Henderson; Flora; and Louis.[9] We are continuing to conduct research to learn more about these individuals.

Nashville Zoo held a reinterment and dedication ceremony at the new cemetery on November 22, 2014. Dr. Learotha Williams, professor of African American studies at Tennessee State University in Nashville, helped develop the content of the ceremony. The Reverend Bruce Maxwell, pastor of Lake Providence

FIGURE 4.3. Tennessee state historian Carroll Van West at the dedication of the new cemetery, November 22, 2014. Courtesy of Nashville Zoo.

Missionary Baptist Church, one of the city's oldest African American congregations, spoke and blessed the cemetery. Tennessee state historian Dr. Carroll Van West spoke about enslaved persons' contributions to Nashville and the South, noting that these individuals were no longer marginalized. This ceremony was held during zoo hours and was open to the public, and about seventy people attended. We hoped that the event showed our respect for the people who had lived, worked, and died at Grassmere and that guests learned a bit more about those enslaved at Grassmere. We were hopeful that members of the descendant community would attend the ceremony, but none came forward to talk to us.

The authors of this chapter, TRC archaeologists, Hodge, and Tung have all published articles and given presentations at the zoo and at local, regional, and national conferences to inform the public about the archaeological and historical research regarding the site and what we have learned about the people enslaved at Grassmere. Presentations at conferences and articles in professional journals have provided us with feedback on our work, allowed us to ask questions of colleagues, and given us ideas regarding how to better communicate with casual visitors to our site. These occasions have also helped us make contacts at other organizations who have subsequently collaborated with us on a variety of projects. For example, collaboration was extremely useful as we planned to move the cemetery and the reinterment ceremony and as we created a new exhibit regarding the relocation.

The Morton Family

Several news outlets covered the story of the cemetery's relocation. In August 2015, Mason received a phone call from Hillman, who said that according to family lore, her great-grandfather, Morton, was a descendant of the enslaved people who had lived at Grassmere. She wondered whether it would be possible to determine if any of the people in the cemetery were her relatives.

Frank Morton (1874–1962); his wife, Agnes Smith Morton (ca. 1874–1930); and their children, Albert (1913–73) and Maude (1909?–70), lived and worked at Grassmere beginning in 1919. Frank took care of crops, livestock, and gardens for the fifth-generation Grassmere owners, sisters Margaret and Elise Croft, as well as doing general farm chores and tending to his personal garden. Agnes helped with the laundry until her death in 1930. Frank stayed and worked at Grassmere for the rest of his life, although his health failed after he suffered a stroke on August 21, 1959. When he died on December 16, 1962, Elise Croft wrote in her diary, "My dear good Frank died this evening at 7:15."[10]

Albert Morton was six years old when his parents moved the family to Grassmere. He helped his father around the farm and later drove Margaret and Elise to the grocery store, the library, and on other errands. When he married, he and his wife, Gertrude, and eventually their children lived at Grassmere for a time but then moved to a home near the Nashville fairgrounds. After Maude died in 1970, he moved back to Grassmere until his death in 1973.[11]

Maude was ten years old when the family moved to Grassmere. When she married, she and her family lived on the Grassmere property in a cabin located about a half mile from the main house. Maude walked to the main house each day to perform household chores for Margaret and Elise. For years she did all of the cooking on the wood-burning stove in the summer kitchen, which is attached to the main house by a covered walkway. According to family lore, Maude finally went on strike until the sisters agreed to put a kitchen in the house with a modern oven, stove, and sink. Maude's husband, Henderson "Shorty" Webb, helped Albert with odd jobs around the farm and sometimes chauffeured Margaret and Elise into the city.[12]

Each member of the Morton family who worked at Grassmere received a salary, and in later years the Croft sisters paid the Mortons' taxes, insurance bills, doctor bills, and various other expenses. Though they were employees, Margaret and Elise also considered them friends, and they were an integral part of life at Grassmere. On February 7, 1970, Elise wrote in her diary, "When Albert came he said Maude had a stroke—much upset—as we are too." Elise noted Maude's death five days later as well as the second anniversary of her passing. On February 2, 1973, Elise recorded, "Albert operated on at 11:30—The growth has spread so much it could not be taken out—so they just sewed him up—The end for him—and us." When he returned to Grassmere just over a week later, ill, weak, and unable to work, she wrote, "Just to have Albert on the place makes us feel better." On December 7, 1973, she sadly recorded, "Paul called me at 5:00 A.M. Albert was dead—The end of so much." Margaret died the following July, and on November 30, 1974, Elise wrote, "What a dreadful year—Albert—Sister." In earlier years, Elise had written about the Mortons almost daily, as they worked alongside her in the gardens or barns or helped her corral escaped cattle.[13]

Prompted by Hillman's question, Mason began conducting research to compile the Mortons' family tree. In addition to Elise's diaries and Grassmere's financial records housed at the Tennessee State Library and Archives, sources including census records, obituaries, city directories, genealogical records, newspaper articles, and oral histories enabled Mason to trace eight generations of Mortons. She determined that Frank was likely not a descendant of people enslaved at Grassmere: his parents and grandparents lived in Nolensville, about fifteen miles south of Nashville in Williamson County, and his grandparents were born in North Carolina and likely were enslaved.

In 2017 Mason shared her research findings with Hillman and eight members of her family, who were overwhelmed and very appreciative of the information. Mason also recognized that the Mortons' contributions had made the existence of Grassmere possible and started planning an exhibit to tell their story.

Mason conducted further research on the Morton family and worked with members of the zoo's education staff to create an exhibit that would be housed where Frank Morton lived—one room of the original cabin on the site. The zoo obtained funding, including a grant from Humanities Tennessee, to create the exhibit.

With Hillman's blessing as well as information, photos, and documents she provided, the exhibit came to life, with photographs and updates occasionally posted on the Grassmere Historic Farm Facebook page. In June 2019, commenters responded to photos of Morton family members by declaring "That was my great grandfather!" and "I'm related to that woman!" Mason thus connected with two more descendants, DeCosta Hastings and Dondrick Jackson, adding them to the Morton family tree and obtaining more valuable family histories. Another descendant, Jerry Morton, was found through a connection to a zoo employee's husband's place of work. Through those three people and Hillman, Mason connected with about 125 living descendants of Frank Morton.

We chose June 19, 2021—Juneteenth—as the grand opening date for the Mor-

FIGURE 4.4.
Frank Morton, n.d.
Courtesy of Dondrick
Jackson.

FIGURE 4.5.
Frank and Albert Morton,
1957. Courtesy of
Tennessee State Library
and Archives.

FIGURE 4.6. Maude Morton Webb, n.d. Courtesy of Tennessee State Library and Archives.

ton Family Exhibit. More than one hundred Morton descendants attended—four generations representing the progeny of three of Frank's children: Maude, Albert, and Rosie. Some of these people had never met each other. The family had two hours in which to view the exhibit privately before it was opened it to the general public. In addition, attendees were encouraged to add to the family tree and to bring photos and documents for us to copy. Williams spoke at the ceremony, and then eight family members cut the ribbon to officially open the exhibit. The event was extremely moving, filled with tears, hugs, and expressions of thanks and gratitude.

When an employee found the Red Goose Shoe token near the cabin where the Mortons lived, Mason sent a picture of it to Hillman. She recalled that her grandparents, Maude and Shorty, would use these promotional tokens when buying Hillman patent leather shoes to wear to church on Easter Sunday. Such small and seemingly insignificant tidbits help give insight into life at Grassmere for a Black tenant family. More important, they give us a direct tie to Frank Morton and his family, bringing them to life.

Our ongoing collaboration and relationship with Morton's descendants was a direct result of an archaeological project that started because Nashville Zoo was growing. We are excited to keep collaborating with the Morton descendants as we continue to do research and expand our interpretation. A single archaeology project involving twenty unknown individuals led us to more than one hundred people who are helping us tell their family's story to Nashville Zoo's visitors.

FIGURE 4.7. Morton descendants in front of the cabin housing the Morton Family Exhibit, June 19, 2021. Courtesy of Nashville Zoo.

FIGURE 4.8. Morton descendants cutting the ribbon to open the Morton Family Exhibit, June 19, 2021. Courtesy of Nashville Zoo.

Notes

1. Veronica A. Riegel, *A Historical, Architectural, and Archaeological Assessment of the Grassmere Property, Nashville, Tennessee* (Nashville: Tennessee Department of Conservation, Division of Archaeology, 1989).

2. Tori Mason and Shannon Chappell Hodge, "The Bitter and the Sweet: Cemetery Relocation at the Nashville Zoo at Grassmere" (paper presented at the Tennessee Association of Museums Annual Conference, Jackson, 2015).

3. Joyce Hillman, personal communication, June 3, 2019.

4. Mason and Hodge, "Bitter and the Sweet"; Michael Cass, "Nashville Zoo Graves Turn Up More Than Expected," *Nashville Tennessean*, May 4, 2014, http://www.tennessean.com/story/news/2014/05/04/zoo-graves-turn-anyone-expected/8705721; Riegel, *Historical, Architectural, and Archaeological Assessment*. Unless otherwise noted, all information in this section is taken from Mason and Hodge, "Bitter and the Sweet."

5. Cass, "Nashville Zoo Graves"; Larry McKee and Hannah Guidry, *Excavation of*

a Mid-Nineteenth Century Cemetery at the Nashville Zoo, Tennessee Archaeology Council, 30 Days of Tennessee Archaeology, Day 18, September 18, 2014, https:// tennesseearchaeologycouncil.wordpress.com/2014/09/18/30-days-of-tennessee -archaeology-day-18/.

6. McKee and Guidry, "Excavation of a Mid-Nineteenth Century Cemetery"; Shannon Chappell Hodge, *Who Was Buried at Grassmere Plantation?*, Tennessee Archaeology Council, 30 Days of Tennessee Archaeology, Day 11, September 11, 2014, https:// tennesseearchaeologycouncil.wordpress.com/2014/09/11/30-days-of-tennessee -archaeology-day-11/; Cass, "Nashville Zoo Graves."

7. Tiffiny A. Tung, Molly Shea, and Larisa DeSantis, "Documenting Forced Movement of African Slaves to the Grassmere Plantation, Nashville, Tennessee, Using Carbon and Oxygen Stable Isotope Analysis of Dentition" (poster presented at the Society for American Anthropology Annual Meeting, San Francisco, 2015).

8. Tung, Shea, and DeSantis, "Documenting Forced Movement."

9. Davidson County, Tenn., Deed Books A–Z, 1–34, 3765, 1784–1866, 1964, Davidson County, Tenn., Will Books 1–19, 150, 1783–1866, 1985, both in Davidson County Archives, Nashville, Tenn.; Kate S. Carney Diary, 1859–76, #139-z, Southern Historical Collection, Wilson Library, University of North Carolina at Chapel Hill; Grassmere Collection, 1786–1985, Microfilm #1071, Tennessee State Library and Archives, Nashville.

10. "Elise Croft on Frank Morton," *Tennessee Virtual Archive*, accessed July 31, 2024, https://teva.contentdm.oclc.org/digital/collection/p15138coll31/id/617/; Elise Croft Diary, December 16, 1962, Grassmere Collection, 1786–1985.

11. Elise Croft Diary, February 12, July 17, 1970.

12. Elise Croft Diary, March 15, September 17, 1960, February 12, July 17, 1970.

13. Elise Croft Diary, February 7, 12, 1970, February 12, 1972, February 2, 10, December 7, 1973, November 30, 1974, and passim.

The Impact of Publicly Funded Archaeology

A Case Study in Prince George's County, Maryland

STEPHANIE T. SPERLING AND KRISTIN M. MONTAPERTO

Prince George's County, Maryland, borders Washington, D.C., to the east and is one of the wealthiest majority-Black counties in the nation. It is served by the Maryland–National Capital Park and Planning Commission (M-NCPPC), a primarily taxpayer-funded government agency that oversees more than twenty-eight thousand acres of public parkland under the management of its Department of Parks and Recreation (DPR). Hundreds of archaeological sites are located on DPR property, and two full-time staff members are assisted by a small part-time staff in the Archaeology Office to preserve, protect, and interpret these belowground cultural resources. In addition, the DPR manages hundreds of aboveground historic resources, including antebellum plantation houses; postbellum African American benevolent lodges, churches, and cemeteries; and twentieth-century manors, among other structures.

The Archaeology Office, established in 1988 and situated within the Natural and Historic Resources Division, has a complex and wide-ranging job, with a focus on public outreach and engagement central to its mission of studying and preserving archaeological resources via excavations, exhibits, and programs for Prince George's County residents. Office personnel take seriously the Society for American Archaeology's Archaeological Ethics Principle 4: "Archaeologists should reach out to and participate in cooperative efforts with others interested in the archaeological record with the aim of improving the preservation, protection, and interpretation of the record. In particular, archaeologists should undertake to: 1) enlist public support for the stewardship of the archaeological record; 2) explain and promote the use of archaeological methods and techniques in understanding human behavior and culture; and 3) communicate archaeological interpretations of the past."[1]

Public excavations, volunteerism, and collaborations with local educational institutions have long been cornerstones of the Archaeology Office, but recent initiatives seek to appeal to hesitant communities, to elevate difficult histories, and to connect with a wide array of internal and external stakeholders.[2] New offerings allow space for discomfort while tackling the legacies of enslavement and colonization, provide unique opportunities to discuss past cultures and environments on innovative tours, and give children hands-on archaeological experiences. Despite the challenges of implementing such programs, we strive continually to demonstrate that the residents of Prince George's County benefit from having a robust public archaeology program as part of their taxpayer-funded park system.

Archaeology Office On-site Programs

The Archaeology Office manages three parks that preserve unique natural and cultural resources: Dinosaur Park, Cherry Hill Cemetery, and Northampton Slave Quarters and Archaeological Park. We also manage and steward the significant archaeological resources at Mount Calvert Museum and Historic Site. In addition, more than one million fossils and artifacts recovered from these and other M-NCPPC properties are curated and stored in the Archaeology Office's climate-controlled collections facility.

Dinosaur Park is the only park of its kind on the East Coast and is home to Maryland's state dinosaur, *Astrodon johnstoni*. This paleontological park contains an open fossil quarry with deposits dating to the Early Cretaceous period—more than 115,000 million years old. The Archaeology Office has managed the park since it was acquired by M-NCPPC in 2007, thereby perpetuating the misconception that archaeologists dig dinosaurs. The park holds popular bimonthly open house events, where participants of all ages are invited to collect fossil remains of ancient plants and animals on the surface. Dinosaur Park staff also provide on- and off-site education programs and have recently developed initiatives including virtual summer camps and small-group excavation days.

Cherry Hill Cemetery, a late nineteenth-century African American cemetery, was established by a formerly enslaved family after the Civil War and served the surrounding community for decades. M-NCPPC acquired the cemetery in 1990 after citizens grew concerned about its treatment. The Archaeology Office staff worked in collaboration with the community association to develop a maintenance plan, but the demographics of the surrounding community changed, and its interpretation and use subsequently have been questioned. We are now working with old and new residents as well as local politicians to keep the park free of purported gang activity and determine the best ways to honor and respect its history while elevating its significance.

Northampton was once a major plantation owned by the Sprigg family, including Samuel Sprigg, who served as Maryland's governor from 1819 to 1822. Among its visitors were such dignitaries as the Marquis de Lafayette and President James Madison. As was the practice on contemporary Prince George's County tobacco plantations, the Sprigg family enslaved countless African Americans for hundreds of years. In the late 1990s, M-NCPPC acquired 12.5 acres of land containing the ruins of the main house and two quarters for enslaved persons as part of the development for the affluent Lake Arbor community. Collaboration with the descendants of those enslaved at Northampton included excavations of the quarters and site interpretation that continued through the early 2000s.[3] Today, the Northampton Slave Quarters and Archaeological Park is situated in the middle of a townhouse development with a majority of African American residents. Within this open-air park, visitors can see the restored foundations of the two quarters and consult interpretive signage.

At Northampton, the Archaeology Office attempted to create a collaboration among staff, historians, descendants, and local residents, but shifting priorities, turnover among homeowners, and the aging of the descendant community left the park without a clear interpretive path. We have recently worked with the Lake Arbor Homeowners Association to reactivate the site and promote its history through an engaging program featuring a Frederick Douglass reenactor who recited his speech "What to the Slave is the Fourth of July?" We have also renewed connections with younger descendants interested in family history. Scholars have noted that this type of engagement cycle is the best chance at keeping parks usable and relevant for years to come, and the changes at Northampton demonstrate the importance of recognizing dynamic community needs and interests.[4]

The seventy-six-acre Mount Calvert Museum and Historic Site possesses one of the most important archaeological sites in Prince George's County.[5] The park overlooks the Patuxent River from a prominent bluff in the middle of the highly significant Jug Bay Complex, which contains more than seventy-five archaeological sites that have been occupied for at least thirteen thousand years.[6] Native people first established base camps near the end of the Pleistocene; by ca. 1100 BCE, they had evolved into major year-round settlements. European colonizers who arrived in the seventeenth century forced the Native people from their lands and eradicated much of this ancient and vibrant civilization. The settlers created a trading port at Mount Calvert and established Charles Town, the first seat of Prince George's County government, in 1696. Several ordinaries, shops, and dwellings were constructed, along with a jail, courthouse, and church, but the town moved in 1721. By the late eighteenth century, Mount Calvert morphed into a tobacco plantation, and hundreds of enslaved workers created a landscape that included the stately brick mansion that still stands on the bluff today. After the Civil War, the property changed hands several times, and twentieth-century owners reportedly allowed collectors to walk away with countless ar-

FIGURE 5.1.
A Frederick Douglass reenactor speaks before local residents at Northampton Slave Quarters and Archaeological Park, 2021. Photo by Stephanie T. Sperling.

tifacts recovered from the farm fields. This practice was halted in 1995 when the M-NCPPC acquired the property.[7]

Archaeologists initially focused their research on the colonial town but beginning in 2013 sought to learn more about the eighteenth- and nineteenth-century enslaved population.[8] The team combined results from a geophysical survey, surface collection, and a shovel test pit survey to pinpoint the location of the quarters where the enslaved people lived approximately six hundred feet from the main house.[9] Through a series of public excavations, staff worked to situate Mount Calvert "within the larger historical context of race relations leading to the county's present political climate," a point that has become increasingly significant as our nation continues to grapple with conversations on ethnic identity and social justice.[10]

The long-standing excavation model at Mount Calvert allowed participants of all ages to join archaeologists as they dug and screened the culturally rich plow zone, allowing countless people to experience a tangible connection to history at the "trowel's edge" and recovering an overwhelming number of artifacts.[11] In 2019 alone, we recovered well over twenty thousand artifacts during three public dig days and several school programs. As Greg Pierce has noted, successful dig programs often come at the cost of processing, researching, and analyzing the collection, but we have recently undertaken new initiatives to engage people in the archaeological process while maintaining the resource in a more responsible way.[12]

Staff began by implementing a series of public lab days, the first of which occurred during Black History Month in February 2020. This program was implemented with the DPR Black History Office and encouraged interaction with and conversations about artifacts from the quarters where Mount Calvert's nineteenth-century enslaved population lived. Several African American families with children aged eight and older participated, and as Stefanie Kowalczyk has pointed out, such programs provide hands-on opportunities to learn difficult histories and encourage critical thinking skills.[13] During our lab days, participants were encouraged to take on the role of archaeologist and determine objects' what, where, when, why, and how, using their knowledge and ideas to "derive meaning from an encounter with archaeology by relating it to their own lives, rather than whether it corresponds to current archaeological consensus," a process that creates a more personal and powerful connection.[14]

FIGURE 5.2. Participants process artifacts at an outdoor archaeology lab at Mount Calvert Historical and Archaeological Park, 2021. Photo by Stephanie T. Sperling.

Each of these outdoor events was filled to capacity. In addition, the Archaeology Office volunteer program has expanded to allow middle and high school students to obtain required service-learning hours by washing and processing artifacts. This initiative provided opportunities for conversations about difficult histories with the students, most of whom are Black and Brown.

Finally, staff implemented other programs that do not focus on excavation or artifact processing. Among them are interpretive walking tours of the property, Patuxent River kayak tours to explore Jug Bay Complex sites from the water, and educational programs featuring atlatl throwing, replica spear hafting, and games like Archaeology Detectives, where children discover modern objects and determine their use.

Programs at these four sites are designed to reach and entertain a broad audience whose members have demonstrated interest in archaeology and history. By engaging with and actively listening to Prince George's County residents, we are better able to preserve and interpret our archaeological and paleontological resources for future generations.

Internal and External Collaborations

Archaeology Office staff routinely support and collaborate with a wide assortment of internal and external colleagues. We engage with stakeholders to determine how our needs align and develop mutually beneficial programming. This type of cooperative ap-

FIGURE 5.3. Kayakers touring the Jug Bay Complex archaeological sites, including Mount Calvert, 2021. Photo by Stephanie T. Sperling.

proach has long been recognized as an effective means of making archaeology more relevant and understood as well as of expanding the message of preservation, protection, and stewardship of subsurface sites.[15]

DPR park managers are often tasked with stewardship of archaeological sites on their properties even though they lack the training needed to understand or appreciate the significance of these sites. Archaeology Office staff attempt to fill that void by creating partnerships and elevating important connections between natural and cultural resources. To that end, several initiatives to locate new archaeological sites have recently been launched with Patuxent River Park (PRP), an expansive nature park encompassing seventy-eight hundred acres of riverside marshes, fields, and forests that includes Mount Calvert. The PRP headquarters is situated on the Prince George's County side of the Jug Bay Complex, where a lack of survey and documentation meant that only three archaeological sites had been identified prior to 2019. In contrast, more than thirty-five sites had been recorded on the Anne Arundel County side of the river. The Archaeology Office, PRP, Anne Arundel County's Division of Cultural Resources, the Lost Towns Project (an Anne Arundel County–based nonprofit organization), and Washington College launched an effort to search for new sites on M-NCPPC property. The team surveyed nearly forty linear miles of Patuxent River bluffs and trails during 2019 and early 2020 and identified eighteen precontact and historic sites in PRP alone.[16] In addition, a shovel test pit survey was conducted on one of the most promising precontact sites in PRP as part of the Washington College field school. This survey provided an excellent opportunity for students to gain archaeological experience while supplying much-needed personnel to complete the undertaking. Currently, Archaeology Office and PRP staff are collaborating on outreach initiatives that include developing signage, hikes, paddles, and classes to highlight the Jug Bay Complex discoveries and expand archaeological interpretations of the region.

Recent excavations at the nearby and understudied Billingsley site also demonstrate the benefits of partnerships. Archaeology Office staff worked in cooperation with the Maryland Historical Trust and the Archeological Society of Maryland to hold the annual Tyler Bastian Field Session at the site in 2019 and 2021. The team was searching for evidence of the contact-period Mattaponi and Patuxent Indians who were recorded as living on the land in the late seventeenth century and were the last known Native residents in the Jug Bay Complex. Only traces of their settlements were recovered from the plow zone during the field sessions, but dozens of volunteers discovered an intact Late Archaic period component on the property: large storage pits, hearths, and thousands of artifacts.[17] This excavation provided a direct connection to local Native culture for modern Prince George's County residents, many of whom had never considered the tremendous significance and longevity of Indigenous people in the region.

These Jug Bay Complex undertakings demonstrate the need to connect with multiple stakeholders on public-facing projects. However, our responsibilities also include working on compliance projects when archaeological sites or cultural resources may be affected by development, maintenance or repair work, or restoration. Working with planners and developers, archaeology staff conduct desk audits in areas of potential effects, undertake pedestrian surveys, and monitor construction. If a job is too large for our office to handle, we recommend that an external consulting firm be hired. New sites identified through this compliance process include a Late Woodland–period base camp found during tree removal at the ca. 1928 Oxon Hill Manor and a mid-nineteenth-century well found while monitoring the installation of a new fiberoptic line at the ca. 1801 Riversdale House Museum. Although compliance work is not always evident or visible to the public, Archaeology Office staff use it to inform, educate, and change attitudes of "the public and government decision-makers on the value and contributions of archaeology."[18]

Artifacts recovered from these and other DPR properties are stored and curated at the Archaeology Office collections facility, which contains nearly a million objects. Our staff assists historic site managers with archaeological programming and recently delivered an unprocessed 1990s-era artifact collection to the Surratt House Museum to assist with its Inclusive Interpretation initiative. The museum is housed in the mid-nineteenth-century home of Mary Surratt, who was executed by the federal government for her role in the Lincoln assassination, but new managers and local residents have expressed interest in redirecting the traditional narrative to focus on the enslaved labor force at the property and in surrounding communities. Not only do the artifacts facilitate these conversations, but a series of hands-on public lab days has brought the added benefit of stabilizing the collection.

We use these and other collections extensively as a means of engagement and outreach. Archaeology Office staff bring artifacts, hands-on activities, and interpretive materials to large events and festivals offered by our DPR colleagues. War of 1812 artifacts provide evidence of British and American troops in Prince George's County for commemorations of the Battle of Bladensburg, while objects from the enslaved persons' quarters at Northampton are displayed at the Black History Office's Juneteenth celebration. The public is also invited to participate in crafts such as creating traditional clay marbles on Juneteenth and constructing Indigenous-style pinch pots at PRP's American Indian Festival. These events expose thousands of people to the rich history of Prince George's County; allow us to build relationships with residents, visitors, and park staff;

and provide "hands-on, experiential learning offered in the fun context of celebration."[19]

The Archaeology Office benefits from taking a collaborative approach in nearly every aspect of our work. By cultivating partnerships and developing allies, we engage with a wide variety of people to consistently demonstrate the value of archaeology. These audiences include Prince George's County residents seeking different types of educational opportunities and upper-level DPR staff who might otherwise question the involvement of cultural resource professionals during the development process. These efforts proved especially important during the COVID-19 pandemic, when much of our park system shifted to a virtual environment.

Public Programming in the Time of COVID-19

Many scholars have noted the benefits of engaging people in creative, accessible, and affordable ways.[20] While this idea has long been a cornerstone of the work undertaken by the Archaeology Office, the COVID-19 pandemic forced staff to find new methods for online engagement.

When the popular American Indian Festival was held virtually in 2020, our office was invited to produce a video highlighting significant aspects of the precontact Jug Bay Complex.[21] We utilized jargon-free language to demonstrate how archaeological discoveries contribute to a more vibrant picture of the Native people who lived along the Patuxent River for countless millennia. It was also important to acknowledge that nearly all the Jug Bay Complex excavations were conducted by white archaeologists, so a non-Native professional provided tactful and empathetic on-screen narration for the video. As Peter Young has suggested, presenting our work in easily digestible ways, telling a story, being authentic, and making ourselves present enables us to better engage our audiences in accessible and entertaining ways.[22] Available on the DPR YouTube page, the video has been viewed and shared hundreds of times.

Archaeology Office staff also participated in virtual camps hosted by the DPR during the summers of 2020 and 2021. Our office had not previously held summer camps, but staff were encouraged to produce remote learning experiences for the community. We actively engaged online with elementary school students, made time for movement breaks, held group discussions, and included hands-on components.

Prior to the camp, we provided parents with the craft materials needed for the projects—for example, glue sticks, crayons, and scissors needed to make replica spear points and bamboo sticks for a hafting exercise. Other activities included at-home scavenger hunts to understand context and online trivia games created with the Kahoot application. We also produced a video, "Archaeology and Stra-

FIGURE 5.4. Archaeology Office staff teaching virtual campers how to draw a replica projectile point, summer 2021.

tigraphy," to demonstrate the process of archaeology.[23] Several of these activities, games, and videos were subsequently adapted for in-person programming when it resumed.

Flexibility was a persistent theme during the COVID-19 pandemic. In September 2019, the Archaeology Office held our first Echoes of the Enslaved event at Mount Calvert. Echoes of the Enslaved was developed in partnership with the Slave Dwelling Project, a South Carolina–based nonprofit that advances awareness of the legacies of chattel slavery.[24] The organization's model of evening fireside conversation circles and overnight sleepovers encourages people to engage in hard discussions about difficult histories. Founder Joseph McGill routinely works with archaeologists to highlight powerful discoveries made from studying the material remains of the enslaved, and our inaugural event series featured evening conversation circles, an overnight campout, morning public excavations of the site where the enslaved people lived, and an off-site panel discussion about the legacies of slavery in Prince George's County. The response to these events was overwhelming, clearly demonstrating that local residents want to participate in frank and honest historical programming. More than one hundred people attended the conversation circles, and nearly seventy stayed for the campout, many with the local chapter of Outdoor Afro, "the nation's leading, cutting-edge network that celebrates and inspires Black connections and leadership in nature."[25]

Building on this success, we planned to host another Echoes of the Enslaved event at the M-NCPPC's Montpelier House Museum in September 2020. Montpelier was built ca. 1780 as a plantation for agriculture and iron production, and records indicate that the wealthy Snowden family enslaved hundreds of laborers to work at these endeavors. With the onset of the pandemic, we transitioned to an almost entirely virtual program. The team worked with DPR photographers to produce and distribute a short video featuring a tour of the historic house with an emphasis on archaeological findings and research on the enslaved. After debating how to hold meaningful conversation circles without an in-person audience, we hired a professional production company to film and livestream on Facebook two consecutive evenings of discussion featuring McGill and a guest in front of a campfire, with viewers encouraged to ask questions. The first night's conversation, "The Legacies of Enslavement," featured McGill and Marvin-Alonzo Greer, M-NCPPC's lead historical interpretation and community engagement officer. The second night, "The Legacies of Colonization," featured McGill and Rico Newman, an elder with the Piscataway-Conoy tribe. Nearly 125,000 people watched the livestreams, and the recordings on the DPR YouTube page have been viewed and shared hundreds of times.[26]

The collaborative approach for programming Echoes of the Enslaved continued in September 2021 at the M-NCPPC's Marietta House Museum. Marietta was once the home of U.S. Supreme Court justice Gabriel Duvall, his family, and the hundreds of individuals they enslaved. This time, the team selected a hybrid model for the two-day event to accommodate both a small live audience and those more comfortable within the virtual world. McGill, descendants of Prince George's County white enslavers and Black enslaved, and an Iraqi immigrant participated in a September 10 panel discussion that included the topics of healing processes, coping with trauma, divergent historical memories, and the implications of buildings eradicated from the landscape. The panel was both livestreamed and recorded, and when it ended, in-person attendees were invited to continue these conversations around campfires in the fields near the historic house. The following morning, the twentieth anniversary of the 9/11 attacks, the Washington Revels Jubilee Voices offered a stirring song and spoken-word performance that incorporated stories of the Marietta enslaved and those lost on September 11. The event concluded with a family-centered archaeology experience that included displays of never-before-seen Marietta artifacts and the

FIGURE 5.5. Echoes of the Enslaved 2021 was filmed and livestreamed from Montpelier House Museum.

opportunity for participants to help process portions of the site's collection.

Echoes of the Enslaved has become a M-NCPPC signature event and has elevated our exposure with upper management. It exemplifies our desire for thought-provoking programming about difficult histories in a majority-Black county and squarely demonstrates the importance of archaeology at each historic site. Taking an interdisciplinary and collaborative approach is a cornerstone of Echoes of the Enslaved, promoting the idea of public archaeology as a conversation between equals rather than a presentation by experts and bridging past and present through a critical archaeological lens.[27]

Conclusion

By developing and implementing innovative programs at the sites managed by the Archaeology Office, initiating and nurturing collaborations with internal and external stakeholders, and making room for flexibility in unsettled times, our staff consistently demonstrates the public benefits of archaeology. New initiatives are expanding our outreach and engagement as we encourage multiple stakeholders to develop the "ability to look at the world in different ways."[28] Following the model outlined by the National Park Service and the Center for Heritage Resource Studies, we seek to "Inform/educate park visitors how and what has been learned from archeological study; Provoke visitors to establish their own intellectual and emotional connections with archeological resources; and Inspire public awareness of and appreciation for cultural resources stewardship."[29] Our recent efforts help people of all backgrounds connect with and discover our shared and turbulent past in unique and tangible ways.

We continue to encourage "thinking beyond the artifacts" and seek to develop hikes and paddles for nature lovers, provide creative uses of the collections we curate, continue our open dialogues with park planners on compliance projects, and sustain healing discourse about the legacies of enslavement and colonization.[30] We make tremendous efforts to meet the needs of many audiences and recognize that "there is no single public and no single past" within an ever-changing environment.[31] The recent Archaeology Office initiatives permit ethical stewardship of Prince George's County archaeological resources while allowing space to evolve as circumstances, funding, and staffing change.

Notes

1. *Ethics in Professional Archaeology*, Society for American Archaeology, 1996, https://www.saa.org/career-practice/ethics-in-professional-archaeology.

2. Michael Lucas, "Applied Archaeology and the Construction of Place at Mount Calvert, Prince George's County, Maryland," in *Places in Mind: Public Archaeology as Applied Anthropology*, ed. Paul A. Shackel and Erve J. Chambers (London: Routledge, 2004), 119–36.

3. Kristin Marie Montaperto, "Public Archaeology and the Northampton Slave Quarters: Community Collaboration" (PhD diss., American University, 2012).

4. Elizabeth Bollwerk, Robert Connolly, and Carol McDavid, "Co-Creation and Public Archaeology," *Advances in Archaeological Practice* 3, no. 3 (2015), https://doi.org/10.7183/2326-3768.3.3.178.

5. Eugene L. Meyer, "State Buying Site of Old P.G. County Seat; After 3 Years of Negotiation, Md. Acquiring Mount Calvert," *Washington Post*, February 2, 1995, https://www.washingtonpost.com/archive/local/1995/02/02/state-buying-site-of-old-pg-county-seat/f5a93e77-55c0-4bc1-aec7-cd5b7ddaadd1/.

6. Stephanie Sperling, "The Pig Point Complex" (paper presented at the Society for American Archaeology Annual Meeting, Washington, D.C., 2018).

7. Lucas, "Applied Archaeology."

8. Michael Lucas, "Negotiating Public Landscapes: History, Archaeology, and the Material Culture of Colonial Chesapeake Towns, 1680 to 1720" (PhD diss., University of Maryland, 2008); Michael Lucas, "Charles Town: The Anatomy of a Public Place in

Early Tidewater Maryland," in *The Archaeology of Colonial Maryland: Five Essays by Scholars of the Early Province*, ed. Matthew D. McKnight (Crownsville: Maryland Historical Trust Press, 2019), 114–30.

9. T. J. Horsley, *Mount Calvert (18PR6), Prince George's County, Maryland: Report on Geophysical Surveys, March & October 2013* (Riverdale, Md.: M-NCPPC, Prince George's County Department of Parks and Recreation, 2014).

10. Lucas, "Applied Archaeology," 130.

11. Laurie E. Miroff and Nina M. Versaggi, "Community Archaeology at the Trowel's Edge," *Advances in Archaeological Practice* 8, no. 4 (2020), doi:10.1017/aap.2020.28.

12. Greg Pierce, "Integrating Research, Outreach, and Education at the Gipson Site," *AP: Online Journal in Public Archaeology* 7 (2017): 54, https://doi.org/10.23914/ap.v7i0.139.

13. Stefanie Kowalczyk, "Excavating the 'Who' and 'Why' of Participation in a Public Archaeology Project," *Advances in Archaeological Practice*, 4, no. 4 (2016): 454–64, https://doi.org/10.7183/2326-3768.4.4.454.

14. Nick Merriman, "Introduction: Diversity and Dissonance in Public Archaeology," in *Public Archaeology*, ed. Nick Merriman (New York: Routledge, 2004), 11.

15. Paul Belford, "Sustainability in Community Archaeology," *AP: Online Journal in Public Archaeology* 1 (2014): 21–44, https://doi.org/10.23914/ap.v4i2.58; Montaperto, "Public Archaeology"; Vergil E. Noble, "Making Connections: Beyond the Confines of Compliance," *Historical Archaeology* 41, no. 2 (2007): 67–71, https://doi.org/10.1007/bf03377007; Margaret Purser, "What This Place Needs Is a Few More Cats," *Historical Archaeology* 41, no. 2 (2007): 62–66, https://doi.org/10.1007/bf03377006.

16. Amelia Chisholm, Stephanie Sperling, Shawn Sharpe, Andrew Webster, Marc Morris, and Patricia Melville, *Archaeological Survey and Evaluation of the Jug Bay Prehistoric Complex* (Crownsville: Maryland Historical Trust, 2019–20).

17. Amanda Gaster, Matthew D. McKnight, Stephanie T. Sperling, Amanda Melton, Celia Engel, W. B. Arnold, and Jeanne A. Ward, *Report on the 2019 Tyler Bastian Field Session in Maryland Archaeology at the Billingsley Site (18PR9)* (Crownsville: Archeological Society of Maryland, 2020); Amanda Melton, *Report on the 2021 Tyler Bastian Field Session in Maryland Archaeology at the Billingsley Site (18PR9)* (Crownsville: Archeological Society of Maryland, 2022).

18. Terry H. Klein, Lynne Goldstein, Deborah Gangloff, William B. Lees, Krysta Ryzewski, Bonnie W. Styles, and Alice P. Wright, "The Future of American Archaeology: Engage the Voting Public or Kiss Your Research Goodbye!," *Advances in Archaeological Practice* 6, no. 1 (2018): 2, https://doi.org/10.1017/aap.2017.34.

19. Eliza Grames and Mary Vitcenda, *Community Festivals—Big Benefits, but Risks, Too*, University of Minnesota Extension, 2012, https://extension.umn.edu/vital-connections/community-festivals-big-benefits-risks-too.

20. Wendy Ashmore, Dorothy T. Lippert, Barbara J. Mills, Mitchell Allen, and Rosemary A. Joyce, "Communicating Archaeology in the 21st Century," in *Voices in American Archaeology* (Washington, D.C.: Society for American Archaeology, 2010), 270–90; Klein et al. "Future of American Archaeology"; William B. Lees and Julia A. King, "Response to Comments by Little, Noble, and Purser," *Historical Archaeology* 41, no. 2 (2007): 80–83, https://doi.org/10.1007/bf03377009; Carol McDavid, "Towards a More

Democratic Archaeology? The Internet and Public Archaeological Practice," in *Public Archaeology*, ed. Merriman, 159–87; Montaperto, "Public Archaeology."

21. "Discovering Archaeological Sites along the Patuxent River with Stephanie Sperling," YouTube, December 17, 2020, https://youtu.be/kt2LtSh97Sw.

22. Peter Young, "The Archaeologist as Storyteller: How to Get the Public to Care about What You Do," *SAA Archaeological Record* 3, no. 1 (2003): 7–10.

23. Stephanie Sperling, "Archaeology & Stratigraphy," YouTube, November 12, 2020, https://youtu.be/PkhRq4MsQBw.

24. Tony Horwitz, *One Man's Epic Quest to Visit Every Former Slave Dwelling in the United States*, Smithsonian.com, October 1, 2013. https://www.smithsonianmag.com/history/one-mans-epic-quest-to-visit-every-former-slave-dwelling-in-the-united-states-12080/.

25. "Closing the Nature Gap—Our Mission—Outdoor Afro," Outdoor Afro, January 25, 2023, https://outdoorafro.org/our-mission/.

26. "Echoes of the Enslaved," YouTube, 2020, https://youtube.com/playlist?list=PLdO4Q48mn1MXFJhAUa8VKiRcgxMnDOOys.

27. Elizabeth Bollwerk, Robert Connolly, and Carol McDavid, "Co-creation and Public Archaeology," *Advances in Archaeological Practice* 3, no. 3 (2015): 178–87, https://doi.org/10.7183/2326-3768.3.3.178; McDavid, "Towards a More Democratic Archaeology?"; Montaperto, "Public Archaeology"; Michael P. Roller, Amanda Tang, Jocelyn E. Knauf, and Mark P. Leone, "Critical Theory in Archaeology," in *Encyclopedia of Global Archaeology*, 2nd ed. (Cham, Switz.: Springer, 2020), 2802–9.

28. Paul Belford, "Sustainability in Community Archaeology," *AP: Online Journal in Public Archaeology* 1 (2014): 40, https://doi.org/10.23914/ap.v4i2.58.

29. *An Inspiring Guide: Effective Interpretation of Archeological Resources, a Four-Part Program for Archeologists and Interpreters*, National Park Service and Center for Heritage Resource Studies, 2004, http://www.heritage.umd.edu/CHRSWeb/nps/guideweb/guidehome.htm.

30. Miroff and Versaggi, "Community Archaeology," 404.

31. Barbara J. Little, "Archaeology as a Shared Vision," in *Public Benefits of Archaeology*, ed. Barbara J. Little (Gainesville: University Press of Florida, 2002), 7.

Public Archaeology over the Long Haul
Education at the Fairfield Plantation Site, Virginia

DAVID BROWN, JESSICA TAYLOR,
ASHLEY MCCUISTION, AND THANE HARPOLE

For more than twenty years, the Fairfield Foundation, an archaeology nonprofit, has built and maintained relationships with students, schoolteachers, summer camps, local businesses, and descendant communities across Virginia's Middle Peninsula and the surrounding region. Founders and codirectors David Brown and Thane Harpole structured the organization with community engagement as a core objective. The Fairfield Plantation archaeological site in Gloucester County provided the opportunity to develop this objective. As an organization using archaeology to confront the complex history of a rural southern community, the foundation built a network of local collaborators and allies committed to interpreting all aspects of the region's past. Building long-term public archaeology programming and place-based collaboration and learning constitutes more than just community service: it is an integral and consistent component of the intellectual and social life for this eastern Virginia community.

This chapter highlights the benefits of place-based archaeology education for K–12 educators and students in high school, college, and graduate school. It also discusses how the Fairfield Foundation engages members of these groups in the study and preservation of local history through active participation in archaeological projects. The Fairfield archaeology site's public programming emphasizes Indigenous cultures, colonization, slavery, and African American life after emancipation, overlapping topics that are integral to eastern Virginia's history and many of which lie at the root of contemporary inequities. The results of a survey of interns and teachers demonstrate how participants in Fairfield Foundation's public programs have used their historical understanding, experience, and long-term contact with the organization to benefit their communities and to pursue careers in education, archaeology, history, and public service. This study found that long-term development of program participants as professionals and citizens relies on playing an individualized role in this programming. These two results of longevity and place-based learning are interre-

FIGURE 6.1.
The Fairfield archaeology site with the York River in the background. Courtesy of Fairfield Foundation.

lated. Young professionals dedicated to cultivating relationships across diverse interests found success through consistent engagement in archaeology grounded in community needs.

Archaeologists increasingly describe public engagement as an expectation of both contract and academic archaeological research.[1] Collaboration through public archaeology ensures that professionals, contractors, community organizations, local residents, and other interested members of the public influence or lead the interpretation of local history. When successful, public archaeology can encourage individuals from these groups to collaborate on truthful stories about the past and correct injustices.[2] Proactive approaches encourage curriculum designers and educators to integrate public archaeological research. Involvement in public archaeology programs—whether in the field or in the classroom—builds skills in public engagement, leadership, and critical dialogue. It encourages reflection on the historical roots of contemporary social injustices and deepens understanding of history for students as early as kindergarten.[3] This understanding is further developed when archaeo-

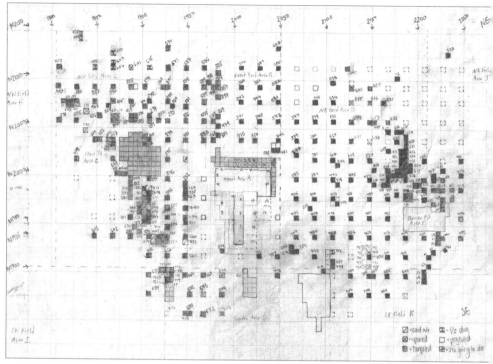

FIGURE 6.2.
Excavation units in the area immediately surrounding Fairfield's ca. 1694 manor house, most of which were excavated with volunteers as part of our public outreach programs. Courtesy of Fairfield Foundation.

logical concepts are integrated into subsequent grade levels through place-based and project-based learning initiatives.[4] Social ties and connections with place deepen when students understand how their communities' heritage shapes their surroundings and perpetuates unresolved inequality, directly informing their positions as researchers, citizens, and heritage stewards.[5]

While successful public archaeology initiatives exist across the country, not all participants have the opportunity to connect with a network of professionals and community members who add value to the experience. Participant engagement is also typically restricted to a short period, limiting opportunities for participants to learn from, collaborate with, and grow with the schools or community organizations that lead these projects. While attending the College of William and Mary (W&M), Harpole and Brown found that few students in the archaeology program had any prior practical experience in the field, and opportunities to gain experience relied on students' ability to dedicate signifi-

FIGURE 6.3. Fairfield's ca. 1694 manor house, 1890s. Courtesy of Virginia Museum of History and Culture.

cant time and resources beyond the classroom. As Harpole and Brown pursued their careers, they became dedicated to making archaeology more accessible to anyone with an interest, establishing the Fairfield Foundation with that principle at its core.

At first glance, the Fairfield archaeological site is a nondescript agricultural field tucked between small housing developments and a Tidewater creek, but its history makes it an ideal site for an education-focused archaeology organization. The property was occupied for long periods from the Archaic period through the early twentieth century, and at its center are the ruins of a massive colonial manor house. The ca. 1694 Fairfield manor, constructed substantially by enslaved Africans, housed multiple generations of the affluent Burwell family. It changed hands several times after the American Revolution and was converted to housing for Black tenants following the Civil War before burning in 1897. Six photographs of the building before the fire indicate the plantation's architectural significance, and its design marks an architectural transition that is of interest to scholars of Chesapeake archaeology and of southern history. Still, the property's historic owners and the enslaved Africans and African Americans who lived and worked there remained largely unknown prior to the Fairfield Foundation's work.

The opportunity was clear: the Fairfield property could both inform our understanding of the most-often-studied aspects of our shared heritage and highlight underrepresented groups and stories in history, connecting people with names, faces, and items in their hands. The site is treated as an outdoor classroom where anyone can excavate alongside professional archaeologists. The Fairfield Foundation collaborates with public and private schools across Virginia, nonprofit organizations, universities, and historical societies to bring these experiences to a broad range of participants.

One of these collaborations, the Fairfield Foundation internship program, serves as a cornerstone for continuing engagement with students. The initial class started work during 2001 with eight interns from W&M and Gloucester High School. Two high school juniors shadowed the codirectors and staff archaeologists. Four high school seniors designed their own projects, which included conducting research on the layout of the eighteenth-century enclosed gardens and Fairfield's surviving architectural fabric, and creating lesson plans for teaching archaeological methods in fourth-grade classrooms. Two W&M undergraduates focused on training to become archaeological field technicians. The codirectors worked with students to craft their internships, focusing on their individual interests and needs and meeting weekly. The internships culminated in public presentations to a community audience of parents, friends, neighbors, and fans of history. This effort marked Fairfield's initial foray into community-focused outreach.

Subsequent years saw the internship program expand and contract as the Fairfield site became a classroom and laboratory. The program averaged eight interns each year. The majority came through W&M's National Institute for American History and Democracy's Pre-College Program in American History. Participants in that program experience a two- to four-hour "dig day," which often constitutes their first opportunity to participate in hands-on archaeology. Many participants have returned for subsequent summers, enrolling in one-, two-, or three-week residential internships focusing primarily on fieldwork. Students work alongside staff to engage visitors, teach new volunteers, and conduct original research. Staff emphasized a "see one, do one, teach one" approach within a professionally supervised environment, working in contexts suitable for hands-on activities with untrained volunteers. Interns not only gain valuable personal experience but also contribute to legitimate archaeological research.

During the program's first decade, most interns chose to shadow professional archaeologists, but a significant minority pursued research projects or learned other skills such as nonprofit management and fundraising. In addition to the summer programs, some interns participated in structured programs offered through their universities during the semester. In 2011, the Fairfield Foundation teamed up with Colorado-based Adventures in Preservation, which offered marketing, models, and support for weeklong preservation experiences for all ages. After offering workshops for students and teachers on architectural restoration in 2010 and 2011, the Fairfield Foundation developed weeklong programs in which participants used new technologies to document archaeological deposits while learning traditional architectural conservation methods. In addition, teachers collaborated on weeklong summer institutes, field trips, and in-class experiences during the school year, eventually adding presentations to schools on archaeology, African American history, and historic preservation. Today, interns ranging in age from teenagers to senior citizens receive and deliver on-site education year-round. They also apprise community members of new interpretations and finds, innovative projects, and changing programs. In 2019, for example, the Fairfield Foundation worked with each of Gloucester County's public and private K–12 schools to provide hands-on archaeology programs, reaching more than twenty-one hundred students.

Teachers and students, mostly from regional public schools and W&M, provided a tangible link between the community and the academy. Staff encouraged students to engage with local residents and institutions as practitioners. Research projects involving writing , repointing bricks, flying drones, 3D printing, recording oral histories, and blogging reflected decades of the broadening definitions of public and community-oriented archaeology. Practitioners note that these experiences promise to create not only community leaders but also bonds between archaeologists and community organizations. Archaeologists also note the tendency to privilege the student experience and the creation of advocates for the field rather than to ask how communities might benefit from or inform place-based education in their schools.[6]

In 2021, we conducted a program assessment survey of teachers and former interns. The survey was publicized via social media, Fairfield Foundation listserv emails, and personal communications. After the survey was completed, individual former interns of varying ages and occupations were asked to complete a ten- to fifteen-minute interview about their career paths and Fairfield programs.[7] About half of our former interns (74 of 150) and 16 teachers answered questions about how working with the Fairfield Foundation influenced their careers, perspectives on history, and orientation toward social justice and leadership. The questions covered community involvement and leadership, professionalization, and ongoing interest in local and national history. The results demonstrate an increased appreciation for American and local history and for the research skills often associated with historians and archaeologists. Regardless of career path or current geographic location, respondents reported increased engagement in conversations about history and involvement in historical organizations and sites. Staff also interviewed six former interns and a current teacher in Gloucester County, revealing how maintaining long-term place-based educational programming contributed to their professional development and career trajectories.

Building Long-Term Relationships as Future Archaeologists

Sierra interviewed with us virtually, from a department lounge in her graduate program's academic building, with shelves of archaeology journals packed to the ceiling. Spending a day digging and screening artifacts alongside other high school students showed her how archaeology creates more inclusive histories: the eighteenth-century site where she worked "doesn't have a history like other plantations and locations in the area, where someone famous lived there, something monumental happened," But instead it provided a glimpse of history divergent from "studying the most famous or the most important." Sierra returned as a college intern and learned from engagement with other interns, talking with the public, and sifting through courthouse records. As a graduate student, Sierra was examining archaeobotanical remains from slave plantation sites across eastern Virginia, including some from Fairfield Plantation. She is one of several students whose relationships with Fairfield and Gloucester County have spanned multiple degrees and projects, moving from student of to collaborator with Fairfield's archaeologists.

While several interns reported that their internship taught them that they did not want to become archaeologists, others found the environment crucial for their professional development. More than thirty former interns mentioned interactions with longtime staff as integral to their education or to their experiences on-site. Specifically, students cited mentorship, intellectual and emotional support during difficult projects, and friendships or collaborations with staff that lasted beyond their internship. In some cases, these interactions resulted in professional connections as students entered careers in archaeology, museums, or government offices. Five respondents explicitly mentioned that their time at Fairfield increased their confidence in their ability to complete research and engage the public. One local K–12 student who later became an intern remembered that a staff archaeologist "sat me down next to someone who showed me how to wash" artifacts. Previously, "I don't think I'd ever really gotten to do something in the community outside of church, school, or camp. Any experience after that with Fairfield—school trips, volunteer nights, . . . interning, etc.—felt like contributing to a community that was raising me at the same time. Fairfield had/has my back, and I'm 100 percent behind them." Similarly, staff understand that the organization depends on engagement and communicating how archaeology can make vital contributions to participants' intellectual enrichment. This mutuality challenges the interns to think about the relevance of their work and priorities and to help the organization adapt as research at the site develops.

Like Sierra, most interns held multiple positions at Fairfield, serving as volunteers, seasonal staff members, Adventures in Preservation participants, or collaborating teachers in educational roles. These experiences heightened awareness of local archaeology and deepened interest in further study. Fairfield internships exposed participants to opportunities provided by the foundation's collections and resources and the methodology and local historical context needed to pursue careers in archaeology. As a result, Sierra developed a concrete research agenda and leveraged her roles within the Fairfield Foundation into a graduate-level thesis project. The combination of Fairfield Foundation's long-term investment in students and flexible programming for adults encourages students-turned-professionals to return to the organization in a capacity that works for them.

Beyond the Field

Another former intern, Chris, observed, "Sometimes little things contribute a lot more to your understanding than you would expect," referring to both archaeological research and data for clinical research trials. Chris completed a high school internship with Fairfield and two archaeology field schools while in college and is currently employed in implementing software and integrating data for oncology studies. He accepted a fellowship to return to the Fairfield Foundation to study Archaic-period Native American materials before joining as a staff member for several years. Like most former interns, Chris did not continue his professional career as an archaeologist, but he nevertheless remains engaged with the Fairfield Foundation and other community organizations. He retains a strong conviction that archaeology can build important skills and promote civic engagement as well as a lasting willingness to engage others in conversations about eastern Virginia and U.S. history.

Genevieve was an enthusiastic undergraduate student interested in research. As a geology major and a Fairfield intern, she examined the sandstone used to construct Menokin, an eighteenth-century plantation house on Virginia's Northern Neck. She noticed parallels between the study of rocks and the study of the past and gained skills that applied to both fields: "Research is the big one, asking questions, finding mentors." With Fairfield staff, Genevieve took part in a transcription project funded by another local organization that resulted in a publication, and she donated the proceeds from its sale to fund future student projects. After a stint as a business analyst and inspired by the transcription project, she returned to school for a master's degree in library science, inspired by that project. She looks forward to engaging more with community history as a graduate student: "I learned that people are important."

Lasting engagement with public archaeology benefits students and changes their perspectives. Most former interns believed that the skills of both archaeologists and historians are important beyond their respective fields, and 39 percent of respondents engaged more often in conversations about American history after their internship. Among those who reported an increase in conversations, 55 percent were not currently working in archaeology. All respondents felt that American history is important, and all but four felt that eastern Virginia's history was important. In sum, archaeological methods promote the importance of history and historical research and encourage students to engage in dialogue about it.

Having gained public engagement and research experience through their internships, respondents extolled the value of those skills and experiences. Many students mentioned that research skills—particularly writing, speaking, attention to detailed data, and critical thinking—were transferable. Twenty respondents discussed how their current work overlapped with archaeologists' and historians' skills overlapped with their current work, even when they were employed in such fields as medicine and therapy. Respondents also noted that enthusiasm for local history was transferrable to other fields: one intern drew on historical work for their legal practice; another delighted her coworkers and clients at a New Orleans real estate agency with architectural history. Wrote one person, "The tools I gained with my very few years in archaeology, e.g. appreciation and respect for other cultures, awareness of racial issues and the historical footprint of these, the impact of poverty, have all helped me be a better social worker to the people I serve." Similarly, those not in archaeology or related fields continued to value the building and maintenance of local community ties.

Regardless of their career paths, Fairfield's former interns see historic sites as crucial to exploring and telling new and diverse stories. Forty-seven respondents reported that their archaeological experience at Fairfield resulted in increased in-person and online visitation, volunteering, donation, and leadership at historical sites. This increased interest extended to small or understudied sites and was shared with their family and friends. According to a former intern who went on to work for the National Park Service, "Prior to my time at William & Mary, I had never heard of Fairfield but was familiar with sites such as Mount Vernon and Monticello. My experience at Fairfield has shown me that these lesser-known sites have just as interesting stories." In their work for the National Park Service, they "try and tell some of those lesser-known stories."

Place-based education and heritage studies encourage students to think critically about their stewardship and about their roles in perpetuating or disrupting systemic inequalities. Further, a small number of respondents foregrounded the role of archaeologists and historians in retelling the history of race in eastern Virginia and highlighted the centrality of race and other social and economic factors in contemporary inequities. One former student who had recently moved to Jackson Ward, a historically Black area of Richmond, Virginia, reported, "I have been incredibly interested in the recent efforts to preserve the history of the neighborhood in the face of gentrification, which I know I am also a part of." As another respondent stated succinctly, "I understand that I can be a participant in and not just a consumer of history and culture." Former interns had the confidence to engage with professionals and the narratives they promoted at other heritage sites. Interns better understood the justifications for the decisions those professionals made, how they communicated with the public, and the stakes of their relationships with residents and others involved.

Teachers Learning through Archaeology

Rhonda, a science and gifted resource teacher with Gloucester County Public Schools, began collaborating with the Fairfield Foundation in 2000 and has worked with the organization on numerous projects over the ensuing quarter century. She described archaeology as "the perfect marriage of history and science—it has elements of both." She felt that Fairfield's programs benefited her students by inspiring interest in history and introducing stories that they would never learn from history books. In her view, students who participate in Fairfield's programs develop a greater interest in history and preservation, and some became history teachers. She also noticed that Fairfield's approach to educational outreach has become more targeted over time and appreciated the importance of place-based learning, transcendent skills, and student-driven activities.

Fairfield Foundation's programs encourage students to actively guide the lesson by asking questions of the instructor, sharing their understanding of the material, and making interpretations about past cultures, events, and environments. Every lesson includes a hands-on component, thereby providing students with tactile and memorable connections to the information: for example, washing artifacts, measuring the bore diameter of tobacco pipe stem fragments to determine their age, or identifying stone tools created by Indigenous peoples who once inhabited the same area. This teaching method acknowledges that every student absorbs and processes information differently and adapts to those differences by giving students agency in how they learn. The Fairfield Foundation seeks to ensure that every participating student leaves with a thorough introduction to the subject and a better appreciation of local history.

In 2016, the foundation's new public outreach coordinator, Ashley McCuistion, expanded collaboration with educators across Virginia's Middle Peninsula and developed lesson plans aligned with the state's K–12 Standards of Learning, integrating archaeology and local history into class curricula while demonstrating how archaeologists use math, science, history, geography, and art to learn about the past. Employing place-based education principles, programs focus on local history, nearby historic buildings, and locally recovered artifacts.[8] This structure helps students develop personal connections to broader historical themes—slavery, colonialism, trade—across the state, country, and globe.

Since the expansion of the Fairfield Foundation's staff and debut of these new lesson plans, Fairfield archaeologists have established annual programs in every public and private school in Gloucester, Mathews, and Middlesex Counties and doubled the number of collaborating schools across the state. During that time, the number of students taught each year has grown by 65 percent, surpassing two thousand. The increase in demand for these programs speaks to their effectiveness in both educating students and adapting to the Virginia education system. Half of the programs presented each year are recurring, demonstrating strong support from both teachers and school administrators. Regular programs for different grade levels in the Fairfield Foundation's primary service area ensure that students participate in hands-on archaeology lessons at least every two years beginning in elementary school.

The responses to Fairfield Foundation's recent survey of teachers were over-

FIGURE 6.4. Senior staff archaeologist Anna Rhodes teaches a young volunteer to identify soil colors and textures, 2012. Courtesy of Fairfield Foundation.

whelmingly positive. Participants agreed that the programs benefited their curriculum, and 71 percent continued to use information presented during the program in their classes. Responses about the long-term benefits of Fairfield's programs varied: half the participants cited learning the value of local history as the greatest long-term benefit, while 43 percent suggested that the hands-on nature of the programs would make the most lasting impact. Other benefits noted included supporting standardized testing in a meaningful and relevant way and offering students cross-curricular activities with relevance beyond a single class. All but one of the teachers described place-based learning as "somewhat important" or "extremely important." According to Rhonda, the COVID-19 pandemic increased the importance of place-based learning, since the lockdown denied students opportunities to interact with their community members or environments. Through these programs, students discover new methods of thinking, career paths in history, and why history and historic preservation matter, especially in local contexts.

Conclusion

The Fairfield Foundation presents public archaeology as a long-term, community-focused opportunity and an essential element in studying the history of a place. It connects people with each other and the past and is clearly a benefit to students and their teachers from K–12 through early adulthood and beyond. Programs are constructed along a trajectory from childhood introductions to concepts and methodologies through sustained engagement on increasingly complex historical questions, leading to independent research and professional development. The programs offer a compelling case study in support of a consistent all-ages approach. By maintaining opportunities for teachers and students over multiple years and at several grade levels, the highest percentage of students benefit, regardless of whether they intend to pursue archaeology as a vocation.

The opinions of teachers and interns over two decades of public outreach revealed that these efforts resulted in consistent and potentially lifelong interest in history and archaeology. Students learned about people in the past, how to research those people and learn from their actions, and how to inspire others to do the same. Places played a prominent role, influencing the value of preserving locally significant and common sites in addition to better-known sites and acknowledging that both are important to our understanding of history. Interns and K–12 students are part of a model focused on long-term connectivity and often took this model to (and sometimes applied it within) their own communities.

Despite the success of the Fairfield Foundation's public archaeology program, there are of course areas that would benefit from improvement. The population of Virginia's Middle Peninsula is predominantly white, and most of the interns and other participants have been white. The Fairfield Foundation consequently has begun to expand programming into communities with higher percentages of people of color. Active recruitment efforts paired with consistent, long-term antiracist archaeology programs committed to these populations are necessary to bring a broader range of students into internships and the field in general. Dynamic public archaeology groups such as Archaeology in the Community have already brought sustained partnerships and programming to schools that serve communities of color.[9] Such programs are models that embrace an antiracist archaeology regardless of the school and population demographics. Public archaeology organizations that have a focus on mentorship, including the Fairfield Foundation, must acknowledge and work to dismantle systems of oppression, actively seek to reconstruct a system with an antiracist core, and collaborate with others who envision creating antiracist archaeologies that would both support our mentees and sustain their continued presence in the discipline.[10] With adequate scaffolding for training and space for student-driven research interests, the possibility of increasing the number of archaeologists of color and thereby increasing the number of diverse voices and overall representation in archaeology is a goal worth pursuing.[11]

If one goal of the program is producing community leaders and engaged citizens, our results are mixed. The internship program clearly inspires participants and helps them develop leadership skills but does not provide them with actual tools or guide them down the path to replicating the best elements of their experiences beyond the Fairfield Foundation's area of service. And while respondents mentioned their greater understanding of, interest in, awareness of, and appreciation for the importance of community engagement and leadership, they did not demonstrate a consistent investment in addressing community concerns. Continued and consistent support is needed so that internships do not just create models of community leadership but provide more opportunities to put these models into practice.

These dilemmas and their solutions are interconnected. If the intent is to provide an organizational example for how to work within and continue to build a community that learns from the past and inspires the future, it is crucial to represent the diversity toward which we aspire and to provide the training and support necessary to achieve these goals beyond our own community. We must make practical changes, such as opening boards and planning meetings to students, collaborating with community partners to devise new programs, and replacing existing programs with innovative ones that respond to changing demographics and interests.[12] In addition, we must institute mentorship opportunities that promote retention of archaeologists of color in a sometimes-hostile academic environment.[13] We must move beyond awareness of social inequality and persuade donors and grant organizations to invest beyond pilot programs into permanent staff.

These solutions require a long-term commitment that consistently demonstrates the essential nature of what we have to offer to a population that seldom sees archaeology as much more than a one-off event. Archaeology must be relevant both now and in the future and cannot depend on a singular defining moment like the discovery of a lost landmark or the recovery of an item of antiquity. Rather, archaeology must be an ongoing process—a perpetual opportunity and an ongoing dialogue within the community that represents our collective goals and aspires to something greater.

Notes

1. Carol McDavid and Terry Brock, "The Differing Forms of Public Archaeology: Where We Have Been, Where We Are Now, and Thoughts for the Future," in *Ethics and Archaeological Praxis*, ed. Cristóbal Gnecco and Dorothy Lippert (New York: Springer, 2015), 159–84.

2. Eleanor M. King, "African Americans, American Indians, and Heritage Education," in *History and Approaches to Heritage Studies*, ed. Phyllis Mauch Messenger and Susan J. Bender (Gainesville: University Press of Florida, 2019), 59–86; Barbara J. Little, "Archaeology and Civic Engagement," in *Archaeology as a Tool of Civic Engagement*, ed. Paul A. Shackel and Barbara J. Little (Lanham, Md.: AltaMira Press, 2007), 1–22.

3. Thomas J. Pluckhahn, "The Challenges of Curriculum Change and the Pedagogy of Public Archaeology and CRM at the University of South Florida," in *Pedagogy and Practice in Heritage Studies*, ed. Susan J. Bender and Phyllis M. Messenger (Gainesville: University Press of Florida, 2019), 72–93; Anne K. Pyburn, "Archaeology for a New Millennium: The Rules of Engagement," in *Archaeologists and Local Communities: Partners in Exploring the Past*, ed. Linda Derry and Maureen Mallory (Charlottesville, Va.: Society for American Archaeology, 2003), 167–84; Sonya Atalay, "Pedagogy of Decolonization: Advancing Archaeological Practice through Education," in *Collaborating at the Trowel's Edge: Teaching and Learning in Indigenous Archaeology*, ed. Stephen W. Silliman (Tucson: University of Arizona Press, 2008), 123–44; Scott A. McLaughlin, "Developing an Archaeology Service-Learning Course," in *Archaeology and Community Service Learning*, ed. Michael S. Nassaney and Mary Ann Levine (Gainesville: University Press of Florida, 2009), 59–78; Paul Shackel, foreword to *Pedagogy and Practice in Heritage Studies*, ed. Bender and Messenger, xi–xii; John L Cotter, "Archaeologists of the Future: High Schools Discover Archaeology," *Archaeology*, January–February 1979, 29–35; John L. Cotter, Daniel G. Roberts, and Michael Parrington, *The Buried Past: An Archaeological History of Philadelphia* (Philadelphia: University of Pennsylvania Press, 1992).

4. Carol Kramer, *Ethnoarchaeology: Implications of Ethnography for Archaeology* (New York: Columbia University Press, 1979); Patrice L. Jeppson and George Brauer, "Archae-

ology for Education Needs: An Archaeologist and an Educator Discuss Archaeology in the Baltimore Country Public Schools," in *Past Meets Present: Archaeologists Partnering with Museum Curators, Teachers, and Community Groups*, ed. John H. Jameson and Sherene Baugher (New York: Springer, 2007), 231–48.

5. Elizabeth C. Reetz, Chérie Haury-Artz, and Jay A. Gorsh, "Strengthening a Place-Based Curriculum through the Integration of Archaeology and Environmental Education," in *Public Engagement and Education: Developing and Fostering Stewardship for an Archaeological Future*, ed. Katherine M. Erdman (New York: Berghahn Books, 2019), 74–108.

6. McDavid and Brock, "Differing Forms of Public Archaeology."

7. This study was IRB exempt through Virginia Tech as a program evaluation.

8. Dominic G. Morais, "Doing History in the Undergraduate Classroom: Project-Based Learning and Student Benefits," *History Teacher* 52, no. 1 (2018): 49–76, https://www.jstor.org/stable/26646473; Somnath Sarkar and Richard Frazier, "Place-Based Investigations and Authentic Inquiry," *Science Teacher* 75, no. 2 (2008): 29–33.

9. Alexandra Jones and Sydney Pickens, "The Power of Community Archaeologists in Uncertain Times," *Journal of Community Archaeology & Heritage* 7, no. 3 (2020): 155–57, https://doi.org/10.1080/20518196.2020.1780051.

10. Ayana Omilade Flewellen, Justin P. Dunnavant, Alicia Odewale, Alexandra Jones, Tsione Wolde-Michael, Zoë Crossland, and Maria Franklin, "'The Future of Archaeology Is Antiracist': Archaeology in the Time of Black Lives Matter," *American Antiquity* 86, no. 2 (2021): 224–43, https://doi.org/10.1017/aaq.2021.18.

11. For more information, see *Striving towards Diversity*, Society for Historical Archaeology, Gender and Minority Affairs Committee, accessed August 2, 2024, https://sha.org/committees/gender-minority-affairs-committee/; *Promoting Academic Excellence and Social Responsibility: About the Society of Black Archaeologists*, Society of Black Anthropologists, accessed August 2, 2024, https://www.societyofblackarchaeologists.com/about.

12. Shannon Lee Dawdy, *Patina: A Profane Archaeology* (Chicago: University of Chicago Press, 2016).

13. Michael L. Blakey, "Archaeology under the Blinding Light of Race," *Current Anthropology* 61, no. s22 (2020): 183–97, https://doi.org/10.1086/710357; Flewellen et al., "Future of Archaeology Is Antiracist."

Putting the Washington Home Back on the Land and the Obstacles to Re-creating a Colonial Virginia Landscape

PHILIP LEVY AND DAVID MURACA

For most of the twentieth century, the land at Ferry Farm, George Washington's childhood home on the Rappahannock River, opposite Fredericksburg, Virginia, had little to impress visitors. Early in the century, the land's owner dusted off tales of hatchets and cherry trees to make a quick sightseer buck, but the working farm had no buildings still standing that dated to the 1740s, when young George walked the acres and dreamed of bigger things. Over time, here and there, a Washington story attached itself to a much-later farm building, but only the truly starstruck found the stories convincing. Most people knew the site was devoid of anything perceived as savable or valuable, and so for decades, despite a few failed preservation attempts, the land remained in private hands, its buildings leased to tenants and its story mostly overlooked.[1]

That changed in 1996, when Walmart announced plans to build a new shopping center on the land where Washington had grown up. A national movement opposed Walmart's plans, and local preservation advocates saved the land from future development. More than anything, though, what saved Ferry Farm was the intersection of Washington's famous name and the promise of archaeology. Even in the absence of surviving Washington-era materials aboveground, a few small-scale excavations had already shown that a significant site existed just below the grass.

More than two decades later, visitors to Ferry Farm can see, enter, and engage with a full-scale interpretive structure that reconstitutes the old Washington home. Completed in 2018, this building was a project of the George Washington Foundation, which owns and curates the property. The new home sits structurally suspended just above the protected subterranean remains of the original and reflects years of archaeological and architectural study at both the site and regional levels. The home is a one-to-one-scale wood, brick, stone, and plaster presentation of evidence. An archaeologically recovered home could be presented to the public through textual description, an artist's

FIGURE 7.1. The archeologically informed rebuild of the Washington home created a stage on which to interpret the eighteenth century and the processes involved in putting a home back on the landscape. Courtesy of Philip Levy.

rendering, or a computer-generated image. At Ferry Farm, those findings are presented in the form of a full-sized rebuild.

Despite the quantity and quality of the evidence that went into creating the structure, building it was no easy feat. The technical side was hard enough. Working out the details of how to move heavy machinery onto vulnerable historical sites, engineering construction so that it did no damage to archaeological features, and locating craftspeople with the correct-to-the-period skills needed takes time and effort, as does obtaining funding. But this chapter explores the less tangible obstacles to rebuilding. Segments of the preservation world have a long-standing hostility to historical reconstructions that remains rather influential. This view is counterproductive and very much out of step with the current level of research that goes into most reconstructions. This hostility also robs archaeology of one of its most effective and engaging ways to present a site's architectural findings. The lingering prejudice against rebuilding does not take into consideration the reality of what historical buildings and landscapes face in an era of rapid-swing climate change. Ferry Farm went from an empty field to the site of an extensive excavation to a full-scale interpretive platform. Recounting what went into taking the rebuilt Washington home from idea to reality shows the state of the reconstruction field, the background to this work, and why, now more than ever, preservationists of all stripes must embrace rebuilding. Reviewing how rebuilding itself has changed over the years offers a long-needed contextual reset for similar projects.

During the planning stages of the rebuild, an attendee at a public talk on the project asked, "Why rebuild at all? What if you get it wrong?" These questions have troubled some preservationists for well over a century. In the middle of the nineteenth century, French art critic and archaeologist Adolphe Napoléon Didron laid out a hierarchy for acts of preservation: "It is better to consolidate than repair, better to repair than restore, better to restore than to reconstruct."[2] For Didron, reconstruction sat at the bottom of the list because it was so fraught with opportunities for error, misrepresentation, and deception. In 1883, that fear led Italian architect Camillo Boito to outline a set of reconstruction principles intended to impose some rigor on the era's rampant and often quite fanciful restoration projects.[3] Boito's framework influenced the 1964 International Charter on the Conservation and Restoration of Monuments and Sites (the Venice Charter), which stipulated that "all reconstruction work" should be "ruled out 'a priori.'"[4] Mexico was the only non-European nation to sign the charter, and it focused only secondarily on architecture. Despite those limitations, there is no sidestepping the fact that serious preservationists looked down on reconstruction.

The fear that a rebuild might blur into forgery or that conjecture would lead to deception has shaken American preservation circles as well. Despite calling rebuilding a "respectable tradition," Calder Loth, former senior architectural historian for the Virginia Department of Historic Resources, lamented that "the reconstruction of destroyed historic and architectural landmarks has long been considered as something less than serious architectural expression."[5] The National Park Service (NPS) rules governing reconstruction projects do not outright preclude reconstruction, as the Venice Charter did, but nevertheless reflect the apprehension regarding conjecture or error to which Loth referred. In the late 1930s, many in the NPS saw "so called restoration" as a "curse" that would inevitably succumb to an "almost irresistible urge to gild the lily."[6] Over time, the NPS reconstruction criteria have softened somewhat, but they still hold rebuilds at arm's length, deeming reconstruction suitable only when "documentary and physical evidence is available to permit accurate reconstruction with minimal conjecture" and when "such reconstruction is essential to the public understanding of the property."[7] A project can move ahead only when following these rules, the NPS has produced many excellent historical reconstructions, including numerous forts, the soldiers' huts at Valley Forge in Pennsylvania, and the Thomas Stone House in Maryland.[8] But the rules do not specify who gets to define *essential* or which public's understandings are privileged. The guidelines also look down on "conjectural designs" or "the availability of different features from other historic properties."[9] While the former is perfectly reasonable, the latter is a bit of catch-22. Informed comparison with surviving or well-documented regional examples is a central part of bringing a lost building from excavation to construction. Denying the legitimacy of comparison at the outset effectively hobbles most archaeologically informed rebuilds. The guidelines also presuppose that rebuilders would be interested primarily in elite or high-style formal architecture, in which each building is (to some extent) its own unique statement. The room for deceptive error there is large. But for more mundane vernacular buildings of the nonelite, the poor, the enslaved, and other previously marginalized people, comparison is invaluable since so many plain buildings and simple homes strongly resembled those of their neighborhoods. A prejudice against informed comparison risks silencing both archaeology and the under-represented people who now often stand at the center of research agendas.

The NPS rules do stem from real experience, some of which hit unnervingly close to home for Ferry Farm. Many preservationists' cold feet regarding re-building were chilled by earlier mistakes—a few high-profile poorly executed examples. And unfortunately for Ferry Farm, one of the most problematic of these projects was also associated with George Washington.

The 1920s and 1930s were the height of what has come to be called the Co-lonial Revival, a romanticized pastiche reinvention of colonial-era styles riding on an industrial age's ability to mass produce and a growing media industries' abilities to influence. The trend was particularly popular among what one of its historians has called "the middle and upper-middle classes."[10] Colonial Revival might take the form of a newly built symmetrical Georgian-style home and ga-rage set on a suburban street or might show itself as a colonial-themed gala in which celebrants put on big wigs and long coats to do country dances and drink punch. Colonial Revival was anywhere Americans invoked the Founding Fa-thers or the revolutionary era with a nostalgic sense of charming lost innocence and much-missed gentility. This spirit crept into many endeavors, but "architec-ture," as William Butler wrote, "was the most effective material manifestation of the Colonial Revival."[11] David Gebhard has argued that a new appreciation for rapidly vanishing colonial-era buildings in the early 1900s gave architects a new appreciation for the old homes. That enthusiasm led architect Ralph S. Fanning to claim as early as 1916 that "this country may almost be said to be undergoing a colonial revival."[12]

Colonial Revival has consistently been something of an object of derision. In its heyday, the movement's detractors thought it ridiculous that one might "park his 1931 Buick in the replica of a Colonial stable" or that there could be a "Georgian country house on Madison Avenue."[13] Other critics simply wished to see Colonial Revival "dead and buried," replaced by something sleeker and more modern.[14] Scholars have seen the revival not necessarily as ridiculous but nevertheless as essentially a dilatory exercise in nostalgia that produced a mis-matched jumble of elements clumsily strung together as practitioners "misread the intentions and realities" of their colonial-era subjects.[15] But a lot of those

FIGURE 7.2. The Memorial House at the George Washington Birthplace National Monument (NPS) is a beautiful if fanciful Colonial Revival home. Its majesty though was more a tribute to Washington than an attempt to understand and interpret the eighteenth century. Courtesy of Philip Levy.

misreads occurred, and they went a long way toward giving reconstruction a bad name in American preservation circles. Preservationists worried that enthusiasm would overtake evidence and lead efforts down what Ivor Noël Hume called "the slippery path of speculation towards the netherworld of fantasy."[16]

A visitor to this netherworld would quickly encounter the George Washington Memorial House, completed in 1931, at the first president's birthplace on Popes Creek off the Potomac River in Westmoreland County, Virginia. This fanciful brick colonial-style home was meant to be a grand tribute to Washington. But in designing it, the commemorators of the Wakefield National Memorial Association (WNMA) relied heavily on Colonial Revival sentimentality instead of evidence, ultimately building an impressive beefed-up copy of the ancestral home of one of the project's main backers.[17] Despite its elegance and style, the house had little to do with what might have stood on the land when Washington was born. The NPS, which manages the site, has spent decades correcting the record and keeping visitors from confusing the tribute with the long-lost original. And the problems of the house caused the NPS and others in the region to take a negative view of rebuilding as a whole rather than of the WNMA's flawed approach and research.

The Memorial House's shadow has reached forty miles up Virginia's Northern Neck to Ferry Farm. Washington's Popes Creek birthplace had already long been confused with his childhood home. The Washingtons left Popes Creek when George was only about two years old, moving first up the Potomac and then over to Ferry Farm on the Rappahannock, and the stories of the three places understandably became blurred and conflated. As early as 1777, visitors to Fredericksburg believed that Washington had been born there. In his much-read 1807 *Life of Washington*, Mason Locke "Parson" Weems noted that early pilgrims to Washington's home were still making the same error. Nineteenth-century artists and lithographers confused the matter further by creating a lineage of images that placed a drawing of a simplified and rather rustic-looking imagined Ferry Farm home on the Popes Creek landscape. Biographers did no better. In the 1920s, the WNMA and project historian Charles Arthur Hoppin, in particular battled the humble-home image made popular by purveyors of commercial art such as Benson Lossing and Currier and Ives. Hoppin saw the drawn home as far too small and crude to have been the birthplace of one so vaunted.[18] Even in 2008, the link between the two sites and the enduring stain of the Memorial House lingered. The public announcement of archaeological finds at Ferry Farm and the plan to rebuild based on those finds touched old nerves for some Didron-inspired preservationists. One of these critics wondered whether a rebuilt Washington home was "really the best way to interpret" the site's story (while offering no viable alternative) and urged using the WNMA's "clumsy handling" of its project as a caution.[19] As Didron himself might have said, *plus ça change*.

But a neo-Didronian outlook does not take into account the dramatic changes that have occurred on rebuilding scene since the beginning of the twentieth century and especially since the turn of the twenty-first. Nor does this hostility take into account the scale and quality of the information about the colonial era that archaeologists and architectural historians have amassed over that time. Ironically, hostility to rebuilding has in its way helped forward these improvements. It has proved itself a valuable nemesis by forcing advocates of rebuilding to make sure their game was in top form to calm the naysayers. What has emerged—particularly over the past four decades or so in the greater Chesapeake region—is something of a unified approach. The projects of this New School (to borrow a term from art history) of rebuilding rely on similar methods and datasets and frequently even the same craftspeople and scholars. Their work also often rests on shared research concerns and frameworks, which have been very powerfully shaped by anthropology's and social and cultural history's concern with revealing the lives of marginalized people too easily overlooked and certainly not made central in Colonial Revival construction. The work of the WNMA and many Colonial Revivalists was self-consciously meant to create shrines to the past. The New School, though, moves outward from a very different starting point. Just as museum planners and interpretive staff at long-established shrines such as Mount Vernon and Monticello have retooled their exhibits and programs to bring the lives of the enslaved into focus, New School rebuilders in Virginia and Maryland have put similar interests at the center of those projects to create spaces that can convey a number of historical stories.

The new approach did not develop overnight. Many important sites pushed the envelope and improved methods to help build the model at work today. Among the standout projects are St. Mary's City, in Maryland, one of the first regional museum environments to rebuild in this new way. A wide range of approaches remain visible across the site, from a Colonial Revival–era brick rebuilt courthouse to a newly reconstructed Catholic church. Rebuilds such as Van Sweringen's Inn, Smith's Ordinary, and the Print House all represent projects in which archaeology took the lead in determining not just where rebuilds would sit but much of how they would look aboveground as well. The regional database of sites has increased considerably since these buildings' excavation and construction; thus, some of the assumptions built into the rebuilds might not stand the test of time. But all of these sites stand out for their willingness to follow the archaeology no matter where it led. If the reconstructions at St. Mary's City were archaeology-centric projects, then the Godiah Spray Tobacco Plantation could be called a project of the social historians. Spray is a fully imaginary re-created seventeenth-century homestead and garden heavily based on the work of Chesapeake School social historians. It is rather like a three-dimensional representation of Lois Green Carr, Russell R. Menard, and Lorena S. Walsh's book, *Robert Cole's World*, set away from the core of town so that it is not mistaken as either original or representing an actual archaeological site.[20] Interpreters plant crops and do other chores while chatting with visitors in a setting filled the clutter of daily life and wandering chickens. Interpretation of plantation life and material culture at Godiah Spray Tobacco Plantation draws on archaeological and documentary findings but also makes clear that nothing there is on a specific site—even the name *Godiah Spray* is fictional. The result is a useful and engaging life-sized gritty interpretive platform.[21]

The St. John's Site Museum strongly represents architectural historians' expertise and is built as a home within a home. Approaching the site, visitors first see a large wooden seventeenth-century-style residence. When they enter, though, they find an open excavation of foundations and cellars—an educational nesting-doll effect. In classic museum style, exhibitors have remade bifurcated walls and flooring so that visitor simultaneously see both the original features in the ground and what historical architecture research shows would have been above.

St. Mary's City's creative and experimentally bold rebuilt environments highlight the different fortes of each of the New School's central research-specialty streams. But these emerging approaches came to bear most dramatically on the lives of marginalized people at Colonial Williamsburg's Carter's Grove Slave Quarter in the 1980s. The site had been excavated in the 1970s, but the foundation subsequently chose to use this site, a few miles east of museum's historical area, to boost its representation of the lives of enslaved people.[22] Archaeologists had located the features and filled in details about the construction of enslaved people's plantation housing but had yet to reach consensus what would have stood aboveground. As a result, the museum's architectural historians used the setting as to reconstruct different styles of home and bounding fences, creating an interpretive space that showcased current understandings about how the enslaved lived in the mid-eighteenth-century Tidewater.

As expected with an often-controversial topic, observers disagreed about the effectiveness of the rebuild. Eric Gable, Richard Handler, and Anna Lawson believed that the site risked perpetuating majority stereotypes about both the enslaved people of the past and their modern descendants. Terrence Epperson, in contrast, viewed the entire project through the lens of Michel Foucault's ideas of space and control and saw the layout of the buildings and their relationship to the "big house" as models of discipline. Maria Franklin saw mostly lost opportunity and outlined a more nuanced and ground-up interpretive program and material culture for the space.[23] The Slave Quarter was an early example of architectural history and archaeology coming together to focus exclusively on marginalized people, and it garnered at best mixed results.[24] But the great success of the rebuild was the discussion it engendered. Rebuilds have always produced some back-and-forth about what rebuilders got right and wrong in the shape, fabric, or stylings of buildings. The Slave Quarter produced something different. It facilitated a deep and robust discussion about the dynamics, meaning, and memory of slavery itself and its museum interpretation. Rebuilders might not have intended this result, but the Slave Quarter might be best understood as a three-dimensional piece of scholarship—an argument and a thesis rendered in wood and metal and placed on the land for visitors to see and scholars to consider. This desire to spark discussion has emerged as a core element of the New School approach and stands in stark contrast to Colonial Revival rebuilders' desire to induce reverential awe.

All of these elements came together in Colonial Williamsburg's rebuilding of the Peyton Randolph House's kitchen and yard. The home is one of the town's fully restored original eighteenth-century buildings, but the layout of its yard and outbuildings had not survived. As a stand-alone home, the Peyton Randolph House told only part of the story of life there. Filling in the missing spaces with newly reconstructed outbuildings linked the lives of enslaved and enslavers and created an in-town setting for interpreting this vital dynamic of eighteenth-century Virginia life. Excavations beginning in the 1930s exposed how the yard had been laid out and had changed over time.[25] Additional excavations in 1978 and 2003 brought a host of new methods and research questions to the site, including new ways to ascertain the sequence of the site's features and buildings.[26] By the late 1990s, architectural historians could draw on a vast trove of knowledge of outbuildings and homes of Virginia's enslaved population to create the aboveground portion of the rebuilding plan. With that information in hand, museum craftspeople and contractors began a full-scale rebuild of the work yard and dependencies.[27] Building directly on the original bricks in situ, workers laid a new foundation and full brick chimney and then erected the wooden two-story combination kitchen-laundry quarter and its contemporaneous granary, smokehouse, dairy, and other dependencies. The result is a set of original and rebuilt structures that combine to make an interpretive space that is greater than the sum of its parts. Current interpretation at the Peyton Randolph House shows how the yard and home functioned in concert and brings into focus the work of specific identified enslaved people. From a visitor-engagement standpoint, the rebuilt yard puts Peyton Randolph himself on equal interpretive footing with the twenty-seven people he enslaved, including Mose, who carted grain between Randolph's properties, and Betty, the primary cook.[28] The approach used at the Peyton Randolph House came to bear on Thomas Jefferson's Monticello and subsequently at James Madison's Montpelier. Reconstructed quarters for enslaved persons there brought together the same mix of archaeological and architectural-history expertise to create interpretive spaces whose previous absence had represented a significant silence.[29]

George Washington's Mount Vernon pushed the envelope even further with its reexcavation and rebuilding of the Washington Distillery, which operated a few miles from the main home lot in the late 1790s. The museum had already done some excellent rebuilding work, but the scale of this rebuild and the intention to have it function as both a distillery and an interpretive environment set a new standard.[30] The rebuilt stone building was set directly on the original stone footers, and the rest of the internal work areas were laid out according to archaeological finds. Because the building would have the quasi-industrial function of making small batches of commercial whiskey, the reconstruction had to follow the rules of the Occupational Health and Safety

FIGURE 7.3.
The reconstructed work yard behind Colonial Williamsburg's Peyton Randolph House is based on state-of-the-art excavation and research techniques and was built by team of researchers and craftspeople, setting the regional standard. Courtesy of Jasperdo, Flickr.com.

Administration, which were not designed to fit well into eighteenth-century spaces. For example, to accommodate the requirement for a large fireproof safety elevator, a concrete tower was constructed on the northern gable end of the building and was clad in the same stone as the rest of the building. A clear and broad line of mortar interrupted the stonework where the archaeologically and architecturally informed reconstruction ended and the safety requirements began, and on-site interpretation calls attention to this boundary to avoid confusion. The result is one of the most impressive rebuilt buildings in the region as well as a graceful solution to addressing the fact that it is not an original.

All of these projects turn research into tactile reality, giving visitors an intimate feel for past places without the distance and delicate handling required to maintain actual historical structures. These rebuilds therefore can be more rough-and-tumble, more hands-on, and more immersive than responsible curation could ever allow for a building that is two or three centuries old. Visitors to Mount Vernon's distillery, for example, often find fires burning in the ovens, steam rising from huge water-filled barrels, and the smell of brewing in the air. At the Godiah Spray Tobacco Plantation, guests' feet crunch on broken and discarded ceramics while walking into a home whose rafters hold drying herbs and whose floors get scratched from time to time by free-range chickens. Rebuilds used this way offer depth and insight into past lives, offering visitors an elusive and hard-to-define sense of the authentic. Such experiences also offer lessons easily recalled when visiting genuine relics. In that way, rebuilds are valuable complements to historical structures, highlighting the care taken to keep the originals in the best shape possible.

Ferry Farm's new interpretive landscape began its life informed by these regional rebuilds and other similar projects. The long-term plan is to reestablish the entire home lot—very much like the Peyton Randolph House—with every building sitting where the original once stood. Ferry Farm sought to create a space for interpreting the lives of the Washingtons and the roughly twenty people they enslaved on the site in the mid-1700s. The home itself—the highest-profile part of

FIGURE 7.4.
The river-facing front of the house at Ferry Farm shows the re-created stonework that went into the foundation. The original home sat on Aquia sandstone blocks much like the ones seen here, but these stones are facers set on a concrete frame. Courtesy of Philip Levy.

the landscape and at the time its best-understood component—was the logical place to start. The rebuilt home was envisioned as a hands-on interpretive stage on which visitors were invited to sit on chairs, lie down on beds, and handle the reproduction ceramics, all of which had antecedents in either documents or excavations. The goal was to show the intertwined nature of the lives of the enslaved and of their enslavers by placing visitors within the spaces of colonial-era daily life. This programming ideal was also being carried out at Kenmore, an extensively renovated original 1773 plantation home in Fredericksburg that is also owned and run by the George Washington Foundation.

Ferry Farm had no Colonial Revival–era buildings: only an 1870s farm office and a few small utility buildings sat anywhere near the Washington homesite. Consequently, reimagining the few acres as a historical setting faced few modern obstacles. The biggest material challenge was that the home itself had left a fairly small footprint, with its shape and location marked only by the stone footers for three chimneys, two unlined root cellars, two large stone-lined cellars, and a few sections of foundation. The lack of bricks on the site indicated that the home was made of wood, and the width of the supporting footers showed that it could not have been more than a story and a half tall. In one earthfast cellar, burned plaster topped by fresh plaster told the story of a small but damaging fire and subsequent repairs. An entryway in the older—and far better-built—of the two cellars showed a central passage that had an "over and under" stairway main entrance on the river-facing side of the house. One side of the house featured a massive chimney for fireplaces in two rooms. On the other side, the chimney was smaller, but the footprint of the hearth was extremely large. The presence of early eighteenth-century trash deposits, combined with a 1733 probate inventory, showed the research team that the structure had originally been L-shaped but was expanded after the fire to make a full rectangle. A new third chimney heated the added room. By 2008, archaeologists knew more about this home than anyone had since the 1830s, when its remnants had been torn down and plowed into the ground.[31]

An extensive review of regional historic architecture produced photographs and drawings of a few contemporary buildings that closely resembled the footprint of the Washingtons' home.[32] One of them, Richmond County's Linden Farm, served as a model for some of the aboveground details at Ferry Farm. In addition, the new home would have to be constructed in a way that not only looked authentic but protected the surviving features. Following normal excavation practice, the team had left large sections intact for future study, and the weight of the new home needed to avoid bearing down on potentially fragile foundations. The solution was to sit the new foundation on dozens of steel rods screwed into the ground in areas that had no intact remains. The entire structure

FIGURE 7.5. The concrete foundation of the Ferry Farm house shows the ledge on which the Aquia sandstone facing will sit. The metal poles in the center will hold the weight of the home so that the entire structure floats above and protects the archaeological resources beneath. Courtesy of Philip Levy.

in effect floats above and has no contact with the original features and touches the ground only in non-load-bearing ways. Explaining to visitors how the building both replicates and preserves the site is part of interpretation.

The 1743 death of George Washington's father, Augustine, occasioned a will and a probate inventory of the home. These records provided some documentary information about the home's rooms and about furnishings and possessions. Craftspeople have made facsimiles of tables and chairs that are distributed among the rooms of the reconstructed home as they are listed in the probate inventory. Interpreters use the furnishings to talk about the probate process and the kinds of documentation created by a wealthy eighteenth-century planter.

However, the records offered no information about the cellar, which was by far the most impressive archaeological feature though it was not designed to be the home's centerpiece. With its carefully faced Aquia sandstone walls and perfectly square corners, the stone cellar is a telling remnant of a gentry home. Visitors cannot enter the cellar but can see into it through a viewport situated beneath the stairway. The cellar is the only place where new construction touches original: as at the Mount Vernon Distillery, a clear and easily interpreted line separates the old stones from the new ones, heralding the cellar as the only eighteenth-century material vestige and calling attention to the rebuilding process. In addition, the line heightens the genuine historicity of material survivors from the distant past, something that visitors to historical sites always want. Rather like the way the St. John's Site Museum uses architecture to encase a site, the walls of the reconstructed Washington home are a sort of elaborate casing for the display of this eighteenth-century relic.

Over time, broken reproduction ceramics will accumulate near windows and doorways, foot traffic will trample grass and leave dirt trails, chickens will walk in and out of doorways, and a host of internal unplanned accidents will leave scratches, burn marks, stains, and muddy footprints in the home and dependencies. As is the case at the Godiah Spray Tobacco Plantation, the goal is to create a living material experiment of the sort that could never take place in an original home but for which rebuilt historical structures are uniquely well suited. The value of this sort of interpretive

FIGURE 7.6.
The hall of the rebuilt Washington home contains reproductions of furnishings and table settings represented in Augustine Washington's wills and inventories or found in the archaeological record. Visitors are invited to sit on chairs and interact with the objects. Courtesy of Philip Levy.

stage is beyond estimation, and there is no question that visitors love a good rebuild. As Loth wrote, "Time has shown that few people regret these resurrected landmarks."[33]

Despite the lingering Didronian hostility to reconstructing, even naysayers have seen its value in one area: the oft-cited example of a sixteenth-century bridge at Mostar, Bosnia. Croatian forces destroyed the bridge's graceful arch in 1993, leading to an international outcry and accusations that the offending officers had committed war crimes. The bridge was rebuilt by 2004.[34] The bridge's wanton destruction made an open-and-shut case under an emerging consensus that such instances not only deserved but even required rebuilding.

U.S. historical sites today are threatened not by artillery but by rapid-onset violent climate change. Buildings constructed for Holocene conditions are not going to fare well in Anthropocene realities: in the Chesapeake region, where many historical sites sit on or close to waterways, rapid coastal erosion is removing sites. Rebuilding serves two purposes in this emerging battle. First, given the need to repair and replace aging buildings, reconstruction projects offer vital laboratories for new techniques and technologies of use well beyond the confines of single rebuild. Second, rebuilding is a valuable tool for calling attention to what the ground holds out of our sight, and that attention can motivate action to save what is rapidly being lost.

Carl Becker's Mr. Everyman cared about the past.[35] Today's Everyperson cares, too, but as was the case for their predecessors, only what fits into their own lives truly matters. Preservationists might love past sites, but saving them requires allies. If Everypeople cannot interact with a place, they cannot appreciate it and they will not endorse the needed legislative, economic, and cultural changes needed to protect it. Rebuilding can be the missing piece.

Notes

1. Philip Levy, *Where the Cherry Tree Grew: The Story of Ferry Farm, George Washington's Boyhood Home* (New York: St. Martin's Press, 2013); Philip Levy, *George Washington Written on the Land: Nature, Memory, Myth, and Landscape* (Morgantown: West Virginia University Press, 2015). See also Philip Levy, "'Crystallized into Solid Reality': How Mason Locke 'Parson' Weems Shaped George Washington's Boyhood Home," *Virginia Magazine of History and Biography* 120, no. 1 (2013): 107–45; Philip Levy, "The Many Houses of Washington's Boyhood Home," in *The Permanent Resident: Excavations and Explorations of George Washington's Life* (Charlottesville: University of Virginia Press, 2022), 39–63.

2. Quoted in Christina Cameron, "Reconstruction: Changing Attitudes," *UNESCO Courier*, July–September 2017, https://en.unesco.org/courier/july-september-2017/reconstruction-changing-attitudes.

3. Cameron, "Reconstruction." See also Lucia Maria Cardos Rosas, "The Restoration of Historic Buildings between 1835–1929: The Portuguese Taste," *Journal of Portuguese History* 3, no. 1 (2005): 5.

4. International Charter for the Conservation and Restoration of Monuments and Sites (Venice Charter 1964), https://www.icomos.org/images/DOCUMENTS/Charters /venice_e.pdf.

5. Calder Loth, *Architectural Reconstructions: A Respectable Tradition*, October 8, 2014, ICAA, https://www.classicist.org/articles/architectural-reconstructions-a -respectable-tradition/.

6. Barry Mackintosh, "National Park Service Reconstruction Policy and Practice," in *The Reconstructed Past: Reconstructions in the Public Interpretation of Archaeology and History*, ed. John H. Jameson (Walnut Creek, Calif.: AltaMira Press, 2004), 67.

7. Mackintosh, "National Park Service Reconstruction Policy," 72; National Park Service, Technical Preservation Services, *Standards for Reconstruction*, https://www.nps .gov/tps/standards/four-treatments/treatment-reconstruction.html.

8. Mackintosh, "National Park Service Reconstruction Policy," 65–76.

9. National Park Service, Technical Preservation Services, "Standards for Reconstruction."

10. David Gebhard, "The American Colonial Revival in the 1930s," *Winterthur Portfolio*, 22, nos. 2/3 (1987): 109.

11. William Butler, "Another City upon a Hill: Litchfield, Connecticut, and the Colonial Revival," in *The Colonial Revival in America*, ed. Alan Axelrod (New York: W. W. Norton, 1985), 19.

12. Ralph S. Fanning, "Some Post-Colonial Remains on Eastern Long Island," *American Architect* 110, no. 2138 (1916): 367. For further definitions, see Richard Guy Wilson, "What Is the Colonial Revival?" in *Recreating the American Past: Essays on the Colonial Revival*, ed. Richard Guy Wilson, Shaun Eyring, and Kenny Marota (Charlottesville: University of Virginia Press, 2006), 1–10; Karal Ann Marling, *George Washington Slept Here: Colonial Revivals and American Culture* (Cambridge: Harvard University Press, 1988), 150; Lydia Mattice Brandt, *First in the Homes of His Countrymen: George Washington's Mount Vernon in the American Imagination* (Charlottesville: University of Virginia Press, 2016), 203.

13. Gebhard, "American Colonial Revival," 110; William B. Rhodes, "The Long and Unsuccessful Effort to Kill Off the Colonial Revival," in *Recreating the American Past*, ed. Wilson, Eyring, and Marota, 14.

14. Rhodes, "Long and Unsuccessful Effort," 13.

15. Carl R. Lounsbury, "Beaux-Arts Ideals and Colonial Reality: The Reconstruction of Williamsburg's Capitol, 1928–1934," *Journal of the Society of Architectural Historians* 49, no. 4 (1990): 373.

16. Marley R. Brown III and Edward A. Chappell, "Archaeological Authenticity and Reconstruction at Colonial Williamsburg," in *Reconstructed Past*, ed. Jameson, 47.

17. Joy Beasley, "The Birthplace of a Chief: Archaeology and Meaning at George Washington Birthplace National Monument," in *Myth, Memory, and the Making of the American Landscape*, ed. Paul A. Shackel (Gainesville: University Press of Florida, 2001), 197–220; Seth Bruggeman, *Here, George Washington Was Born: Memory, Material Culture, and the Public History of a National Monument* (Athens: University of Georgia Press, 2008); Charles E. Hatch Jr., *Popes Creek Plantation: Birthplace of George Washing-*

ton (Washington Birthplace, Va.: Wakefield National Memorial Association in Cooperation with the National Park Service, 1979); David Rodnick, "Orientation Report on the George Washington Birthplace National Monument, Westmoreland County, Virginia" (report prepared for the National Park Service, October 17, 1941). See also Philip Levy, Amy Muraca, and Alena Pirok, "George Washington Birthplace National Monument, Westmoreland County, Virginia, Summer 2013 "Building X" Archaeological Reassessment Report" (report prepared for National Park Service, George Washington Birthplace National Monument National Park, Colonial Beach, Va., 2014); Elizabeth Sargent, "George Washington Birthplace National Monument National Park: Provenance of a Colonial Revival Commemorative Landscape," in *Recreating the American Past*, ed. Wilson, Eyring, and Marota, 216–36.

18. For more on this subject, see Levy, *Where the Cherry Tree Grew*; Levy, "Many Houses."

19. Seth C. Bruggeman, *Don't Build on a Cherry-Tree Myth—Again*, History News Network, July 25, 2008, https://historynewsnetwork.org/article/52782. See also Seth C. Bruggeman, "Hard Time," Bruggeman's personal blog, August 3, 2008, https://sites.temple.edu/sethbruggeman/category/ferry-farm/.

20. Lois Green Carr, Russell R. Menard, and Lorena S. Walsh, *Robert Cole's World: Agriculture and Society in Early Maryland* (Chapel Hill: University of North Carolina Press, 1991).

21. Henry Miller, "When the Digging Is Over: Some Observations on Methods of Interpreting Archaeological Sites for the Public," in *Past Meets Present: Archaeologists Partnering with Museum Curators, Teachers, and Community Groups*, ed. John H. Jameson Jr. and Sherene Baugher (New York: Springer, 2007), 42–43. See also Julia A. King and and Henry M. Miller, "The View from the Midden: An Analysis of Midden Distribution and Composition at the van Sweringen Site, St. Mary's City, Maryland," *Historical Archaeology* 21, no. 2 (1987): 37–59. The St. Mary's City website offers excellent maps and information about the museum's sites and landscape. See *Interactive Map*, Historic St. Mary's City, accessed January 23, 2022, https://www.hsmcdigshistory.org/the-experience/interactive-map/.

22. David Muraca, *The Carter's Grove Museum Site Excavation: Carter's Grove Archaeological Report, Block 50 Building 3* (Williamsburg, Va.: Colonial Williamsburg Foundation Library, 1989). See also Mary A. Stephenson, *History of Carter's Grove Plantation, Carter's Grove Historical Report, Block 50 Building 3* (Williamsburg, Va.: Colonial Williamsburg Foundation Library, 1964).

23. Eric Gable, Richard Handler, and Anna Lawson, "On the Uses of Relativism: Fact, Conjecture, and Black and White Histories at Colonial Williamsburg," *American Ethnologist* 19, no. 4 (1992): 791–805; Terrence W. Epperson, "Race and the Disciplines of the Plantation," *Historical Archaeology* 24, no. 4 (1990): 29–36; Maria Franklin, "Rethinking the Carter's Grove Slave Quarter Reconstruction: A Proposal," *Kroeber Anthropological Society Papers* 79 (1995): 147–64.

24. The project came to an unceremonious end when Carter's Grove was closed to the public and eventually sold. See Gregory Connolly, "Colonial Williamsburg Sells Carter's Grove to Chicago-Based Preservationist Businessman," *Williamsburg Yorktown Daily*, September 19, 2014, https://wydaily.com/news/local/2014/09/19/colonial-williamsburg-sells-carters-grove-to-chicago-based-preservationist-businessman/.

25. Marley R. Brown III and Andrew C. Edwards, "Re-excavation: Reflexivity and Responsibility at Colonial Williamsburg," in *Between Dirt and Discussion: Methods, Methodology, and Interpretation in Historical Archaeology*, ed. Steven N. Archer and Kevin M. Bartoy (New York: Springer, 2006), 169–82; Francis Duke, *Peyton Randolph House Archaeology Report: Block 28 Building 6 Lot 236* (Williamsburg, Va.: Colonial Williamsburg Foundation Library, 1939).

26. Brown and Edwards, "Re-excavation," 174.

27. Mark Kostro, *The 2003 Archaeological Excavations at the Peyton Randolph Property, Williamsburg, Virginia* (Williamsburg, Va.: Colonial Williamsburg Foundation Library, 2010); Marc Heller, "Building on the Past," *Newport News Daily Press*, January 22, 1997, https://www.dailypress.com/news/dp-xpm-19970122-1997-01-22-9701220092 -story.html. See also *Reconstruction Underway at the Peyton Randolph House*, Colonial Williamsburg, https://www.slaveryandremembrance.org/Almanack/places/hb /hbranout.cfm.

28. For a digital version of the current interpretive program, see *Our Lives, Our Stories: Legacy of the Randolph Site Virtual Tour*, Colonial Williamsburg, accessed January 20, 2022, https://virtualtours.colonialwilliamsburg.org/randolph/.

29. Gardiner Hallock, "Mulberry Row: Telling the Story of Slavery at Monticello," *SiteLINES: A Journal of Place* 14, no. 2 (2019): 3–8; Gardiner Hallock, "*Object Lesson*: 'Build the Negro Houses near Together': Thomas Jefferson and the Evolution of Mulberry Row's Vernacular Landscape," *Buildings and Landscapes: Journal of the Vernacular Architecture Forum* 24, no. 2 (2017): 22–36; *Rebuilding a Difficult Doorway, Montpelier's Digital Doorway*, Montpelier.org, accessed January 25, 2022, https://digitaldoorway .montpelier.org/project/the-south-yard-dwellings/. See also James L. Nolan and Ty F. Buckman, "Preserving the Postmodern, Restoring the Past: The Cases of Monticello and Montpelier," *Sociological Quarterly* 39, no. 2 (1998): 253–69.

30. Esther White, "'As You See It So It Was'? Reconstructing Historic Built Environments in the USA: The Case of Sites Associated with George Washington" (PhD diss., University of Leicester, 2008), 202–22; Dennis Pogue, *Founding Spirits: George Washington and the Beginnings of the American Whiskey Industry* (Buena Vista, Va.: Harbor Books, 2011).

31. David Muraca, Paul Nasca, and Philip Levy, *Report on the Excavations at the Washington Farm: The 2006 and 2007 Field Seasons* (Fredericksburg, Va.: George Washington Foundation, 2010).

32. Architect Mark Wenger conducted the architectural study and produced a large and detailed report in preparation for the Ferry Farm building project. See Mark Wenger, *A Proposal for the Reconstruction of George Washington's Ferry Farm* (Williamsburg, Va.: Mesick Cohen Wilson Baker, Architects, 2011).

33. Loth, *Architectural Reconstructions*.

34. Christina Cameron. "From Warsaw to Mostar: The World Heritage Committee and Authenticity," *APT Bulletin: The Journal of Preservation Technology* 39, nos. 2/3 (2008): 19–24; Judith Bing, "Ideas and Realities: Rebuilding in Postwar Mostar," *Journal of Architectural Education* 54, no. 4 (2001): 238–49.

35. Carl Becker, "Everyman His Own Historian," *American Historical Review* 37, no. 2 (1932): 221–36.

The Future of Collection Stewardship and Exhibition in Small-Town Museums

A Case Study from Southeastern Utah

TARA BERESH

"Small Museum, Big Stories" is the adopted brand for the Moab Museum, a recently remodeled and revitalized rural nonprofit institution nestled in the southeastern Utah town of Moab. In 2018, the Moab Museum shifted to a new strategy, engaging with the public through in-depth and authentic storytelling rather than prioritizing the quantity of objects exhibited. Its succinct mission statement—"Share stories"—requires staff to develop programming and interpretive features to carry out this goal. Of course, substantial resources are needed to support a nonprofit organization with the humble vision to "change how we see the world around us, from here to beyond, for everyone who calls here home or is just passing through, building pride, compassion and humility along the way."[1] The Moab Museum serves as a case study in the challenges rural museums face. Such museums house some of the most valuable and irreplaceable historic objects of our nation's history, many of them provided by trusting community donors and founding families, but these institutions often lack the resources to care for these collections in a manner consistent with the best practices required by accredited museum standards. In addition, rural museums tend to lack professionals experienced in tribal consultation and community-outreach principles, a gap that can easily damage an institution's reputation. These practices, among others, require trained and educated staff and contractors, archival-quality materials, and controlled storage environments as well as a consistent revenue stream from audiences and sustaining donors. As the stewards of many rare objects, rural museums can better preserve, protect, and share American history as well as educate and inspire the public when they have support from key stakeholders.

Background

Like many museums rooted in rural towns, locals recall the Moab Museum, formerly the Museum of Moab and the Dan O'Laurie Museum, as more of a cabinet of curiosities than an institution resembling those accredited by the American Alliance of Museums.[2] Visitors have long enjoyed the institution's mishmash of artifacts, which range from pre-Hispanic ceramics and sandals to early twentieth-century baby dolls and inoperative Geiger counters. Until recently, however, many of these items lacked more than a passing reference to any deeper significance in the context of local history. Area residents who visited the museum often believed that one visit was enough—they had already "seen" the museum. A community engagement assessment conducted as part of planning for a 2018 remodel found that locals could recall a lot of "stuff" on display but struggled to provide the stories that stuff represented.[3] The reimagined Moab Museum seeks to remedy this problem, appeal to a broader audience, and increase visibility by focusing more on facilitating source-based storytelling/programming and less on showcasing an arbitrary cornucopia of objects. To that end, the Moab Museum has sought to improve on four of the most common issues confronting rural museums: the curation of sizable, poorly provenanced, and inadequately documented collections with limited cohesion and clear relevance; inadequate training of staff in modern museum practices and problems with employee retention; limited access to funding to properly manage collections and conduct outreach activities, including repatriation; and limited engagement with patrons in a way that promotes repeated visits and historical retrospection. In this chapter, I use the term *artifacts* to refer to objects produced and used by ancestral Native inhabitants of the Moab area as well as more recent inhabitants. However, this archaeological term fails to encapsulate the contemporary cultural meanings embodied within individual artifacts for descendant Native communities.

Extensive but Poorly Integrated Collections

Historically, rural museums develop from the ideas of well-intentioned community members who have a sense of pride in hometown history yet lack professional experience with object accessioning and collection-management policies. The Moab Museum had its origins in a literary club's 1958 "community achievement project" to preserve, display, and interpret the various archaeological, paleontological, geological, historical, and mineralogical resources abundant in the area.[4] At its inception, the museum was run by a committee of five local women in a residential home allocated for the storage of the community's trove of artifacts. A handful of impassioned members of the community without any training in object conservation subsequently operated what became a nonprofit county-supported museum. The institution grew to curate thousands of donated objects without any policy or protocol for acceptance or accessioning. Most of these objects lacked relevance or documentation, preventing current and future museum staff from delivering accurate or authentic stories that integrated such objects. The result was an eclectic collection of unprovenanced items. But to tell historically relevant stories for the greater benefit of the public, the Moab Museum needed to give more attention to fewer objects—specifically, those with documentation that established their place in Moab's history.

In 2017 the museum hired an experienced museum executive to transform the organization from a typical rural museum to one operating according to professional standards. The transformation would prioritize gathering authentic stories via face-to-face conversations and oral history archives over speculating on the regional significance of rusty farm implements and spurs or typed placards summarizing broad accounts of the past. Two years later, the museum hired a licensed archaeologist, who highlighted that the inadequately documented collections demonstrated how the power of an object is only as great as its context. Whether written or oral, the story associated with an object increases its historical value. When an archaeologist surveys a tract of land looking for clues about past cultures, the context of a corroded pile of tin cans or of a scatter of lithic flakes indicates how they might have been situated within the environment or served their users, thus demonstrating their role in history. In many cases, the context outweighs the value of any individual artifact or assemblage. The same holds true for objects donated to a museum: the context provided by the donor enables curators to accurately explain the object's significance. And because rural museums have limited resources with which to employ professionals, staffers are commonly enthusiasts who graciously accept all objects offered or items that they personally find appealing. Despite their good intentions, these staff members lack the training to prioritize legal transfer of ownership, object history documentation, and collection relevance as outlined in a collections statement policy. Consequently, such museums frequently become glorified—and exorbitantly expensive—storage spaces for random objects.

Limited Funding, Limited Expertise

Rural museums are often underfunded and outdated and commonly maintain extensive displays of ancient relics with vague or inaccurate signage about the cultures the objects represent. Locals routinely donate baskets, ceramics, sandals, bows and arrows, projectile points, and other objects, leaving curators and collection managers to weigh the ethical stipulations, past land management questions, and tribal consultation that are part and parcel of the responsible acquisition of objects of unknown provenance. Some donors are uncomfortable about possessing these items and fear being implicated in unlawful collecting. Others, equally problematic, are oblivious to the issue. Visitors as well as state and federal authorities typically hold urban institutions to a higher standard, so they are more careful about displaying and caring for objects as well as about consulting with Native

American tribes. These institutions want to maintain their reputations. Moreover, they typically have greater funding and can employ trained professionals with the skill sets to establish policies, conduct consultations, and allocate resources for foundational archival needs, aspects of museum management whose importance may not be fully understood by employees of lesser-known rural museums. As a consequence of the complexity and costs of inventory and compliance requirements under the Native American Graves Protection and Repatriation Act (1990), the federal government has provided grants to enable poorer institutions to meet their obligations. The availability of similar funding resources to enable small museums to support technical and/or tribal consultations would significantly improve professionalization. The Moab Museum was fortunate to have a Native American employed as a Bureau of Land Management archaeologist serve as board president and diligently address any residual repatriation needs in the museum's collection. Most rural museums do not have this luxury.

Training, Professionalization, and Staff Retention

Funding limitations; facilities that expose artifacts to such damaging factors such as pests, light, and temperature fluctuations; and a lack of professionally experienced or trained staff often mean that rural museums often are less aware of and do not follow best practices, including tribal consultation. Museums that are professionally managed according to American Alliance of Museum standards can readily cultivate working relationships with other institutions, take on loans, and accept new collections for new exhibits—because best practices equate to having established policies and environments conducive to caring for valuable objects. Rural museums that have working relationships with other institutions, especially prominent ones, have increased access to collections beyond their own, can develop higher-caliber exhibits, and receive increased public support, which translates into funding, success, and longevity. Increased funding, in turn, enables small museums to retain trained professionals; otherwise, those professionals may leave for higher-paying opportunities at larger institutions. And when they do, systems established for the preservation of objects and stories tend to break down. A generous endowment from a private donor has recently enabled the Moab Museum to provide competitive compensation and benefits to attract and retain professionals, but most rural museums struggle in this area.

Grants Are Available but Inaccessible

Although entities such as Utah Humanities and the Institute of Museum and Library Services distribute funding via grants, the obstacles to securing those grants can prove insurmountable for understaffed institutions. In the absence of trained professionals, the grant application process can prove daunting if not impossible. Furthermore, at small rural institutions that do have trained professionals, they may be overextended with their other duties—managing front-end operations, curating exhibits, developing revenue-generating interpretive programming, and addressing collections care needs and digitization. Applying for and administering grants of even small amounts of money is time-consuming, requiring not only hours of preparation and number-crunching but also the writing of reports. Small rural museums seldom have the staff time and expertise to research, draft, edit, and submit grant applications; in contrast, many urban institutions have a staff member hired specifically for grant writing.

Rural museums can, however, take advantage of some resources. The American Association of State and Local History offers training in membership development and fundraising for historical societies, history museums, and historic homes and sites. Some state and regional museum associations offer scholarships for staff professional-development activities. In 2019, after developing its new strategy, the Moab Museum identified and applied for funding to put it into practice. The museum has received grants from the Utah State Historical Records Advisory Board, the Utah Department of Arts and Museums, and Utah Humanities that have enabled it to significantly elevate collections care, digitize deteriorating archives, and develop public programming.

A Load Basket, the "Old" Moab Museum, and Inadequate Tribal Consultation

In July 1990, three teenagers hiking in the canyons near Moab discovered an ancient load basket tucked under a cliff ledge. Their families notified the Bureau of Land Management, which took possession of the cone-shaped basket constructed of yucca fiber and split willow and authorized the Moab Museum to exhibit it. The museum displayed the basket alongside a plethora of pre-Hispanic ceramic vessels, farming implements, and other baskets. The label copy for these items contained few if any Native American narratives about these objects: members of local Native tribes were rarely asked to contribute to the interpretation of these artifacts, and when they were asked, the objects were exhibited before the tribes had time to respond.

As a result of these practices, Euro-American museum visitors viewed the artifacts as abandoned relics from long ago. But many ancient objects curated by the Moab Museum relate to ancestral Native peoples whose descendants are very much alive in Moab and across the southwestern United States. These descendants often have unique cultural understandings of these objects and can articulate from oral traditions the sacredness or cultural significance of an object. In addition, the descendants can raise legitimate concerns regarding the treatment of their ancestors' belongings. According to some Native teachings, the presence of ancestral objects is not only offensive but physically and spiritu-

FIGURE 8.1.
The interpretive text for a pre-Hispanic artifact on display at the revamped Moab Museum has been derived from tribal consultations, and tribal members reviewed the text for accuracy before the object was displayed. Photo by Tara Beresh. Courtesy of Moab Museum.

ally harmful. It is also widely known that most artifacts on display at museums were acquired through systematic archaeological removal or wholesale looting. Groups that perceive ancestral sites as living spaces may object to bearing witness to objects violently uprooted from ancestral lands. Individuals from the Diné, Ute, Paiute, and other Native American tribes with ancestral ties to the Moab area often avoid visiting many museums for this reason. Productive tribal consultation can reduce or eliminate such conflicts.

Reimagining the Moab Museum

In the mid-1800s, direct trade between early settlers and the Diné and Ute was common, and locals legitimately came to possess Native American objects. However, settlers also scoured the canyons for ancient objects and then traded them for food, medical services, and other necessities, especially during hard times. Moab's first doctor, J. W. Williams, acquired many ancestral objects in this way and later contributed his private collection to the National Park Service (NPS) and the Moab Museum. The United States eventually enacted laws prohibiting the collection of pre-Hispanic items (for example, the Antiquities Act of

1906), but these laws have lessened rather than completely halted artifact looting and do nothing about those materials that are already in private hands. The items in some of these private collections were illegally looted, while others were removed from scientifically documented archaeological sites on public lands in the interests of preservation, research, or loss prevention. Even in such cases, the objects were removed from living spaces that descendants of the region's First Peoples consider sacred, meaning that even if their removal was legal, it was culturally inappropriate. People who inherit private collections may be uncomfortable about possessing the artifacts and often donate them to museums but typically lack information about the context where the items were found.

In February 2020, the collections manager for the NPS's Southeast Utah Group reached out to the Moab Museum about exhibiting two pre-Hispanic vessels collected to prevent their loss. One of these vessels is a storage jar found in the mid-1970s in an alcove along Salt Creek in Canyonlands National Park alongside a corrugated cooking vessel and a basketry fragment. Another ancient vessel is a water container that NPS archaeologists date to between 1200 and 1300 CE. Ancient Native inhabitants cached the water container above Cataract Canyon of the Colorado River in Canyonlands National Park alongside two large corrugated vessels beneath an overhang with a crack leading to a river overlook. A visitor removed the vessel in 1992 but returned it when instructed to do so. Nevertheless, NPS rangers, archaeologists, and officials determined that recovery of the vessel was necessary.

In earlier years, the Moab Museum would have welcomed a loan of these vessels, which feature striking painted designs and other unique elements that would attract visitor interest. However, museum professionals find themselves in an ongoing ethical shift in which, in the words of Raney Bench, they "are purposefully working to incorporate Native people and perspectives into all aspects of their work with the intent of improving their own interpretive processes."[5] In that light, NPS and museum personnel consulted with area tribes to learn their perspectives on the vessels and views about displaying them in the museum. This consultation took two years but resulted not only in a consensus in favor of displaying the vessels and an accurate and culturally appropriate interpretive story but also relationships between the museum and several tribal communities.

Consultation between the NPS and the Hopi Cultural Preservation Office, for example, shed light on Hopi perspectives regarding their connections to early cultural groups in Canyonlands National Park and to the objects found there. The Hopi consider the archaeological sites and artifacts of their ancestors to be "footprints" and traditional cultural properties:

Hopi migration is intimately associated with a sacred Covenant between the Hopi people and Màasaw, the Earth Guardian, in which the Hopi people made a solemn promise to protect the land by serving as stewards of the Earth. In accordance with this Covenant, ancestral Hopi clans traveled through and settled on the lands in and around Canyonlands National Monument [Park]—during their long migration to Tuuwanasavi, the Earth Center on the Hopi Mesas. The land is a testament of Hopi stewardship through thousands of years, manifested by the "footprints of ancient villages, sacred springs, migration routes, pilgrimage trails, artifacts, petroglyphs, and the physical remains of buried Hisatsinom, the 'People of Long Ago,' all of which were intentionally left to mark the land as proof that the Hopi people have fulfilled their Covenant."[6]

Canyonlands National Park, therefore, is not simply an isolated park managed by the NPS but one piece in a vast, intricate cultural landscape. Other tribes shared similar views of the park. According to the Navajo Nation's tribal historic preservation officer, Richard M. Begay, "There are long-time Native people that lived here, and continue to come back, and they still remember these places." Canyonlands "figures predominantly in people's stories, songs, [and] prayers, today. It helps bridge 'the past' with people's daily lives today. It is part of a larger cultural landscape of people that are still alive. Cultural materials are still alive. It would be preferable to have modern material displayed. The materials used to make these pots came from the landscape, are put on the land with intention, and should stay on the land, because this is a way to remember where people came from."[7] The tribal historic preservation officer for the Pueblo of Laguna, Richard Smith Sr., asserted that "sites still have life based on our connections to those locations. The deities that are in those areas are called on constantly. Some pots are used for specific purposes, and what may be a seed jar by our interpretation may be something else to another pueblo or tribe. That's why it would be best to hear from other tribes."[8] In 2021, the Moab Museum installed the two ancient vessels recovered by the NPS, with interpretive text derived from and approved by the tribal representatives consulted.

Ethnographic research and collaboration are essential to preserve, manage, and interpret cultural and natural resources in an effective, culturally informed manner. The presence of Native artifacts in a museum setting without the consultation of local tribes and alongside speculative and often inaccurate signage can be a source of contention within and among regional Native communities. Today, museums managed by non–Native Americans are seeking new ways to share the diverse stories of the region while honoring the variety of cultures that comprise our collective history. Approaching this task will require that to the best of our ability, we tell full, complex truths about our region's history without glossing over the parts that negatively portray Euro-American settlers or

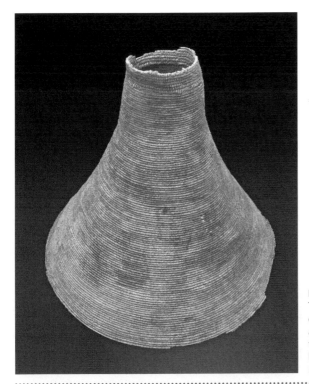

FIGURE 8.2.
The ancient load basket discovered in Moab in 1990 as it appears on display at the Moab Museum. Photo by Jonathan Till. Courtesy of Moab Museum.

contemporary inhabitants. The Moab Museum's proactive consultation with descendant Native communities has provided the public with multifaceted perspectives on the past and the ways that choosing artifacts and their accompanying interpretation impacts our perceptions of past lifeways, especially ancestral Native ones.

During the remodel of the reimagined Moab Museum, trustees and staff consulted with members of the Ute and Hopi tribes to hear authentic perspectives on how to tell Native stories in the new galleries. The Moab Museum recorded valuable teachings that have guided the installation of a First Peoples exhibit as well as incorporated Native voices throughout the region's complex historical timeline. The museum continues to consult with and build relationships with regional tribes to cultivate a positive space in which people from all cultures feel welcome and respected.

Conclusion

Rural as well as urban museums are engaged in a larger discourse regarding the interpretation of history. This discussion encompasses many additional questions: How much contextual information should a museum require before accepting an object of unknown historic value into perpetual stewardship? Should the museum focus on telling an accurate version of history or on entertaining visitors with a bounty of visual stimulation? Should museum professionals accept objects in haste when they appear compelling or require provenance information to be passed on to future generations? The answers to these questions boil down to the age-old issue of quality versus quantity. Managing museum accessions requires the ability to diplomatically refuse gifts from eager donors. Acquiring an object makes an institution responsible for its physical preservation, and choosing to exhibit an object makes the curator responsible for its impacts on the people who interact with it. Artifacts can inspire, provoke, and influence but can also cause pain and reinforce inequality, bring people together or drive people apart. The way in which we accumulate and share must thus be considered carefully.

Notes

1. Tara Beresh, *Moab Museum Scope of Collections Statement, Moab, Utah* (Moab, Utah: Moab Museum, 2022), 3–4.

2. Forrest Rodgers, *Community Engagement Assessment, Museum of Moab, Moab, Utah* (Moab, Utah: Rodgers & Associates, 2017), 6–7.

3. Rodgers, *Community Engagement Assessment*, 6–7.

4. Beresh, *Moab Museum Scope of Collections Statement*, 3.

5. Raney Bench, *Interpreting Native American History and Culture at Museums and Historic Sites* (Lanham, Md.: Rowman & Littlefield, 2014), 7.

6. Stewart B. Koyiyumptewa, interim manager, Hopi Cultural Preservation Office, to National Park Service, June 25, 2018.

7. Richard M. Begay, "Island in the Sky Visitor Center Exhibit Project, Canyonlands National Park," online presentation, December 17, 2018.

8. Richard Smith Sr., "Island in the Sky Visitor Center Exhibit Project, Canyonlands National Park," online presentation, December 17, 2018.

From Santa Barbara to Gila River
Multisited Histories and Collaborative Archaeology

KOJI LAU-OZAWA

Public archaeology is a practice that has multiple different meanings. In one, it is an archaeology that collaborates with public groups—that is, an archaeology with the public. Under this rubric, a large number of approaches to archaeological methods are applied, such as community-based research paradigms and decolonizing methodologies. Key aspects of these techniques include identifying and working with nonarchaeological stakeholders to develop project parameters, research questions, methodologies, and outputs. A second understanding of public archaeology focuses on the dissemination of project results and data to the public. In this application, archaeological research is presented to public audiences rather than in strictly academic journals and monographs or in the vast arena of technical and compliance reports in gray literature intended for bureaucratic regulators. Here, nonspecialists are framed as having a key interest in the outcome of archaeological projects. The two understandings, of course, involve large amounts of overlap. For instance, community-based research paradigms often center the importance of disseminating results to communities impacted or scrutinized in the process of research.

However, tensions also arise in the scope of archaeology for the public, particularly because no single public exists; rather, there are multiple publics, especially in cases involving multisited histories—those that span multiple geographic and temporal spaces. Such breadth increases the number of publics that can and should be engaged. This chapter focuses on a project tracing the impacts of Japanese American incarceration during World War II.[1] With few exceptions, archaeological work on Japanese American incarceration has focused on the spaces of camps of confinement, with less attention paid to the communities where Japanese Americans came from and to which they returned in many cases. At the same time, it is clear that the camps themselves were put not into terra nullius—spaces devoid of history and social and cultural meanings—but rather into places connected to communities and people. Consequently, a publicly engaged archaeology must consider these diverse strains tied together by the process of the forced removal and incarceration.

Multisite Histories mean Multicommunity Engagements

For many people, the practice of archaeology is predicated by deep-seated interest and in the best cases a commitment to all communities touched by the parameters of a particular project. These qualities—interest and care—are integral to producing an archaeology that can benefit publics, broadly defined. My own relationship to the archaeology of the Gila River Incarceration Camp has another layer applied to it—members of my family, including my grandparents, were incarcerated there from August 1942 to August 1944. From my early childhood, I remember hearing stories of "camp" and "Gila," never really apprehending the meanings behind these vague allusions until I was much older. Members of my family often used these terms solely as markers of time: "That was before camp"; "No, it was after Gila." As I learned more about the subject of Japanese American incarceration, the legacies of confinement became clearer, revealed as much from the stories told as from the silences on the subject. Consequently, I approached the archaeological study of the camp that had such an impact on my family with great apprehension in 2013.

At that time, only a handful of archaeological studies of the Gila River Incarceration Camp had taken place, and most of them existed in cultural resource management reports from the 1980s and early 1990s.[2] The most recent assessment had been produced more than a decade earlier as part of a National Park Service survey of Japanese American incarceration. This report indicated that extensive archaeological remains were present, more so than many of the other incarceration camps. The report also noted that the camp had been constructed on the land of the Gila River Indian Community, a reservation of Akimel Oʼotham (Akimel Oʼodham)and Pee Posh (Pipaash) peoples.[3] After a series of introductions from colleagues of colleagues, I was put into contact with the Gila River Indian Community Cultural Resource Management Program (GRIC-CRMP) and proposed a survey of the remains of garden ponds, features that previous reports suggested might be accessible for documentation with minimal impact. This effort began my collaborative relationship with archaeologists at GRIC-CRMP, which has continuously shaped my approach to doing archaeology for the public.

At the same time, I began contacting Japanese American community and heritage organizations, each of which had its own internal dynamics, politics, interests, and desires.[4] The mechanics of World War II incarceration compounded the geographic dispersion of such communities related to Gila River. Rather than a population from a single area being incarcerated at Gila River, people were taken from more than three hundred cities and towns, primarily from the Southern California coast, the greater Los Angeles area, the San Joaquin Valley, and the San Francisco Bay Area.[5] After the war, with many people returning to the general areas from which they had been removed, they formed separate communities in these locales, at times with limited exchange between organizations and groups.

The heritage landscape of Japanese American incarceration is geographically complex, multisited, and diachronic because people moved through the apparatus of the camp system. While some scholars have referred to this complexity as an eventscape (a dispersed landscape connected by a historical event), the impacts to communities with histories before and after incarceration calls for a framing that extends through time, preceding and following the event of mass removal and incarceration.[6] Further, pursuing a practice of archaeology committed to and for various publics means that projects must seek out and engage with multiple communities touched in different ways by the history of incarceration. Such engagements are not easy or fleeting but instead necessitate long-term relationships best suited to practices advocated by slow archaeologies, antiracist archaeologies, and community-based praxis.[7]

The remainder of this chapter details a portion of what multicommunity engagement has looked like in my work at Gila River. In particular, I focus on how my collaboration with GRIC-CRMP has shaped my research methodologies and my understandings of what it means to do an archaeology for multiple publics as well as on my work with the Santa Barbara Nihonmachi community, one of the many Japanese American communities whose members were sent to Gila River. I came to be involved with the Santa Barbara Japanese American community in 2018, after a colleague, Stacey Camp, followed a series of citations in gray literature referring to archaeological materials from Santa Barbara and came into contact with the Santa Barbara Trust for Historic Preservation.[8] Working with Camp and trust archaeologist Mike Imwalle, I met with several Japanese American families whose members were part of Santa Barbara's vibrant prewar Japanese American community. Many of the accounts and details of Santa Barbara's Japanese American history come from discussions with these families.

I am also cognizant that despite my own relationship to the Gila River Incarceration Camp as a descendant of former incarcerees, I am not a member of either the Gila River Indian or Santa Barbara community. My family members lived in Pasadena before and after their incarceration. I emphasize this fact here as throughout my work, I have tried to respect both my nearness to the history of World War II incarceration as well as my distance from some of the communities with which I work. Remembering my positionality has pushed me to consider whose histories are represented in the work that I do and perhaps just as importantly whose histories I am not in the position to tell.

Different Sites Brought Together

The decision to incarcerate all people of Japanese ancestry on the U.S. West Coast was made in early 1942, though its roots reach much further back. After the Japanese Empire's December 7, 1941, attack on the military base at Pearl Harbor in Hawai'i, white supremacist pressure groups on the West Coast advocated the mass removal of all people of Japanese ancestry. President Franklin Roosevelt, who had expressed racist attitudes toward Japanese American communities, became receptive to the argument that it was impossible to assess the loyalty of Japanese Americans and that they therefore represented a threat to national security. In February 1942 he issued Executive Order 9066, which created a military exclusion zone that encompassed sections of Oregon, Washington, and Arizona and all of California. The Western Defense Command, led by General John L. DeWitt, was empowered to remove all people deemed a security risk. Over the next several months, plans were put into place and subsequently implemented to remove all people of up to one-sixteenth Japanese ancestry living in the exclusion zone. Most were first sent to temporary detention facilities (often quickly converted parade grounds and racetracks) and then to ten purpose-built incarceration camps: Poston and Gila River in Arizona, Tule Lake and Manzanar in California, Jerome and Rohwer in Arkansas, Amache in Colorado, Heart Mountain in Wyoming, Minidoka in Idaho, and Topaz in Utah. All told, more than 120,000 people—two-thirds of them U.S. citizens—were sent to these camps.[9]

The Gila River Incarceration Camp opened in the summer of 1942 on the land of the Gila River Indian Community in southern Arizona. The decision to place the camp on reservation land stemmed in part from John Collier, commissioner of the Bureau of Indian Affairs, who advocated placing all of the incarceration camps on reservations not only to improve infrastructure but also because of the "Indian Service's long experience in handling a minority group."[10] Ultimately only the two camps in Arizona—Poston on the Colorado River Indian Community Reservation and Gila River—were placed on reservation land. The Gila River Indian Community objected to the camp's construction, voting twice against the plan, but were ignored by the Bureau of Indian Affairs, the Western Defense Command, the Department of the Interior, and the newly created War Relocation Authority, which administered the camps. Only in October 1942, after most of the incarceration camp had been constructed and thousands of Japanese Americans transported there, did the Gila River Indian Community Tribal Council approve a permit to lease the land to the federal government. The council did so by a narrow five-to-four margin after reservation superintendent

A. E. Robinson made it clear that the camp would continue operating with or without the permit and that the tribe was losing $387.60 per day in leasing fees.[11]

The first Japanese Americans arrived at Gila River in July 1942, and the camp operated until November 1945. The population peaked at 13,348 people, with a total of about 16,000 Japanese Americans passing through. The camp was divided into two subcamps: Butte Camp housed approximately 8,500 people, while Canal Camp housed approximately 4,800. The footprint of the two sub-camps and their surrounding agricultural fields totaled about 17,000 acres, with 540 barracks, 72 latrines, 36 washrooms and laundry rooms, 36 recreation halls, 36 mess halls, and dozens of administrative, military, and storage buildings. Heat and dust featured prominently in my grandmother's memories of camp. The temperatures at Gila River ranged from close to freezing in the winter to well over 100°F in the summer—much hotter than most California residents were used to.[12] In addition, the clearing of vegetation for the construction of the camp exacerbated the area's frequent dust storms, with dust entering the barracks through gaps left by the shrinkage of cheap green lumber in the floorboards and covering everything in the small, cramped apartments.[13]

Santa Barbara County sent the majority of its Japanese American residents to Gila River. Sitting on the Southern California coast approximately eighty miles northwest of Los Angeles, between San Luis Obispo and Ventura Counties, most of Santa Barbara County's urban area was concentrated relatively close to the Pacific Ocean in the area bounded by the San Rafael and Santa Ynez Mountains. Japanese Americans in Santa Barbara County have a rich history, particularly in northwestern towns such as Santa Maria and Guadalupe, where much of the Japanese American population was concentrated in the first half of the twentieth century. Just as important, though less well known, the city of Santa Barbara had a neighborhood known as Nihonmachi (Japantown).[14] Located downtown on the north side of the 100 block of East Canon Perdido Street between Anacapa and Santa Barbara Streets, Nihonmachi stood on the northern footprint of the El Presidio de Santa Barbara, one of four fortified Spanish military bases in California. El Presidio was constructed in 1783 midway between the town's mission and the Pacific Coast. As control over El Presidio transitioned from Spain to Mexico in 1822 and then to the United States in 1846, the buildings fell into disrepair, degraded by exposure to the elements, lack of repair, and a series of earthquakes. As the structures of El Presidio came down, new buildings were constructed atop the ruins of the old fortification. By 1886, the 100 block of East Canon Perdido Street retained only one building from the El Presidio era, the Cañedo Adobe, which still stands today.[15]

The first Japanese migrants to live in Santa Barbara were not recorded in the U.S. Census until 1900 and in the Japanese Association of America's *History of*

Japanese in America until about 1901.[16] By 1910, the Nihonmachi area was home to 33 Japanese migrants; a decade later, that number had grown to 210, and the neighborhood had a Japanese Christian church and a Buddhist temple as well as a boardinghouse, grocery store, and hotel. Over successive years, the Nihonmachi remained an economic and social hub, with businesses and churches anchoring the community even as Japanese migrants moved to other parts of the city. Unlike the relatively nearby Santa Maria and Guadalupe Japanese diasporic communities, which dominated the vegetable industry and created an economically stratified social structure, the residents of Santa Barbara's Nihonmachi worked primarily in racially segregated professions such as gardening and domestic labor.[17] The development of Santa Barbara's community did not differ greatly from that of other Japanese communities in the United States before World War II.

Japanese migration to the United States began in the late 1860s with the onset of the Meiji era (1868–1912) and the expansion of the Japanese Empire. The kingdom of Hawai'i and the United States became prime destinations for migrants, many of whom left Japan as a result of economic hardship, political instability, violence, and a lack of perceived opportunity.[18] While migrants moved across and throughout the Pacific, many maintained transnational connections with families, friends, businesses, and other institutions both within the spheres of the Japanese Empire and in other parts of the diaspora in North, Central, and South America.[19] In the western United States, Japanese American communities concentrated in major urban cores such as San Francisco, Seattle, and Los Angeles as well as in small farming, mining, and lumber towns. Though many migrants initially worked in transient labor occupations, many transitioned to agriculture by the 1920s, becoming a major political and economic force on the California landscape.[20] At the same time, Japanese Americans faced intense prejudice, with states passing racist and white supremacist laws restricting opportunities for migrants from Asia to naturalize as U.S. citizens, work in particular fields, and buy or lease property. Furthermore, throughout the western states, anti-Asian and particularly anti-Japanese violence increased in places where the success of these communities was considered a threat to white laboring communities.

The residents of Nihonmachi included the Fukushima family at 129½ East Canon Perdido Street, next to the Buddhist temple. Kinzo and Fuji Fukushima were migrants from Kumamoto-ken who were living at that address by 1910. Kinzo served as the sixth president of the Japanese Association of Santa Barbara; his successor was another prominent longtime Nihonmachi resident, Sentaro Asakura, who ran the Asakura Hotel at 111 East Canon Perdido. Kinzo Fukushima worked as a gardener in Santa Barbara, while Fuji ran a grocery store and boardinghouse. Kinzo and Fuji had enjoyed relatively high social status in

Japan: according to their granddaughter Hideko, they were well educated and practiced calligraphy, and Fuji regularly traveled back and forth to Japan. One of their daughters, Shigeko born in 1914 and known as Shige, married Hideo George Nishihara, and the two continued their lives at 129½ East Canon Perdido, raising Hideko and her sisters, Valentine and Yoshiko.

Down the street from the Fukushima-Nishihara family were the Asakuras. The Asakura Hotel featured rooms for

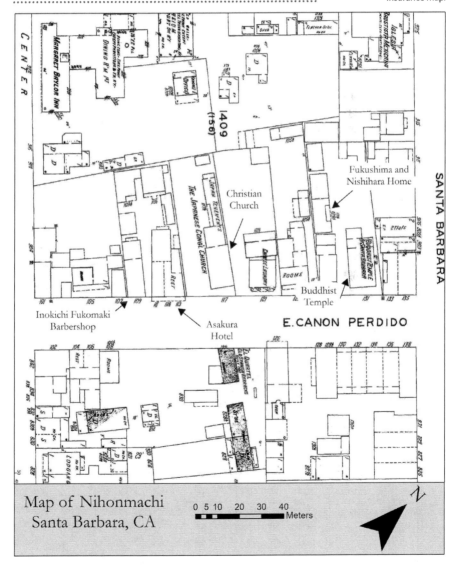

FIGURE 9.1. Map of the Nihonmachi neighborhood of Santa Barbara. Adapted by Koji Lau-Ozawa from 1940 Sanborn Fire Insurance map.

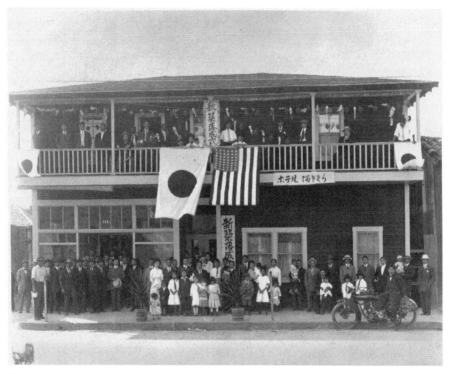

FIGURE 9.2.
Asakura Hotel, ca. 1910. Binder 1.1.3, Presidio Neighborhood Photograph Collection, Presidio Research Center, Santa Barbara California. Courtesy of Santa Barbara Trust for Historic Preservation.

both short-term visitors and longer-term boarders as well as a bathhouse, a grocery store, and a restaurant. The hotel was a cornerstone of the community along with the Christian Church and Buddhist Temple, as one of the first buildings built by the Japanese American community in Nihonmachi. At 109 East Canon Perdido, next door to the hotel, was a barbershop run by Inokichi Fukomaki. These institutions were important not only for the residents of Nihonmachi but also for Japanese Americans living in the surrounding communities, who would come into town to attend religious services, shop at the stores, and eat at the restaurants. One pair of sisters who grew up in eastern Santa Barbara before the war fondly remembered attending the Christian church and Japanese language school in Nihonmachi and buying sweets after class. The community provided spaces for Japanese Americans to come together. During World War II, most of Santa Barbara's Japanese American community was sent to the Tulare Detention Facility in Central California and then on to Gila River.

The Nihonmachi community never recovered from the mass removal. Some families returned to East Canon Perdido, but most were forced to move to other parts of the town. The Asakura Hotel was demolished and replaced by a parking lot in the early 1960s, and the house at 129½ East Canon Perdido soon followed. Today, there are no visible remnants of the Japanese American neighborhood: the block is dominated by the reconstructed chapel and buildings of El Presidio de Santa Barbara.

Designing a Project

In thinking through how to research the archaeology of the Gila River Incarceration Camp, close collaboration with GRIC-CRMP was essential. This collaboration brought to light two major concerns. The first was minimizing the impact of any archaeological work on the site itself. It was clear that excavation would not be an option, nor would the removal of objects or any kind of destructive analysis. Consequently, we decided over a series of conversations that intensive survey, mapping, and aerial photography would provide an understanding of the landscape yet have minimal impact. Working with GRIC-CRMP archaeologists, I mapped landscaping features and created high-resolution unmanned aerial vehicle orthomosaics and digital elevation models of four residential blocks from the Gila River Incarceration Camp, including two that had housed residents from Santa Barbara. Following work pioneered by collaborative archaeologists Kent Lightfoot and Sara Gonzales at Fort Ross in California and Bonnie Clark at the Amache Incarceration Camp in Colorado, I also conducted a catch-and-release analysis of artifacts left at a trash deposit.[21] Catch-and-release analysis involves removing artifacts from their provenance, photographing and analyzing them on site, and then returning them. This allowed for a great amount of data to be collected while respecting the need for minimal impact at the site.

The second concern was the potential that work would attract trespassers onto Gila River Indian Community land. Nonmembers of the Gila River Indian Community must apply for permission to enter tribal land, but that sovereignty is not always respected. Trespassers, including Japanese Americans, often are either ignorant of their transgressions or attempt to minimize the meaning of such intrusions. Several of the people I have interviewed and spoken to throughout the course of my research have admitted to both, though as awareness grows, more descendants of Gila River incarcerees are affirming a commitment to respect the rights of the Gila River Indian Community. Consequently, publicizing the results of my research runs the risk of revealing sensitive location data and encouraging trespassing. This problem is not unique to Gila River: many vulnerable archaeological sites require limitations on publicly available geographic data. The ethics of such research, especially in collaboration with Indigenous communities, is actively debated, and the desires of the Japanese American communities that actively seek such spatial data and representations complicate the question of how to navigate the desires of multiple communities.[22] To provide former incarcerees and their descendants with information while simultaneously minimizing the risks of trespassing, I minimize the amount of geographic data published and presented publicly and omit most real-world geographic references when presenting maps.

To supplement the data collected at Gila River, I examined materials excavated at Nihonmachi. By 1964, the land was owned by the Santa Barbara Trust for Historic Preservation, which conducted archaeological excavations to discover the remnants of the El Presidio buildings.[23] In addition to materials from the eighteenth- and nineteenth-century Spanish and Mexican periods, significant amounts of material from the Nihonmachi period were discovered. Since 2009, further excavations in the El Presidio courtyard have revealed a series of trash pits related to the residents of Nihonmachi, providing a glimpse into the material lives of its residents.

Communities Connected through Confinement

The use of noninvasive mapping has allowed for a better appreciation of what life was like in the camps for those who lived in Nihonmachi. Hideko Nishihara Malis described her block at Gila River as located near the road, hot and dry, and infested by large black and red ants. Born in 1935, she was seven years old when she was incarcerated and lived in a barracks apartment with five family members—her two younger sisters, her parents, and her grandfather. Her father built a little deck outside their barracks that was reached by a few stairs, and she would sit there during hot days. Malis stayed in touch with friends from the Nihonmachi neighborhood, though they were in other blocks.

When she and her sisters were ill and confined to their room, they would wave to their friends from the window. A woman in the apartment next door ran a beauty shop where she would give perms to women. According to Malis, gardens were small private areas between barracks, with little rocks and gates around them and often with water features. She emphasized that such gardens were to be looked at rather than played in.

People from Nihonmachi were fairly dispersed across the Butte Camp but were nevertheless concentrated in certain areas. Hideko's memories suggest that despite this dispersion, community members maintained close ties. In addition to the barracks, the block featured six ponds. My survey also found the remains of about ten entryway platforms, several fencepost lines demarcating garden areas, and seventeen depressions—likely basements beneath barracks. Utilizing a

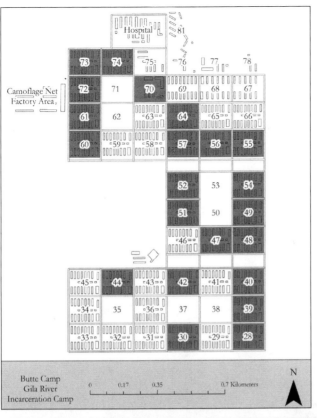

FIGURE 9.3.
Map of the Butte subcamp of the Gila River Incarceration Camp, with shaded blocks indicating where members of the Nihonmachi community lived. Map by Koji Lau-Ozawa.

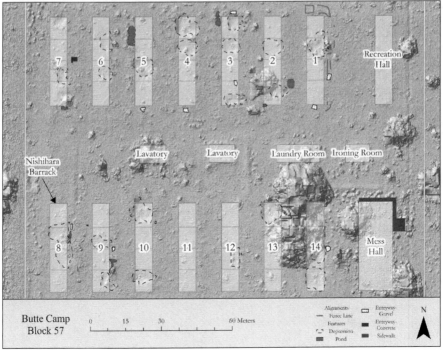

FIGURE 9.4.
Block 57 of the Butte subcamp, where the Nishihara family lived, showing depressions, ornamental ponds, and other landscaping features. Map by Koji Lau-Ozawa.

FIGURE 9.5. Feature 63 at Gila River, the remains of a small concrete pond ornamented with granite and quartz stones located across from the Nishihara family's apartment. Photo by Koji Lau-Ozawa.

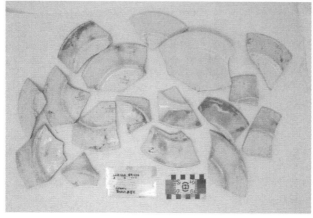

FIGURE 9.6. Hotelware dishes manufactured by the Homer Laughlin Company and documented on-site at the Gila River Incarceration Camp. Photo by Koji Lau-Ozawa.

digital elevation model derived from unmanned aerial vehicle photographs, the contours of the depressions are clearly visible.

A trash deposit at Gila River contained large numbers of ceramic sherds, including hotelware ceramics—that is, mass-produced durable white ironstone dishes often found in institutional settings.[24] Feature 3 exclusively held these hotelwares, while Feature 1 contained a mixture of ceramics, glass, and other materials. After hotelware, the most prevalent ceramics were porcelains. Twelve of the seventy porcelain vessels had marks indicating the country of manufacture: eleven were made in Japan, while one was made in China. The deposition of these features suggests that Feature 3 holds material from the camp's mess halls, likely discarded after the camp closed, while Feature 1 likely contains refuse discarded from the barracks during the camp's operation. Since these features represent community-wide consumption patterns, analysis of individual household behaviors is extremely challenging.[25] However, when these items are viewed alongside materials from prewar contexts, interesting patterns emerge.

In 2009, archaeologists from the Santa Barbara Trust for Historic Preservation uncovered a small trash deposit likely related to a single household from the Nihonmachi period. Analysis shows that this material was dominated by porcelains imported from Japan, followed by a small number of European-produced items. The relative proportions of holloware (bowls and cups) and flatware (plates and dishes) from the Gila River and Santa Barbara assemblages are very similar. This finding suggests that camp authorities supplied incarcerees with slightly more holloware than flatware. In contrast, more than twice as many hollowares than flatwares were present among the porcelain vessels found in Feature 1, a proportion roughly the same as found in the Santa Barbara deposit. In the context of Japanese American table settings, this is not surprising: a typical meal uses a large number of bowls. This finding may suggest that incarcerees attempted to continue their prewar consumption practices despite the structures of the institution, as was the case in other Japanese American incarceration camp contexts.[26]

The features at Gila River contained no matching sets of porcelains, only individual items. The Santa Barbara assemblage, in contrast, contained multiple sets of matching ce-

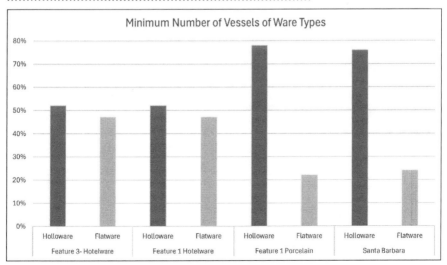

FIGURE 9.7. Proportions of holloware and flatware from Features 1 and 3 at Gila River and from the Santa Barbara deposit.

ramics. This discrepancy may reflect the rapidity with which people packed their possessions for camp, limitations on the ability to bring relatively heavy items (many incarcerees could bring only what they could carry), or difficulty in procuring sets of ceramics while in camp.

An Archaeology for Multiple Publics

The positioning of the Gila River Incarceration Camp as a site of removal, both in the sense of a place to which communities (Japanese Americans) were removed and as a landscape removed from control of a people (the Gila River Indian Community), entails an approach that respects the different yet intertwined levels of violence inflicted on those communities. There is no easy way to contend with this fact when the wishes and beliefs of multiple community perspectives come into contact with one another through the act of research. As Reinhard Bernbeck contends, the practice of archaeology is embedded within structures of violence, and it is difficult to untangle the discipline from its extractive and invasive nature.[27] The dual conceptions of public archaeology demand an acknowledgement of the legitimate concerns of external parties— a public defined as outside of the discipline. When such acknowledgments are made, control is ceded, a movement along what Chip Colwell-Chanthaphoh and T. J. Ferguson describe as the collaborative continuum.[28] This chapter briefly sketches out one such approach.

I worked with GRIC-CRMP and the Gila River Tribal Historic Preservation Office to create a research design that respected the site's sensitivity and limited the potential physical impact of my archeological research. At the same time, I worked with former incarcerees and their descendants to understand both the impact of incarceration and the desire to know more about their history. I have discussed the results of my research with Santa Barbara's Japanese American community as well as organizations such as the Santa Barbara Trust for Historic Preservation. I have also given talks on the subject, published articles in local journals, and worked with director Barre Fong to produce a short documentary film, *Sonzai: Japantown in Santa Barbara*.[29] At the same time, I have worked to limit the way in which I share my data in an attempt to limit the risk that directing the archaeological gaze on a site might have in increasing its vulnerability. This approach has not limited the ability to do good archaeology or good science but instead, I believe, has made the research at Gila River stronger. Important insights can be gained by working with different communities and noninvasive methodologies. After acknowledging the existence of multiple publics, public archaeology must then seek to work with and for such publics. Long-term collaboration, dialogue, experimentation, and trust building are all facets of this process. Working as a descendant of incarcerees, I am all too aware of the anger, sadness, and pain the discussion of histories of violence brings to the fore. It is my hope that taking seriously such concerns can perhaps work to make a better archaeology for many publics.

Notes

1. See Raymond Y. Okamura, "The American Concentration Camps: A Cover-Up through Euphemistic Terminology," *Journal of Ethnic Studies* 10, no. 3 (1982): 95–109; Roger Daniels, "Words Do Matter: A Note on Inappropriate Terminology and the Incarceration of the Japanese Americans," in *Nikkei in the Pacific Northwest: Japanese Americans and Japanese Canadians in the Twentieth Century*, ed. Louis Fiset and Gail Nomura (Seattle: University of Washington Press, 2005), 183–207; Japanese American Citizens League, *Power of Words Handbook: A Guide to Language about Japanese Americans in World War II* (San Francisco: Japanese American Citizens League, 2013), https:// thentheycame.org/wp-content/uploads/2019/03/Power-of-Words-Handbook-JACL.pdf. I use the term *Japanese American incarceration*. While *Japanese American internment* may be more familiar to many readers, *internment* refers to a specific legal category of the detainment of enemy aliens and is not appropriate for this case in which two-thirds of those incarcerated were U.S. citizens.

2. Richard W. Effland Jr. and Margerie Green, *Cultural Resource Assessment for the Gila River Farms Indian Community, GRIC* (Phoenix, Ariz.: Archaeological Consulting Services, 1983); Mary Sullivan, Monique Sawyer-Lang, Richard W. Effland Jr., and Margerie Green, *An Archaeological Survey of the Gila River Farms Expansion, Pinal County, Arizona* (Tempe, Ariz.: Archaeological Consulting Services, 1987); Monique Sawyer-Lang, *Recovery of Additional Information from the Gila River Farms Expansion Area: A Study of a Japanese-American Relocation Center* (Tempe, Ariz.: Archaeological Consulting Services, 1989); Orit Tamir, Scott C. Russell, Karolyn Jackman Jensen, and Shereen Lerner, *Return to Butte Camp: A Japanese-American World War II Relocation Center* (Tempe, Ariz.: Archaeological Consulting Services, 1993).

3. Jeff F. Burton, Mary M. Farrell, Florence B. Lord, and Richard W. Lord, *Confinement and Ethnicity: An Overview of World War II Japanese American Relocation Sites* (Tucson, Ariz.: Western Archaeological and Conservation Center, National Park Service, 1999).

4. Koji Ozawa, Chip Colwell, Kerry Thompson, Laura Jones, Claudia Nissley, Barbara J. Little, Paul A. Shackel, and Thomas Gates, "Thinking through 'Community' in Archaeological Practice," *Practicing Anthropology* 40, no. 1 (2018): 53–57, https://doi.org /10.17730/0888-4552.40.1.53.

5. Gordon G. Brown, "Final Report: War Relocation Authority, Gila River Project, Rivers, Arizona, Community Analysis Section," *Applied Anthropology* 4, no. 4 (1945): 1–49, https://doi.org/10.17730/humo.4.4.87814670744lko76; U.S. War Relocation Authority, *Final Accountability Rosters of Evacuees (Gila River)* (Washington, D.C.: War Relocation Authority, 1946); final accountability rosters of evacuees at relocation centers, 1944–46, microfilm publication M1965, Records of the War Relocation Authority, Record Group 210, National Archives and Records Administration.

6. Nicole L. Branton, "Landscape Approaches in Historical Archaeology: The Archaeology of Places," in *International Handbook of Historical Archaeology*, ed. D. Gaimster and T. Majewski (New York: Springer, 2009), 51–65; Stacey Lynn Camp, "Landscapes of Japanese American Internment," *Historical Archaeology* 50 (2016): 169–86, https://doi.org/10.1007/BF03377183.

7. Sonya Atalay, *Community-Based Archaeology: Research with, by, and for Indigenous and Local Communities* (Berkeley: University of California Press, 2012); Jerimy J. Cunningham and Scott MacEachern, "Ethnoarchaeology as Slow Science," *World Archaeology* 48, no. 5 (2016): 628–41, https://doi.org/10.1080/00438243.2016.126004 6; William Caraher, "Slow Archaeology, Punk Archaeology, and the 'Archaeology of Care,'" *European Journal of Archaeology* 22, no. 3 (2019): 372–85, https://doi.org/10.1017/eaa.2019.15; Kisha Supernant, Jane Eva Baxter, Natasha Lyons, and Sonya Atalay, eds., *Archaeologies of the Heart* (Cham, Switz.: Springer International, 2020); Ayana Omilade Flewellen, Ayana Omilade, Justin P. Dunnavant, Alicia Odewale, Alexandra Jones, Tsione Wolde-Michael, Zoë Crossland, and Maria Franklin, "'The Future of Archaeology Is Antiracist': Archaeology in the Time of Black Lives Matter," *American Antiquity* 86, no. 2 (2021): 224–43, https://doi.org/10.1017/aaq.2021.18; Kelly N. Fong, Laura W. Ng, Jocelyn Lee, Veronica L. Peterson, and Barbara L. Voss, "Race and Racism in Archaeologies of Chinese American Communities," *Annual Review of Anthropology* 51 (2022): 233–50, https://doi.org/10.1146/annurev-anthro-041320-014548.

8. Julia G. Costello and Mary L. Maniery, *Rice Bowls in the Delta: Artifacts Recovered from the 1915 Asian Community of Walnut Grove, California* (Los Angeles: Institute of Archaeology, University of California, Los Angeles, 1988).

9. Roger Daniels, *Concentration Camps, North America: Japanese in the United States and Canada during World War II* (Malabar, Fla.: R. E. Krieger, 1981); Greg Robinson, *By Order of the President: FDR and the Internment of Japanese Americans* (Cambridge: Harvard University Press, 2001); Greg Robinson, *A Tragedy of Democracy: Japanese Confinement in North America* (New York: Columbia University Press, 2009); Tetsuden Kashima, *Judgment without Trial: Japanese American Imprisonment during World War II* (Seattle: University of Washington Press, 2003); Eric L. Muller, *American Inquisition: The Hunt for Japanese American Disloyalty in World War II* (Chapel Hill: University of North Carolina Press, 2007); Masumi Izumi, *The Rise and Fall of America's Concentration Camp Law: Civil Liberties Debates from the Internment to McCarthyism and the Radical 1960s* (Philadelphia: Temple University Press, 2019).

10. Alison R. Bernstein, *American Indians and World War II: Toward a New Era in Indian Affairs* (Norman: University of Oklahoma Press, 1991), 83.

11. Tamir et al., *Return to Butte Camp*, 103–8.

12. Karl Lillquist, *Imprisoned in the Desert: The Geography of World War II–Era Japanese American Relocation Centers in the Western United States* (Ellensburg: Central Washington University, Geography and Land Studies Department, 2007), 465.

13. Milton Thomas Madden, "A Physical History of the Japanese Relocation Camp Located at Rivers, Arizona" (master's thesis, University of Arizona, 1969); Lillquist, *Imprisoned in the Desert*.

14. *Nihon* (日本) means "Japan," and *machi* (町) means "town" or "village."

15. Anne Salsich, "The Architecture of the Presidio, 1880–1890," in *Santa Barbara Presidio Area, 1840 to the Present*, ed. Carl V. Harris, Jarrell C. Jackman, and Catherine Rudolph (Santa Barbara: University of California, Santa Barbara Public Historical Studies and Santa Barbara Trust for Historic Preservation, Presidio Research Center, 1993), 17–26.

16. Koji Ozawa, Tim Yamamura, and Kaoru "Kay" Ueda, eds., *Zaibei Nihonjin Shi: History of Japanese in America*, trans. Seizo Francis Oka (San Francisco: Zaibei Nihonjinkai, 1940), https://hojishinbun.hoover.org/?a=d&d=hja19401220-01.1.1&l=en.

17. Kent Haldan, "'Our Japanese Citizens': A Study of Race, Class, and Ethnicity in Three Japanese American Communities in Santa Barbara County, 1900–1960" (PhD diss., University of California, Berkeley, 2000); Naomi Hirahara, *An American Son: The Story of George Aratani, Founder of Mikasa and Kenwood* (Los Angeles: Japanese American National Museum, 2001).

18. Yuji Ichioka, *The Issei: The World of the First Generation Japanese Immigrants, 1885–1924* (New York: Free Press, 1988); Daniel M. Masterson, *The Japanese in Latin America* (Urbana: University of Illinois Press, 2004); Eiichiro Azuma, *Between Two Empires: Race, History, and Transnationalism in Japanese America* (New York: Oxford University Press, 2005); Sidney Xu Lu, *The Making of Japanese Settler Colonialism: Malthusianism and Trans-Pacific Migration, 1868–1961* (Cambridge: Cambridge University Press, 2019).

19. Eiichiro Azuma, *In Search of Our Frontier: Japanese America and Settler Colonialism in the Construction of Japan's Borderless Empire* (Oakland: University of California Press, 2019); Iijima Mariko, "Coffee Production in the Asia-Pacific Region: The Establishment of a Japanese Diasporic Network in the Early 20th Century," *Journal of International Economic Studies* 32 (2018): 75–88, https://doi.org/10.15002/00014590; Mariko Iijima, "Sugar Islands in the Pacific in the Early Twentieth Century," *Historische Anthropologie* 27, no. 3 (2019): 361–81, https://doi.org/10.7788/hian.2019.27.3.361.

20. Ichioka, *Issei*; Azuma, *Between Two Empires*.

21. Sara L. Gonzalez, Darren Modzelewski, Lee M. Panich, and Tsim D. Schneider, "Archaeology for the Seventh Generation," *American Indian Quarterly* 30, nos. 3/4 (2006): 388–415; Sara L. Gonzalez, "Indigenous Values and Methods in Archaeological Practice: Low-Impact Archaeology through the Kashaya Pomo Interpretive Trail Project," *American Antiquity* 81, no. 3 (2016): 533–49, https://doi.org/10.1017 /S000273160000398X; Kent G. Lightfoot, "Collaborative Research Programs: Implications for the Practice of North American Archaeology," in *Collaborating at the Trowel's Edge: Teaching and Learning in Indigenous Archaeology*, ed. Stephen W. Silliman (Tucson: University of Arizona Press, 2008), 211–27; Bonnie J. Clark, *Finding Solace in the Soil: An Archaeology of Gardens and Gardeners at Amache* (Louisville: University Press of Colorado, 2020).

22. Dylan S. Davis and Matthew C. Sanger, "Ethical Challenges in the Practice of Remote Sensing and Geophysical Archaeology," *Archaeological Prospection* 28, no. 3 (2021): 271–78, https://doi.org/10.1002/arp.1837; Dylan S. Davis, Danielle Buffa, Tanambelo Rasolondrainy, Ebony Creswell, Chiamaka Anyanwu, Abiola Ibirogba, Clare Randolph, Abderrahim Ouarghidi, Leanne N. Phelps, Francoise Lahiniriko, Zafy Maharesy

Chrisostome, George Manahira, and Kristina Douglass, "The Aerial Panopticon and the Ethics of Archaeological Remote Sensing in Sacred Cultural Spaces," *Archaeological Prospection* 28, no. 3 (2021): 305–20, https://doi.org/10.1002/arp.1819; William T. D. Wadsworth, Kisha Supernant, and Vadim A. Kravchinsky, "An Integrated Remote Sensing Approach to Métis Archaeology in the Canadian Prairies," *Archaeological Prospection* 28, no. 3 (2021): 321–37, https://doi.org/10.1002/arp.1813.

23. Brian Fagan, *Archaeology of the Chapel Site* (Santa Barbara, Calif.: Santa Barbara Trust for Historic Preservation, 1976); Harris, Jackman, and Rudolph, *Santa Barbara Presidio Area.*

24. Adrian Myers, "The Significance of Hotel-Ware Ceramics in the Twentieth Century," *Historical Archaeology* 50, no. 2 (2016): 110–26.

25. Barbara L. Voss, "Between the Household and the World System: Social Collectivity and Community Agency in Overseas Chinese Archaeology," *Historical Archaeology* 42 (2008): 37–52.

26. Nicole L. Branton, "Rice Bowls and Resistance: Cultural Persistence at the Manzanar War Relocation Center, California" (master's thesis, University of Arizona, 2000); Stephanie A. Skiles and Bonnie J. Clark, "When the Foreign Is Not Exotic: Ceramics at Colorado's WWII Japanese Internment Camp," in *Trade and Exchange: Archaeological Studies from History and Prehistory*, ed. Carolyn D. Dillian and Carolyn L. White (New York: Springer, 2010), 179–92.

27. Reinhard Bernbeck, "Violence in Archaeology and the Violence of Archaeology," in *Archaeologies of Violence and Privilege*, ed. Christopher N. Matthews and Bradley D. Phillippi (Albuquerque: University of New Mexico Press, 2020), 15–38.

28. Chip Colwell-Chanthaphoh and T. J. Ferguson, eds., *Collaboration in Archaeological Practice: Engaging Descendant Communities* (Lanham, Md.: AltaMira Press, 2008).

29. Barre Fong, dir., and Koji Lau-Ozawa, prod., *Sonzai: Japantown in Santa Barbara* (San Francisco: Barre Fong Designs, 2021); Koji Lau-Ozawa, "Material Markets of the World: Early Finds in the Nihonmachi Archaeology Collection," *La Campana* 47, no. 1 (2021): 5–14.

Teaching Middle School Students about Migration Using Archaeological Inquiry

An Evaluation of the Investigating Migration Curriculum Project

ELIZABETH C. REETZ, KATHERINE HODGE,
JEANNE M. MOE, AND ERIKA MALO

10

Project Archaeology: Investigating Migration, a new curriculum by Project Archaeology (PA) for grades 7–8, uses archaeological inquiry, primary sources, and geographic information systems (GIS) to investigate the topic of migration, focusing on the Overland Trail. Investigating Migration provides an educational curriculum regarding national historic trails, other trails, roads, railroads, and other avenues for the migration of people, promoting public awareness and stewardship of these cultural resources across public lands. This curriculum was modeled on Project Archaeology: Investigating Shelter and Project Archaeology: Investigating Food and Land using Understanding by Design methodologies developed by Grant P. Wiggins and Jay McTighe.[1]

PA piloted the curriculum in early 2021 with four teachers from Montana and Wyoming. These teachers and their students represented two urban and two rural schools, two science and two history/social studies classes, and grades 6, 8, and 9. An external evaluation assessed whether the curriculum met short-term and medium-term outcomes and identified areas for improvement. The PA staff and its network of educators will also use the results to share program outcomes with stakeholders, encourage support from program funders, and identify new funders.

Background

PA is a national archaeology education program founded by the U.S. Bureau of Land Management for educators and their students. According to its website, "Project Archaeology uses archaeological inquiry to foster understanding of past and present cultures; improve social studies, science, and literacy education; and enhance citizenship education to help preserve our archaeological legacy."[2] The program began in Utah in 1990 to combat vandalism and looting of archaeological sites. Over the next few years, PA expanded and laid the groundwork for a national education program. From 2001 to 2022, the national office was located at Montana State University, where it operated under a partnership between the Department of Sociology and Anthropology and the Bureau of Land Management. PA has served more than 17,000 educators and reaches an estimated 340,000 students each year.[3] PA has been established in thirty-nine states and has grown to encompass four integral components: high-quality grade-level and regionally appropriate curricular materials, professional development for formal and informal educators, continuing professional support, and national network of archaeology educators.

All PA curricular materials and professional development for educators are based on four "enduring understandings that encompass what students need to understand and remember long into the future:

1. Understanding the past is essential for understanding the present and shaping the future.
2. Learning about cultures, past and present, is essential for living in a pluralistic society and world.
3. Archaeology is a systematic way to learn about past cultures.
4. Stewardship of archaeological sites and artifacts is everyone's responsibility."[4]

Curriculum Overview

Investigating Migration consists of seven standards-based lessons and a final performance of understanding that create a cohesive unit using archaeological inquiry, primary sources, and GIS maps to investigate the topic of migration, later focusing on the Overland Trail. Teachers and students query GIS databases to learn more about the physical evidence of the trails, including settlements, trail stations, artifacts travelers left behind, immigrant demographics, and route topography. Students use primary sources such as diaries, census data, and historic photographs to analyze and interpret archaeological data, learn GIS mapping techniques, and build their own StoryMaps.

Investigating Migration fulfills many common core state standards in English language arts and mathematics, the C3 Framework for citizenship and social studies, and Next Generation Science Standards. Because the curriculum includes a significant GIS database and instruction is technology based, it helps teachers meet science, technology, engineering, and math standards.

As with all PA curricular materials, archaeologists developed this unit by working with descendant community members, a model tested and revised over three decades. In this case, the collaborators included Crystal C'Bearing, Northern Arapaho tribal historic preservation officer, and another Northern Arapaho representative, Benjamin Ridgely, who created a written narrative featuring C'Bearing's perspective as well as GIS maps illustrating the movement of the Northern Arapaho.

Archaeologists in the PA network researched site data in the Wyoming region of the Overland Trail. PA wanted to feature different sites around the area that captured various aspects of life in the West, including mountain sites with multiple occupations and conflict sites such as Sand Creek. To protect site locations, PA worked with a GIS contractor, SEARCH Inc., to place map points at general locations rather than at specific coordinates. The maps were also designed to prevent students from zooming in close enough to see revealing geographic information.

The Evaluation

In addition to rigorous reviews, all PA materials undergo some form of systematic evaluation.[5] In the field of public archaeology, where funding for engagement and outreach is limited and personnel often conduct education as an add-on to their primary archaeological job responsibilities, systematic external evaluation is rare. There is little holistic discussion of the best approaches to use in specific types of situations and little assessment of best practices. Archaeologists and educators consequently must spend time reinventing the wheel, and programming may satisfy archaeologists and the organizations for which they work but does not necessarily reach the intended audience.[6] Archaeologists are beginning to build a research base, but internal forms of assessment primarily limit success and impact metrics to attendance and number of events.[7] Effectively measuring programmatic impact through evaluation requires training and experience as well as sufficient funds to hire evaluation experts. However, these efforts are worth the investment.

Evaluation provides data-driven insights into impact and success. When evaluation constitutes a regular part of public archaeology programming, the result is a dataset showing how goals and outcomes are met or exceeded or whether a pivot is necessary. Understanding the benefits of investment with personnel and funding clearly demonstrates whether program methods, activities, and resources are being used effectively and efficiently.[8] Success backed by data results in more powerful grant applications. In short, sustainable programming in public archaeology cannot exist without the systematic integration of evaluation.

The PA national office contracted an external evaluation of the curriculum pilot to help stakeholders better understand whether program outcomes were being achieved and identify areas for improvement. During the planning process, the evaluation team established measurable short-term and medium-term outcomes focused on what students were expected to learn and what pilot teachers were expected to accomplish. The outcomes are outlined in the logic model and drive a series of evaluation questions addressed by the data analysis. Long-term impacts included in the logic model were not assessed in this evaluation but provide a base for more longitudinal studies of the curriculum.

Evaluation Design and Data Collection

The evaluation conducted for PA draws on a single group pretest/posttest study, a single group posttest focus group, and classroom observation data. The evaluation used logic modeling to relate the pilot activities to short-term goals and some medium-term goals. We developed evaluation questions to align with logic model outcomes and created a research matrix to align indicators, data sources, and tools with the evaluation questions. Data were gathered from students and pilot teachers between January and March 2020.

To provide additional evidence that the original pilot students experienced a statistically significant improvement between their pre- and posttest scores, we recruited a control group. The treatment group for the curriculum pilot consisted of four classrooms, with forty-three students participating in the study and thirty-three completing both pretests and posttests that consisted of sixteen questions related to migration, primary sources, maps, and archaeology. A one-classroom control group of twenty students completed the pretest and posttest but did not learn the curriculum. The control group consisted of students in one of the pilot teacher's classes from the 2021–22 school year, whereas her 2020–21 class participated in the treatment group.

A rubric with values 0 (nonexistent), 1 (underdeveloped), 2 (minimally developed), 3 (well-developed), and 4 (highly developed/outstanding) was used to score the quality of student responses and convert qualitative answers into quantitative data. Zeros thus do not reflect missing data. Students were instructed to leave a question blank if they did not know the answer, which provided insight about which questions the students struggled to answer. All student questionnaire responses were scored by four independent coders, with those scores averaged for the results.

A focus group interview involved a single group posttest of four pilot classroom teachers who were voluntary respondents, with no sampling. Qualitative analysis resulted in the generation of five themes: teachers' curricular needs; classroom needs and students' learning abilities; feedback on curriculum and lessons; teachers' observations on student learning; and curriculum value and knowledge gained. Analysis of each of these themes aligned with logic model outcomes and evaluation research questions. Teachers' observations on student learning addresses student learning outcomes, while the other four themes address pilot teacher outcomes.[9]

LIMITATIONS

The results of this evaluation are specific to this curriculum pilot case study and are not transferable or generalizable. The timing of the pilot during the first winter of the COVID-19 pandemic may have affected the results. Some classes were taught completely in person, while others were virtual and/or hybrid.

Student Questionnaire

1. What reasons might people migrate (move) from one country or place to another?

2. Give one example of people migrating in the 1800s.

3. Give one example of people migrating today (in the present day).

4. How has migration impacted the United States?

5. Name two types of primary sources we could use to learn about people's migration experiences.

6. Select the best fit answer. The relationships between historic Native Americans and early European/American settlers were: Circle one

    A. Positive   B. Negative   C. Both

Briefly explain your answer:

7. Rate yourself on a scale of 1 to 5: How confident are you with reading and using maps? Circle one

    1   2   3   4   5

No, not at all ←——————————————————→   Yes, very strongly

8. List three types of information a map could provide:

9. Have you ever created your own map using a digital resource (website, software, GIS, mobile app): Circle one

    YES   NO

If YES, rate yourself on this scale of 1 to 5: How confident are you with your digital map making skills?

    1   2   3   4   5

Not confident at all ←——————————————————→   Very confident

10. How can a map tell a story or help to solve a problem?

11. What is the main job of archaeologists and why is this job important?

12. Archaeologists collect data while investigating archaeological sites. How might an archaeologist use this data with modern mapping technology to learn even more about the past?

13. Name 2 things you think people should do if they find or visit an archaeological site.

    Explain your answers. Why should people do these things?

14. Name 2 things you think people should not do if they find or visit an archaeological site.

    Explain your answers. Why should people not do these things?

15. How does learning about past people and cultures benefit us today or in the future?

16. Explain the relationship between the following words: human migration, maps, archaeology:

FIGURE 10.1.
Student questionnaire.

The curriculum was developed to be taught in a typical in-person classroom, and it is not known how some of the lessons translated into virtual teaching.

EVALUATION FINDINGS

Each data-collection method yielded unique results, but space permits us to provide only a general overview of how the student questionnaire results aligned with logic model outcomes.

A Comparison of Treatment Group and Control Group Questionnaire Results

After the evaluation was submitted, we added a pretest/posttest study with a control group to take a deeper look at the student questionnaire data. On the pretest, the average rubric score for the treatment group ranged from 0.20 (where a student started but did not complete the questionnaire) to 2.36, with an average of 1.62. The control group average rubric score ranged from 1.36 to 2.22, with an average of 1.74. On the posttest, treatment group average rubric scores ranged from 0.77 to 2.70, with an average of 2.11, while the control group ranged from 1.23 to 2.38, with an

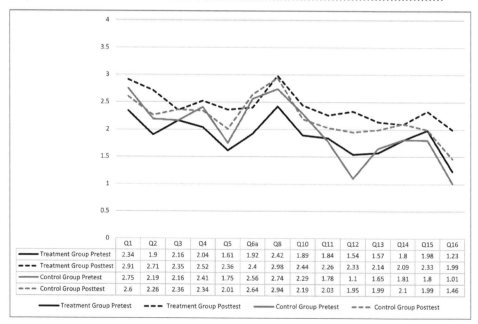

FIGURE 10.2.
Average rubric score per question comparing the treatment group and control group pretest and posttest.

TABLE 10.1
Two-Sample *T*-test Assuming Unequal Variances Comparing Pretest and Posttest
for the Treatment Group and Control Group

	CONTROL	TREATMENT
Mean	0.1845	0.497273
Variance	0.056321	0.22707
Observations	20	33
Hypothesized Mean Difference	0	
df	50	
t Stat	−3.17622	
P(T≤*t*) two-tail	0.002557	

average of 1.93. Treatment group rubric scores increased an average of 0.5 points
from the pretest to posttest, while control group scores increased an average of
0.18 points.

The test scores show that the control group had a higher baseline on the pretest, meaning that its members showed stronger prior knowledge than the members of the treatment group. However, the treatment group outperformed the
control group on the posttest. The treatment group also showed a more consistent increase in scores across each question. The control group scored higher
than the treatment group on the posttest question regarding the relationship
between Native Americans and settlers. We know from the focus group that this
particular teacher teaches a homesteading unit each year, so recent exposure to
these lessons may have affected these answers.

To measure statistical significance, we conducted a two-sample *t*-test assuming unequal variances to compare the difference between pretest and posttest
scores among the treatment group and control group. The null hypothesis as-
sumes that no difference exists among the students who learned the curriculum
and those who did not. The hypotheses are:

H_0: No difference exists in the improvement of pretest and posttest scores between the treatment and control groups.

H_1: A difference exists in the improvement of pretest and posttest scores between the treatment and control groups.

The probability value (p-value) is 0.002557. Because this value is less than 5
percent, the null hypothesis is rejected, and the test is statistically significant.
This means that there is strong evidence that the teaching intervention improved the students' scores between the pretest and posttest.

The biggest gains for the treatment group are noticeable on questions 2, 5, 8,

10, 12, and 16. In questions 2 and 5, students demonstrated knowledge gained by using vocabulary and examples taken directly from the curriculum. The least improvement between pretest and posttest average rubric scores was seen in question 3. The responses were largely similar on the pretest and posttest, and several students conflated the concepts of migration and moving, viewing the question at a more individual or family level than a societal level. At least 30 percent of students scored well-developed responses on the posttest on questions 1, 2, 5, 8, 10, 12, and 15. Question 8 received the highest score on the pretest, with 27 percent of students scoring a well-developed response.

STUDENT OUTCOMES

The summaries presented here are synthesized from the results of the student questionnaire for the treatment group, teacher focus group, and classroom observations.

MIGRATION

On the student questionnaire, four questions asked the students specifically about migration. Students demonstrated through their posttest improvements that they have a basic understanding of the different types of migration and that they learned people have different reasons for migrating. They also demonstrated through improvements in rubric scores that they learned that migration is a human action that leaves tangible evidence on the land that archaeologists can study. They did not demonstrate that they could relate movement and migration in U.S. history to modern-day issues. However, the questionnaire did not specifically ask them to address this relationship.

Teacher focus group feedback provides more insight. One teacher noted that the students struggled with their written communication, which could affect survey answers, but verbally demonstrated material retention. According to the teachers, many students initially did not view themselves or their immediate family as migrants but did make connections between movement and migration from U.S. history to the modern day. The classes had discussions of modern-day moving, which may have affected students' answers, which focused on reasons for migrating, including jobs and weather. The conversations reported by the teachers did not mention other contemporary migration issues such as those involving conditions in Mexico and Central America, but the students communicated these topics in their questionnaire responses.

RELATIONSHIPS BETWEEN NATIVE AMERICANS AND EUROPEAN AMERICAN SETTLERS

One question on the student questionnaire specifically asked students to select the best-fit answer (positive, negative, or both) regarding the relationships between historic Native Americans and early European American settlers and to explain the choice of response. Individual opinions remained largely the same before and after the classroom experience. Students who thought that the relationship was both positive and negative cited trade and assistance as well as attacks, killing, and forcibly taking land. This was the extent of the complexity that they communicated. Because their pretest and posttest opinions were largely the same, it is hard to say definitively that the students met this logic model outcome. They gained knowledge regarding the forcible removal and migration of Native Americans and some of the atrocities related to that removal but did not demonstrate an awareness of complexity or of the challenges of learning about this topic. However, this question was not written in a way that could capture their emotions or feelings regarding this topic.

The focus group data lends more insight into the awareness gained by students. Some students had prior knowledge about these relationships through units on homesteading. Others had classroom discussions on these relationships. One teacher said that students "asked good questions [but] didn't really seem to have so many opinions on what was right and what was wrong yet." Although the focus group data provided insight into challenging conversations that addressed understanding, it is not possible to measure whether the students felt increased respect or empathy toward other peoples.

MAPPING AND GIS

The students showed notable gains in the questions pertaining to mapping, including the types of information maps can provide and how maps can tell a story or solve a problem. A look at individual pretest and posttest ratings show that 42.4 percent of students had increased confidence in their digital mapping skills after completing the intervention. The data from the teacher focus group highlighted students' struggles with accessing the technology, and some schools restricted students' ability to make accounts for the StoryMaps website. Some classes did these activities as a group, watching the teacher project the technology. The teachers described the GeoDig component as one of the most engaging parts of the curriculum, and many students accomplished this lesson without problems. However, other teachers described having to "hold hands" and "spoon-feed" the students to get them through many of the GIS and StoryMaps assignments.

Students improved their ability to use maps to support arguments, with an overall average rubric score of 0.55 points; the number of well-developed responses increased from 3 percent to 36 percent. Many of the students' posttest responses cited trails, patterns, and movement and migration routes among the types of information maps provide and as ways that archaeologists use maps as tools. The students connected the types of information maps provide to migration, but it cannot be determined to what extent GIS and StoryMaps affected this knowledge.

ARCHAEOLOGY

All of the lowest-scoring questions on the student questionnaire pertained to archaeology, including the four questions where at least 20 percent of students answered "I don't know" or failed to answer on the pretests. Although some questions received lower scores in part due to students' failure to answer multiple-part questions, the responses showed that some students still struggled to communicate what archaeologists do and what people should do if they find or visit an archaeological site. Many of the students demonstrated the connections between maps and the archaeological study of migration. They reported that maps could be used to document archaeological sites and that archaeologists could look for patterns, trails, and other landmarks that tell stories about movement and migration.

During the focus group, the teachers shared observations on the lesson about archaeological survey that largely focused on logistics and modifications but did not share any other observations about student learning regarding archaeology or the other archaeology-related lessons. Teachers did not address stewardship topics. The classroom observation of the stewardship lesson showed that the teacher steered the conversation to mass tourism, stranger danger, and photography etiquette.

Archaeology is primarily used in this curriculum as a contextual tool to teach mapping and migration by focusing on what tools, resources, and approaches archaeologists use. Archaeology is not the central focus of the curriculum; in fact, it is one of the more abstract topics covered. Teachers' previous levels of knowledge about archaeology are unknown, and focus-group participants generally did not indicate that they had gained any new knowledge of the subject, though one teacher mentioned learning about archaeological legislation. The teachers did discuss having previously taught homesteading and migration and created maps. It is possible that their lack of prior knowledge about archaeology or teaching archaeology affected their approaches to and teaching of lessons with strong archaeological content. For example, one teacher modified the stewardship lesson to focus on etiquette at national parks because that issue resonated more with their prior knowledge.

Previous studies have also documented that students do not always grasp the basic concepts of archaeology even when it is the primary lesson focus.[10] For example, assessment of a five-week unit on archaeology in Kentucky revealed that students struggled to understand the role of context in building archaeological interpretations and lacked a direct mental connection between material objects and culture. However, they still understood the importance of preserving archaeological sites and artifacts.[11]

SYNTHESIZING KNOWLEDGE

The lowest-scored question was the summary/final question. We expected the scores to be low on the pretest because this question asked for a summary or synthesis of the main topics covered in the curriculum. We hoped that student answers on the posttest would not only build on prior knowledge and demonstrate new knowledge but express the interrelatedness of these topics. There was a 0.76-point improvement in the scores from the pretest to the posttest, primarily because most students felt confident enough to provide an answer on the posttest. About two-thirds of the posttest responses scored between minimally developed and well developed, demonstrating that the students had gained some knowledge on the topic. Many students' posttest responses referred to archaeologists using or making maps to study migration.

Teachers valued the curriculum for the connectedness of the topics and for the big picture it provided but did not communicate observations about the students' synthesis of knowledge regarding these topics.

Pilot Teacher Outcomes

COMPLETING THE PILOT

The four teachers who completed the pilot had a variety of challenges regarding the amount of time it took to teach the curriculum, primarily influenced by the COVID-19 pandemic and last-minute changes between virtual and in-person learning. One teacher did some lessons out of order as a result of class attendance issues and a desire to optimize times for group work and discussions. Teachers also modified archaeological survey components in response to severe cold weather conditions and a lack of indoor space for social distancing. One teacher showed a YouTube video about an archaeological survey instead of doing the activity. The two rural teachers noted that the technology sections were difficult for their students: one of these teachers spent 1.5 weeks on the GIS lessons alone. They estimated that without those challenges, the entire curriculum would have taken between 2.5 and 3 weeks.

KNOWLEDGE GAINED

When asked to indicate what new knowledge had been gained by teaching the curriculum, one teacher cited the laws protecting archaeological sites. Teachers also said that the curriculum affected their understanding of GIS and StoryMaps as teaching tools by prompting them to become familiar with otherwise-intimidating technology.

USING GIS AND STORYMAPS

Aside from the teacher who said that the curriculum impacted their understanding of GIS and StoryMaps as teaching tools, the teachers did not discuss whether their understanding of using GIS and StoryMaps as teaching tools had increased. However, they did express enthusiasm for the content and particularly for the GIS and technology pieces. The teachers also discussed the challenges of using technology in the classroom, such as limited access to websites requiring accounts, poor internet service, and students with lower technological skills.

TEACHER FEEDBACK

Teachers had no critical concerns about the content aside from the fact that some students lacked the prior historical knowledge to understand the background content. One teacher described the curriculum content as "thoughtful, well produced, explicitly explained, solid material. The course of study was clear." Teachers sometimes found organizing instructional materials confusing and time-consuming. Three of the teachers expressed a desire for more direction about what materials to print for their students for each lesson. Feedback on the use of technology was viewed as favorable despite the issues already noted. And in spite of students' struggles with the mapping lessons, they remained among the favorite lessons for both teachers and students. All the teachers chose the debate activity for their final performance of understanding. Feedback regarding the debate varied. One teacher thought that it was a great lesson for higher learners and that several students excelled at it, but it was more challenging for students with behavioral issues. Another teacher chose the activity because debates are not used as a teaching tool at that school.

USING THE CURRICULUM

The teachers felt comfortable teaching the curriculum as written but made many modifications. Teachers may perceive modifications as a standard part of teaching any lesson or curriculum and consequently did not view modifying the curriculum as different from teaching it as written.

Virtual learning necessitated some modifications. Three teachers taught parts of the curriculum virtually; only one teacher taught entirely in person. Some modifications were contextual. One social studies teacher had previously taught similar content in a homesteading unit, so those students had prior knowledge that enabled them to move quickly through the lessons. Two teachers had students who lacked a strong history background and consequently spent a significant amount of time discussing historical context. Further, the lack of prior knowledge meant that their students found the historical background information overwhelming.

PERCEIVED VALUE

The teachers valued the curriculum, as evidenced by their comments about how they loved it, its connections to their teaching, and intention to use the curriculum with future classes. When communicating value, teachers touched on the big picture and connectedness that the curriculum explores. It ties together content they are already teaching along with both history and current events. In addition, the curriculum connects to life in Montana at the same time that it helps students learn about life in other places.

The teachers had differing opinions about whether the curriculum was appropriate for science classrooms. According to the science teachers, it worked with their curricular needs and aligned with some of their standards. One of the history teachers fit the unit into a U.S. history course but did not see its applicability to other grades, and the science teacher at that school did not teach the curriculum because it was "too much history." A third teacher appreciated the interdisciplinary content.

Conclusions

Overall, the students and pilot teachers met the majority of the researchers' short- and medium-term goals. The teachers enjoyed using the curriculum, and all said that they would use it again in the future. The students' scores improved across all questions, and this improvement is statistically significant. However, there is room for improvement regarding archaeological content: the evaluation advised strengthening the narrative regarding what archaeologists do and how they use GIS and maps as tools. This finding supports those of previous assessment studies and PA evaluations, which have noted the abstract nature of teaching archaeology and have revealed mixed opinions regarding archaeology's applicability to social studies and science.

Teachers' positive responses to the curriculum are a testament of PA's three-decade model of success, which involves constant evaluation and revision and input from archaeologists, educators, and descendant community members and which clearly works for teachers.

The availability of data-driven evidence to support the efficacy of the curriculum pilot is critical. The PA can use this data not only for future research studies but also to support grant proposals and other funding opportunities.

Notes

1. Cali A. Letts and Jeanne M. Moe, *Project Archaeology: Investigating Shelter* (Bozeman: Montana State University, 2012); Erika Malo, Jeanne M. Moe, and Cali A. Letts, *Project Archaeology: Investigating Food and Land* (Bozeman: Montana State University, 2018); Grant P. Wiggins and Jay McTighe, *Understanding by Design*, 2nd ed. (Upper Saddle River, N.J.: Pearson, 2005).

2. Project Archaeology website, accessed August 4, 2024, https://projectarchaeology.org/.

3. Jeanne M. Moe, "Archaeology in Schools: Student Learning Outcomes," in *Archaeologists and the Pedagogy of Heritage: Theory and Practice*, vol. 2, ed. Phyllis M. Messenger and Susan J. Bender (Gainesville: University Press of Florida, 2019), 10.

4. *Resources: For Teachers*, Project Archaeology website, accessed August 4, 2024, https://projectarchaeology.org/teachers/.

5. Michael Brody, Jeanne M. Moe, Joelle Clark, and Crystal B. Alegria, "Archaeology as Culturally Relevant Science Education: The Poplar Forest Slave Cabin," in *Public Participation in Archaeology*, ed. Suzie Thomas and Joanne Lea (Woodbridge, U.K.: Boydell Press, 2014), 89–104; Jeanne M. Moe, "Archaeology Education for Children," *Advances in Archaeological Practice* 4, no. 4 (2016): 441–53; Nichole Tramel, "Formative Assessment of 'Project Archaeology: Investigating Food and Land'" (paper presented at the Society for American Archaeology Annual Meeting, Albuquerque, N.M., 2019).

6. Eleanor M. King, "Systematizing Public Education in Archaeology," *Advances in Archaeological Practice* 4, no. 4 (2016): 416.

7. Linda S. Levstik, A. Gwynn Henderson, and Jennifer S. Schlarb, "Digging into the Deep Past: An Archaeological Exploration of Historical Cognition," in *Understanding History: Recent Research in History Education*, ed. R. Ashby, P. Gordon, and P. Lee (London: Routledge-Falmer, 2005), 4:37–53; King, "Systematizing Public Education in Archaeology," 415–24; Moe, "Archaeology Education for Children"; Moe, "Archaeology in Schools," 9–29; Jeanne M. Moe, "Best Practices in Archaeology Education: Successes, Shortcomings, and the Future," in *Public Engagement and Education: Developing and Fostering Stewardship for an Archaeological Future*, ed. Katherine M. Erdman (New York: Berghahn Books, 2019), 215–36.

8. Julie A. Ernst, Martha C. Monroe, and Bora Simmons, *Evaluating Your Environmental Education Programs: A Workbook for Practitioners* (Washington, D.C.: National Association for Environmental Education, 2009).

9. All data is on file electronically at the University of Iowa Office of the State Archaeologist and is available for researchers upon request.

10. M. Elaine Franklin and Jeanne M. Moe, "A Vision for Archaeological Literacy," in *The Oxford Handbook of Public Archaeology*, ed. Robin Skeates, Carol McDavid, and John Carman (Oxford: Oxford University Press, 2012), 556–80.

11. Levstik, Henderson, and Schlarb, "Digging into the Deep Past"; A. Gwynn Henderson and Linda S. Levstik, "What Do They Remember? Assessing the Impact of an Archaeology Unit on School Children's Knowledge and Experience" (paper presented at the Society for American Archaeology Annual Meeting, Vancouver, B.C., 2008); Jeanne M. Moe, "Conceptual Understanding of Science through Archaeological Inquiry" (EdD diss., Montana State University, 2011).

Water Heritage of the Mountain West

Integrating Public Archaeology with Multidisciplinary Approaches to Water Research

11

MOLLY BOEKA CANNON AND ANNA S. COHEN

As the second-driest state in the United States, Utah faces extraordinary water challenges, many of which are also experienced by communities across the globe. To meet these challenges, we need novel technological solutions from engineering, innovative agriculture, and sociocultural perspectives on water use. The Water Heritage Anthropological Project (WHAP) explores the relationship between people and water through multidisciplinary approaches that examine the utility of long-term records for water management and consumption as well as by documenting the legacies of these practices and the implications for contemporary sustainable water management. The WHAP creates a space for community members, water managers, and users to come together and share water perspectives.

Our goals for the WHAP are multitiered. As water heritage scholars, we contextualize the material culture and built environment surrounding water management across time and space, contributing to a growing body of research on water heritage worldwide.[1] Archaeological research from across the Mountain West demonstrates that adaptive strategies to water resource management drive technological innovations and play important roles in social adaptations to changing climatic conditions and increased population.[2] Archival, sociological, and ethnographic studies demonstrate the continuity of climate-adaptive innovation by people in the Mountain West today.[3] As public archaeology scholars, we engage communities in our work through mentorship, outreach, and co-creation.[4] Members of the public—who may include schoolchildren, college students, and people over age fifty-five, among others—does not want just to consume information; rather, they want to actively participate in the process of building knowledge across disciplines.[5] Such participation in archaeological fieldwork and research encourages cultural heritage advocacy and can facilitate public-led initiatives on conservation and preservation.[6]

This chapter shows how our public archaeology addresses multifaceted dimensions of water heritage such as cross-cultural research, climate change and technology, and the role of long-term records in understanding current and future challenges in water management. Water research benefits from a nested outreach framework for the development of comprehensive and effective digital tools, enhanced student training, and building community. Public archaeology must be among the novel multidisciplinary solutions for addressing water use and conservation.

Dimensions of Water Heritage

Water heritage highlights the significance of water; the infrastructure to harvest and manipulate water, including consumption, rituals, and traditions; and the historical narratives that connect people to particular communities. Our research concentrates on three dimensions of water heritage.

First, we employ ethnography and cross-cultural research to illustrate the critical relationship between water and culture in the western United States as well as from a global perspective. Numerous ethnographic studies demonstrate that water and water-management features such as canals and reservoirs constitute significant aspects of the political, economic, and ritual life of communities.[7] Cross-cultural comparisons can connect sociocultural contexts, demonstrating that water serves as a key thread in the human experience. Such comparisons show that multiple perspectives are necessary to examine water economics, resiliency and sustainability in water systems, the breadth of environmental injustices surrounding water, and the meanings that water holds in everyday life.[8] People living in the Mountain West face many of these issues today.[9]

Second, we focus on the relationship between climate change and technology. Archaeologists in the Mountain West and elsewhere regularly evaluate the effects of changing climatic conditions on technological innovation and agricultural adaptations.[10] Some of this work informs research that applies archaeological methods, datasets, and theoretical frameworks to understand contemporary management issues, including conservation biology, heritage preservation, and natural resource and landscape management. Connecting this body of work with water heritage studies is important for understanding how societies can and should adapt to changing environmental, climatic, and social situations in the future.

Finally, we use long-term records from prehistoric through contemporary periods to evaluate changes in water management locally and to document the differing approaches that communities take toward water issues. A long-term cultural view on water management is critical as the Mountain West faces an uncertain water future with pressures from development and agriculture. With only a handful of prehistoric water management systems documented in Utah, the WHAP adds to our understanding of past water use through an interdisciplinary water-focused approach.[11] Archaeological datasets and methods offer unique opportunities to study the long-term intersections of ecological and social systems.[12] The WHAP illustrates the utility of incorporating data from ancient, historic, and modern water management to assess the nexus of these dimensions, highlighting the impact of ethnographic, archaeological, and historical approaches to water management.

Multiscalar, interdisciplinary research generates complex datasets and theoretical frameworks that can be difficult to articulate to nonacademic audiences, sometimes leaving the public uncertain about the meaning, impact, or value of water heritage studies.[13] Consequently, we have incorporated public archaeology into project inception and research design, into grant applications, and in our research products. We strive for meaningful engagement with the public across all aspects of our water heritage project.

Public Archaeology and Water Heritage

Water research not only must be interdisciplinary but must also incorporate the perspectives of water users, including children, college students, and potentially all community members. Our approach to public archaeology involves more than science communication and speaking *to* members of the public. Rather, we strive to speak *with* members of the public by including them in the process of science, engaging them directly in research and decision making.

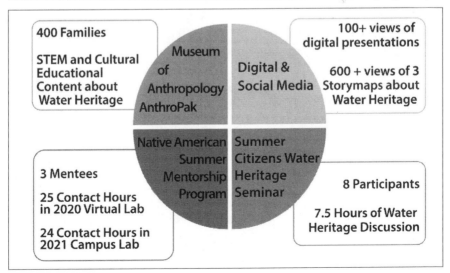

FIGURE 11.1. The impact of outreach initiatives for the Water Heritage Anthropological Project.

While there is a tradition of public engagement in archaeological projects, scholars argue that we should do more by offering opportunities for true collaboration, in which the community helps to shape research and is actively involved in all aspects of the project from research design to data collection to interpretation.[14] Since water is important from both natural resource and sociocultural perspectives, water heritage research presents an opportunity to develop community archaeology for multiple publics. The WHAP outreach program connects scholarship through a series of digital and tangible engagement tools that are geared toward audiences from young children to older adults.

Digital Storytelling to Engage Distant Audiences

Stories hold the power to transform, to move us from one point in time to another, to alter an emotional state, and to pass knowledge from one generation to the next. Our project systematically collects stories about water that inform our academic discourse as well as deepen the public's understanding of water, water heritage, and historic waterways. One way that the WHAP presents stories is by using ArcGIS StoryMaps, a medium focused on digital images and maps that enables us to share our research about water heritage with people living in northern Utah and elsewhere in the West. For example, the series Water Heritage in the West collates a series of ArcGIS StoryMaps that examine water management and water heritage infrastructure.[15] In the story "What Is a Canal Company?" viewers learn about the history of water management and the commodification of water in northern Utah via archival photographs and diary entries and read excerpts from our ethnographic work with canal managers. We examine the historical significance of a local water feature in Cache Valley in the story "A Historical Overview of Cutler Dam, Utah." Known by the indigenous Shoshone as Sihiviogoi (Willow Creek or Willow River), the landscape of Cache Valley, dominated by wetlands, rivers, and streams, offers refuge from the surrounding arid regions of the Great Basin.[16] In the nineteenth century, Euro-American settlers began harvesting water for culinary and agricultural purposes; by the early twentieth century, water was used as a powerful form of currency.[17] The Water Heritage in the West StoryMap series offers viewers who might not otherwise utilize archives digital access to historical narratives and photographs.

Our collection of water stories also assists us in contextualizing quantitative assessments of water heritage, humanizing water features, and illuminating the meaning of water in daily life for individuals and for communities. As one interviewee recalled,

> Every spring we would gather down in the island, 'cause the ditch came off the Logan River, just below where the water research lab is, and wound behind people's houses and that would get it to the edge of River Heights up at the top

of the hill. We had to clean it out every spring, so a family down there would have hot chocolate and donuts and you [would] bring your trimmers and your shovels and rake. It was all, well, pretty much like the pioneers, I suppose. Everybody needed [to] turn out to produce the sweat equity to get the ditch cleaned out from the winter and get it ready to go. As the years went by, fewer and fewer people came: that was also part of the annual ritual.

While documentation of historic water infrastructure such as mapping and quantifying canal lengths helps in assessing the impact of water-management systems, this narrative account highlights the role of social infrastructure, including community participants, the importance of seasonality, and the social practices that bond a community to harvest and manage water.

The ability to document stories and present them in a digital format became particularly important during the COVID-19 pandemic. Museums and cultural organizations have long relied on social media for communication, but with the onset of the pandemic, those digital tools were used to engage communities in new ways, such as via live video tours and conferencing. The pandemic certainly forced adjustments in teaching, research, and public engagement, requiring us to find creative ways to connect and to maintain partnerships.[18] For many cultural institutions, these adaptations have opened access to diverse audiences that academics are increasingly incorporating into their community-engaged research.[19] The WHAP integrates a suite of digital formats not only to offer content but also to engage in water heritage research with our community. During the pandemic lockdown, we relied on digital technologies for ethnographic data collection and used video to share research with our audiences at presentations at professional conferences, in university courses and public seminars, and on social media.[20] StoryMaps, video productions, and podcasts offer unique approaches to digital storytelling, connecting audiences to water heritage research.

Museum Partnerships to Engage Young Audiences

The WHAP works in partnership with local museums and community organizations to collaborate with young audiences. Since museums have a long-standing relationship with public engagement and the communication of complex research, partnering with them offers key advantages for public archaeology. Museums regularly assess impacts (including educational gains, knowledge transfer, engagement, and audience fatigue) and are responsive to public interests, expectations, and needs.[21] The Utah State University (USU) Museum of Anthropology responded to the COVID-19 pandemic and lockdown by creating AnthroPaks—take-home kits that explore different themes within anthropology. To maintain community connections, the museum developed seven different AnthroPaks—Ancient Egypt, World Games, World Music, Connections between Worlds, Solstice, Valentines, and Black History—and handed out more than seven hundred of them. Recognizing the value of museum partnerships, one community partner remarked, "We strive to connect refugees with their local community, and we have been without our typical connection points for the past several months. USU's AnthroPaks have provided a creative way to deliver a fun and educational activity that has enabled us to maintain connections with kids while also engaging with a new community partner."

Drawing on the Museum of Anthropology's experience in developing community partnerships and remote education tools, the WHAP developed a twenty-eight-page water-themed AnthroPak. It contains information about water features such as *acequias* (irrigation channel), canals, dams, *chinampas* (floating fields or gardens), step wells, and aqueducts. The AnthroPak also conveys local statistics about water consumption, management strategies, and conservation steps and includes activities that impart the engineering, science, and traditional knowledge that underlie ancient

FIGURE 11.2.
Excerpts from the Water AnthroPak developed by the Water Heritage Anthropological Project for the Utah State University Museum of Anthropology. Courtesy Utah State University Museum of Anthropology.

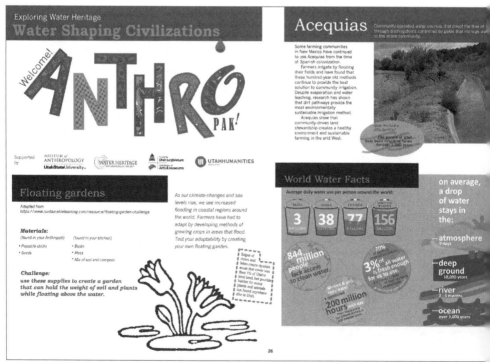

and contemporary water-management practices, using examples from Indigenous societies in Central America, the Mediterranean, and Southeast Asia as well as local communities. One activity, for example, prompts users to create a model Roman-style aqueduct; another offers instructions for creating miniaturized floating gardens modeled after *dhap*, the traditional floating gardens of Bangladesh.[22] In addition to serving the museum's visitors, the AnthroPak serves as a means outreach to local schools, delivering STEM-focused content about water heritage to hundreds of families across our community.

Mentorship and Community Science to Engage Diverse Audiences

Among the WHAP's priorities are ensuring that our programs, research practices, and student training are available to diverse audiences and maintaining community engagement statewide. In the summers, we work with Native students via USU's Native American Summer Mentorship Program (NASMP), which offers multiple weeklong laboratory experiences at the main USU campus in Logan to Native students from our Blanding campus location.[23] Education and other researchers have noted that Native students face challenges in accessing and continuing in higher education as well as in scientific engagement.[24] The NASMP and similar programs show the significant benefits of mentorship on Native and other students.[25]

Beginning in 2020, the WHAP employed active learning, scaffold assignments and tasks, and peer-to-peer mentorship for two NASMP water heritage labs, initially adapting our course to a format that enabled students to participate in the mentorship program during the pandemic.[26] We were able to offer the lab in person in 2021, and students spent time with us on campus, learning about water heritage and our multidisciplinary approaches to water research in anthropology. Our seminar format differed slightly for the in-person and virtual mentees. We met for shorter periods throughout the day via Zoom with the virtual students and provided step-by-step assignments for them to complete independently. For the in-person seminar, we typically spent mornings discussing our personal relationships with water, reading materials, and water heritage research and methodologies. The afternoons then featured hands-on laboratory assignments or field trips to local water features. For example, one afternoon we walked along the Canyon Road Canal, viewing the historic portions of the canal and its associated infrastructure that are visible on the surface. This experience provided the opportunity to talk about the presence of historic cultural resources on today's landscape and about how historic water features can be adapted to contemporary situations and needs. Mentees from both 2020 and 2021 contributed to our research by collecting archival information, compil-

FIGURE 11.3.
Molly Boeka Cannon and a Native student mentee discuss water heritage along the Crocket Canal in Logan, Utah. Photo by Anna Cohen.

ing geospatial information, and producing drafts of digital StoryMaps that we use for public outreach.

In addition to engaging and working with younger audiences, the WHAP developed outreach tools for people over age fifty-five and offered a seminar on Anthropological Perspectives on Water Heritage through USU's Summer Citizens Program. For half a century, the Summer Citizens Program has offered older people opportunities to explore northern Utah's entertainment and education via connections with research and teaching faculty.[27] Such programs offer faculty and research teams the chance to contribute to lifelong learning and to develop "age-friendly" campuses.[28] Our seminar featured lectures, walks, and lab activities and generated important discussions about water use and misuse in the western United States, especially when participants (many of whom lived in the arid Southwest) shared personal experiences. In labs, participants explored water heritage digital archives, collected ethnographic interview data using the WHAP protocol, and examined digital stories using the Water Heritage in the West StoryMaps.

Finally, we have found water's quotidian role and seeming ubiquity in the United States means that it is often underappreciated or unnoticed in our built environment. A walking tour of our campus during which we identified water features in our everyday surroundings proved a particularly insightful activity during both the NASMP and Summer Citizens programs. Participants actively engaged with the water features and connected this tangible resource with heritage and conservation issues.

Conclusion

Humans interact with water across several domains of daily life. An anthropological approach to water, its history, and its meaning for people must approach water heritage through a multidisciplinary lens. Such a holistic approach documents both human and ecological dimensions. Social and natural scientists often note that water studies lack a human or anthropological dimension and/ or historic or prehistoric long-term datasets.[29] Anthropologists have the tools to study water infrastructure and management from different scales and using different techniques via spatial analysis, materials analysis, and ethnographic accounts. Water heritage, which combines tangible aspects of cultural heritage such as the built environment and water infrastructure with intangible aspects such as a sense of place and traditional knowledge can engage a range of audiences—rural and urban, youth and adult, distant and local—with the archaeology of water.[30]

Our experiences are helping us to develop best practices for involving the public in archaeological research. First, public archaeology needs to be integrated into research programs from their outset. The initial design phases of our proposed research for the WHAP included outreach and public engagement so that they would occur simultaneously throughout the project. Communities are thus integrated into all phases, including data collection, analysis, and interpretation.

Second, much like other forms of scholarship, we need to know the audience. While many people can relate to water and make connections with their own experiences, not everyone will relate to the same delivery of the research content. Yet as public scholars, we must make our research accessible to multiple audiences. We integrate public outreach into our ongoing research program by developing programming for younger and older adult audiences, using digital tools to reach remote audiences, and offering mentorship to Native college students.

Finally, public engagement must be considered active participation in research rather than simply the public-focused circulation of information. Contemporary archaeological research strives to contribute to the grand challenges that we face today by providing insight from the past.[31] Natural-resource and heritage management exemplifies relevant research that needs not only to reach public audiences but also to cause a shift in their mindsets and behaviors. Participants who engage in this research are more likely to engage in conservation and sustainability practices and programs.[32] We must develop opportunities for participants to gather data, shape project outcomes, and engage in discussions and interpretations about water in our communities.

Notes

1. Andrea Ballestero, "The Anthropology of Water," *Annual Review of Anthropology* 48 (2019): 405–21, https://doi.org/10.1146/annurev-anthro-102218-011428; Carola Hein, ed., *Adaptive Strategies for Water Heritage: Past, Present and Future* (Cham, Switz.: Springer Nature, 2020), https://library.oapen.org/handle/20.500.12657/22917; William Kelly, "Concepts in the Anthropological Study of Irrigation," *American Anthropologist* 85, no. 4 (1983): 880–86; Fandi P. Nurzaman, "Irrigation Management in the Western States" (master's thesis, University of California, Davis, 2017).

2. Shannon A. Boomgarden, Duncan Metcalfe, and Ellyse T. Simons, "An Optimal Irrigation Model: Theory, Experimental Results, and Implications for Future Research," *American Antiquity* 84, no. 2 (April 2019): 252–73, https://doi.org/10.1017/aaq.2018.90; John M. Marston, "Archaeological Approaches to Agricultural Economies," *Journal of Archaeological Research* 29, no. 3 (2021): 327–85, https://doi.org/10.1007/s10814-020 -09150-0; Steven R. Simms, Tammy M. Rittenour, Chimalis Kuehn, and Molly Boeka Cannon, "Prehistoric Irrigation in Central Utah: Chronology, Agricultural Economics, and Implications," *American Antiquity* 85, no. 3 (July 2020): 452–69, https://doi.org /10.1017/aaq.2020.25.

3. Leonard J. Arrington and Dean May, "'A Different Mode of Life': Irrigation and Society in Nineteenth-Century Utah," *Agricultural History* 49, no. 1 (1975): 3–20; Shannon M. McNeeley, Candida F. Dewes, Crystal J. Stiles, Tyler A. Beeton, Imtiaz Rangwala, Michael T. Hobbins, and Cody L. Knutson, "Anatomy of an Interrupted Irrigation Season: Micro-Drought at the Wind River Indian Reservation," *Climate Risk Management* 19 (2018): 61–82, https://doi.org/10.1016/j.crm.2017.09.004.

4. Sonya Atalay, *Community-Based Archaeology* (Oakland: University of California Press, 2012); Joshua Gisemba Bagaka's, Natale Badillo, and Irina Bransteter, "Exploring Student Success in a Doctoral Program: The Power of Mentorship and Research Engagement," *International Journal of Doctoral Studies* 10 (2015): 323–42, http://ijds.org /Volume10/IJDSv10p323-342Bagaka1713.pdf; Stephen Brighton, "Applied Archaeology and Community Collaboration: Uncovering the Past and Empowering the Present," *Human Organization* 70, no. 4 (December 2011): 344–54, https://doi.org/10.17730 /humo.70.4.w0373w8655574266.

5. Elizabeth Bollwerk, Robert Connolly, and Carol McDavid, "Co-creation and Public Archaeology," *Advances in Archaeological Practice* 3, no. 3 (August 2015): 178–87, https:// doi.org/10.7183/2326-3768.3.3.178; Monica L. Smith, "Citizen Science in Archaeology,"

American Antiquity 79, no. 4 (October 2014): 749–62, https://doi.org/10.7183/0002
-7316.79.4.749.

6. Ipsos, *American Perceptions of Archaeology*, 2018, https://documents.saa.org
/container/docs/default-source/doc-publicoutreach/ipsos_poll2018.pdf?sfvrsn
=a1f0921e_4; Franklin H. Price, "Florida's Underwater Archaeological Preserves: Public
Participation as an Approach to Submerged Heritage Management," *Public Archaeology*
12, no. 4 (2013): 221–41, https://doi.org/10.1179/1465518714Z.00000000045; Maria Ramos
and Duganne David, *Exploring Public Participation and Attitudes about Archaeology*,
Harris Interactive, 2000, http://faculty.washington.edu/plape/pubarchspr14
/READINGS/nrptdraft4.pdf.

7. David Guillet, "Reconsidering Institutional Change: Property Rights in Northern
Spain," *American Anthropologist* 102, no. 4 (2000): 713–25, https://doi.org/10.1525
/aa.2000.102.4.713; J. Stephen Lansing and James N. Kremer, "Emergent Properties of
Balinese Water Temple Networks: Coadaptation on a Rugged Fitness Landscape," *American Anthropologist* 95, no. 1 (1993): 97–114, https://doi.org/10.1525/aa.1993.95.1
.02a00050; William P. Mitchell, "Irrigation and Community in the Central Peruvian
Highlands," *American Anthropologist* 78, no. 1 (1976): 25–44, https://doi.org/10.1525
/aa.1976.78.1.02a00030; Olivia Molden, "Water Heritage and Urban Development: Lessons from Nepal's Kathmandu Valley," *Journal of Heritage Management* 4, no. 2 (2019):
176–91, https://doi.org/10.1177/2455929619890512; Michael J. Sheridan, "An Irrigation
Intake Is Like a Uterus: Culture and Agriculture in Precolonial North Pare, Tanzania,"
American Anthropologist 104, no. 1 (2002): 79–92, https://doi.org/10.1525/aa.2002
.104.1.79; Veronica Strang, "Common Senses: Water, Sensory Experience and the Generation of Meaning," *Journal of Material Culture* 10, no. 1 (2005): 92–120, https://doi.org
/10.1177/1359183505050096; Paul Trawick, "The Moral Economy of Water: Equity and
Antiquity in the Andean Commons," *American Anthropologist* 103, no. 2 (2001): 361–79,
https://doi.org/10.1525/aa.2001.103.2.361.

8. Melissa Beresford, "The Embedded Economics of Water: Insights from Economic
Anthropology," *WIREs Water* 7, no. 4 (2020): e1443, https://doi.org/10.1002/wat2.1443;
Leslie Sanchez, Eric Edwards, and Bryan Leonard, "The Economics of Indigenous Water Claim Settlements in the American West," *Environmental Research Letters* 15, no. 9
(2020), https://doi.org/10.1088/1748-9326/ab94ea.

9. Courtney G. Flint, Xin Dai, Douglas Jackson-Smith, Joanna Endter-Wada, Sara K.
Yeo, Rebecca Hale, and Mallory K. Dolan, "Social and Geographic Contexts of Water
Concerns in Utah," *Society & Natural Resources* 30, no. 8 (2017): 885–902, https://doi.org
/10.1080/08941920.2016.1264653; Caroline Lavoie and Ole Russell Sleipness, "Fluid
Memory: Collective Memory and the Mormon Canal System of Cache Valley, Utah,"
Landscape Journal 37, no. 2 (2018): 79–99, https://doi.org/10.3368/lj.37.2.79.

10. Jago Cooper and Matthew Peros, "The Archaeology of Climate Change in the Caribbean," *Journal of Archaeological Science* 37, no. 6 (June 2010): 1226–32, https://doi.org
/10.1016/j.jas.2009.12.022; Jade d'Alpoim Guedes and R. Kyle Bocinsky, "Climate Change
Stimulated Agricultural Innovation and Exchange across Asia," *Science Advances* 4, no.
10 (2018): eaar4491, https://doi.org/10.1126/sciadv.aar4491; Judson Byrd Finley, Erick
Robinson, R. Justin DeRose, and Elizabeth Hora, "Multidecadal Climate Variability

and the Florescence of Fremont Societies in Eastern Utah," *American Antiquity* 85, no. 1 (January 2020): 93–112, https://doi.org/10.1017/aaq.2019.79; David Kaniewski, Nick Marriner, David Ilain, Christophe Morhange, Yifat Thareani, and Elisa Van Campo, "Climate Change and Water Management in the Biblical City of Dan," *Science Advances* 3, no. 11 (2017): e1700954, https://doi.org/10.1126/sciadv.1700954; Peter J. Richerson, Robert Boyd, and Robert L. Bettinger, "Was Agriculture Impossible during the Pleistocene but Mandatory during the Holocene? A Climate Change Hypothesis," *American Antiquity* 66, no. 3 (2001): 387–411, https://doi.org/10.2307/2694241; Arlene Miller Rosen, *Civilizing Climate: Social Responses to Climate Change in the Ancient Near East* (New York: AltaMira Press, 2007).

11. Duncan Metcalfe and Lisa V. Larrabee, "Fremont Irrigation: Evidence from Gooseberry Valley, Central Utah," *Journal of California and Great Basin Anthropology* 7, no. 2 (1985): 244–54; Floyd W. Sharrock, David S. Dibble, and Keith M. Anderson, "The Creeping Dune Irrigation Site in Glen Canyon, Utah," *American Antiquity* 27, no. 2 (1961): 188–202, https://doi.org/10.2307/277834; Simms et al., "Prehistoric Irrigation in Central Utah."

12. Marcy Rockman and Carrie Hritz, "Expanding Use of Archaeology in Climate Change Response by Changing Its Social Environment," *Proceedings of the National Academy of Sciences* 117, no. 15 (2020): 8295–8302, https://doi.org/10.1073/pnas.1914213117.

13. Arjo Klamer, "The Values of Archaeological and Heritage Sites," *Public Archaeology* 13, nos. 1–3 (2014): 59–70, https://doi.org/10.1179/1465518714Z.00000000054.

14. Neil Faulkner, "Archaeology from Below," *Public Archaeology* 1, no. 1 (2000): 21–33, https://doi.org/10.1179/pua.2000.1.1.21; C. R. McGimsey, *Public Archaeology* (New York: Academic Press, 1973); Gabriel Moshenska, "What Is Public Archaeology?" *Present Pasts* 1, no. 1 (2010), https://doi.org/10.5334/pp.7; Anne K. Pyburn, "Engaged Archaeology: Whose Community? Which Public?," in *New Perspectives in Global Public Archaeology*, ed. Katsuyuki Okamura and Akira Matsuda (New York: Springer, 2011), 29–41; Lorna-Jane Richardson and Jaime Almansa-Sánchez, "Do You Even Know What Public Archaeology Is? Trends, Theory, Practice, Ethics," *World Archaeology* 47, no. 2 (2015): 194–211, https://doi.org/10.1080/00438243.2015.1017599; Gemma Tully, "Community Archaeology: General Methods and Standards of Practice," *Public Archaeology* 6, no. 3 (2007): 155–87, https://doi.org/10.1179/175355307X243645.

15. Water Heritage Anthropological Project at Utah State University, "Water Heritage in the West," May 13, 2021, https://arcg.is/0zOObH1.

16. Darren Parry, *The Bear River Massacre: A Shoshone History* (Salt Lake City, Utah: Common Consent Press, 2019); Mae Parry, "The Northwestern Shoshone," in *History of Utah's American Indians*, ed. Forrest S. Cuch (Louisville: University Press of Colorado, 2000), 25–72; Paula Watkins and Timbimboo Madsen Patti, *From NEWE to Northwestern Shoshone: An Exploration* (Brigham City, Utah: Northwestern Shoshone Cultural Department, 2019).

17. Reed R. Murray and Ronald Johnston, "History of the Central Utah Project: A Federal Perspective" (paper presented at the USCID Water Management Conference, Denver, 2001), 87.

18. Lynn H. Gamble, Cheryl Claasen, Jelmer W. Eerkens, Douglas J. Kennett, Patricia

M. Lambert, Matthew J. Liebmann, Natasha Lyons, Barbara J. Mills, Christopher B. Rodning, Tsim D. Schneider, Stephen W. Silliman, Susan M. Alt, Douglas Bamforth, Kelley Hays-Gilpin, Anna Marie Prentiss, and Torben C. Rick, "Finding Archaeological Relevance during a Pandemic and What Comes After," *American Antiquity* 86, no. 1 (2021): 21; Magdalena Góralska, "Anthropology from Home: Advice on Digital Ethnography for the Pandemic Times," *Anthropology in Action* 27, no. 1 (2020): 46–52, https://doi.org/10.3167/aia.2020.270105; Jose Leonardo Santos, "Special Issue: Teaching and Learning Anthropology in the Time of COVID-19," *Teaching and Learning Anthropology* 4, no. 1 (2021), https://doi.org/10.5070/T34154172; Arpit Sharma, "Finding Community during a Pandemic," *Science* 368, no. 6487 (2020), https://www.science.org/doi/full/10.1126/science.368.6487.206.

19. Michela Magliacani and Daniela Sorrentino, "Reinterpreting Museums' Intended Experience during the COVID-19 Pandemic: Insights from Italian University Museums," *Museum Management and Curatorship* 37, no. 4 (2021): 353–67, doi:10.1080/09647775.2021.1954984.

20. Utah State University Libraries, *Water Heritage Anthropological Project*, https://digitalcommons.usu.edu/water_heritage/.

21. *Briley Rasmussen and Scott Winterrowd, "Professionalizing Practice," Journal of Museum Education* 37, no. 2 (2012): 7–11, https://doi.org/10.1080/10598650.2012.11510726; American Alliance of Museums, *Museum Facts*, 2019, https://www.aam-us.org/wp-content/uploads/2019/02/Museum-Facts-2019.pdf; Jennifer Barrett, *Museums and the Public Sphere* (New York: John Wiley & Sons, 2012); Carol Scott, "Museums and Impact," *Curator: The Museum Journal* 46, no. 3 (2003): 293–310, https://doi.org/10.1111/j.2151-6952.2003.tb00096.x; Carol Scott, *Museums and Public Value: Creating Sustainable Futures* (New York: Routledge, 2016); Susie Wilkening, *Museums and Trust*, 2021, https://www.aam-us.org/wp-content/uploads/2021/09/Museums-and-Trust-2021.pdf.

22. Tawhidul Islam and Peter Atkins, "Indigenous Floating Cultivation: A Sustainable Agricultural Practice in the Wetlands of Bangladesh," *Development in Practice* 17, no. 1 (2007): 130–36.

23. Utah State University, MESAS, Proposed Native American Cultural Center, *Native American Summer Mentorship Program*, accessed July 27, 2024, https://www.usu.edu/mesas/nasmp/.

24. Ahmed Al-Asfour and Marry Abraham, "Strategies for Retention and Persistence for Native American Students in Higher Education," *Tribal College and University Research Journal* 1, no. 1 (2016): 46–56; Cary Michael Carney, *Native American Higher Education in the United States* (New York: Routledge, 2017).

25. J. V. Berrett, C. S. Armstrong, and C. G. Frazier, "Native American Mentorships: Industry's Next Step to Assist Native Americans' Transition into STEM Careers?" (paper presented at the ASEE Annual Conference, New Orleans, 2016), https://peer.asee.org/native-american-mentorships-industry-s-next-step-to-assist-native-americans-transition-into-stem-careers.pdf; Maija Holsti, Edward B. Clark, Simon Fisher, Sam Hawkins, Heather Keenan, Steven Just, Jaymus Lee, Ed Napia, Jose E. Rodriguez, Franci Taylor, Richard White, Scott Willie, and Carrie L. Byington, "Lessons from the First Decade of the Native American Summer Research Internship at the University of Utah," *Academic*

Medicine 96, no. 4 (2021): 522–28, https://doi.org/10.1097/ACM.0000000000003759; Richard S. Mosholder, Bryan Waite, Carolee A. Larsen, and Christopher Goslin, "Promoting Native American College Student Recruitment & Retention in Higher Education," *Multicultural Education* 23, nos. 3–4 (2016): 27–36; Timothy C. Thomason and Hanna Thurber, *Strategies for the Recruitment and Retention of Native American Students* (Flagstaff: American Indian Rehabilitation and Training Center, Northern Arizona University, Institute for Human Development, 1999).

26. Bagaka's, Badillo, and Bransteter, "Exploring Student Success"; David F. Feldon, Kaylee Litson, Soojeong Jeong, Jennifer M. Blaney, Jina Kang, Candace Miller, Kimberly Griffin, and Josipa Roksa, "Postdocs' Lab Engagement Predicts Trajectories of PhD Students' Skill Development," *Proceedings of the National Academy of Sciences* 116, no. 42 (2019): 20910–16, https://doi.org/10.1073/pnas.1912488116; Scott Freeman, Sarah L. Eddy, Miles McDonough, and Mary Pat Wenderoth, "Active Learning Increases Student Performance in Science, Engineering, and Mathematics," *Proceedings of the National Academy of Sciences* 111, no. 23 (2014): 8410–15, https://doi.org/10.1073/pnas.1319030111; German Mora, "Effect of Fading Scaffolds on the Mastery of Scientific Abilities in Inquiry-Based Laboratory Exercises of a College-Level Environmental Science Course," *Journal of Geoscience Education* 67, no. 1 (2019): 50–63, https://doi.org/10.1080/10899995.2018.1542475; Jenny Olin Shanahan, Elizabeth Ackley-Holbrook, Eric Hall, Kearseley Stewart, and Helen Walkington, "Ten Salient Practices of Undergraduate Research Mentors: A Review of the Literature," *Mentoring & Tutoring: Partnership in Learning* 23, no. 5 (2015): 359–76, https://doi.org/10.1080/13611267.2015.1126162; Molly Boeka Cannon, Anna S. Cohen, and Kelly N. Jimenez, "Connecting Native Students to STEM Research Using Virtual Archaeology: A Case Study from the Water Heritage Anthropological Project," *Advances in Archaeological Practice* 9, no. 2 (May 2021): 175–85, https://doi.org/10.1017/aap.2021.2.

27. Utah State University, Event Services, *Summer Citizens*, accessed July 27, 2024, https://summercitizens.usu.edu.

28. Jason Dauenhauer, Afeez Hazzan, Kristin Heffernan, and Chantré M. Milliner, "Faculty Perceptions of Engaging Older Adults in Higher Education: The Need for Intergenerational Pedagogy," *Gerontology & Geriatrics Education* 43, no. 4 (2022): 1–22, https://doi.org/10.1080/02701960.2021.1910506; Craig A. Talmage, "Age Friendly Universities and Engagement with Older Adults: Moving from Principles to Practice," *International Journal of Lifelong Education* 35, no. 5 (2016): 19; Sun Joo Yoo and Wenhao David Huang, "Engaging Online Adult Learners in Higher Education: Motivational Factors Impacted by Gender, Age, and Prior Experiences," *Journal of Continuing Higher Education* 61, no. 3 (2013): 151–64, https://doi.org/10.1080/07377363.2013.836823.

29. Emily G. Bradshaw, Anne Birgitte Nielsen, and N. John Anderson, "Using Diatoms to Assess the Impacts of Prehistoric, Pre-industrial and Modern Land-Use on Danish Lakes," *Regional Environmental Change* 6, nos. 1–2 (2006): 17–24, https://doi.org/10.1007/s10113-005-0007-4; J. A. Dearing, R. W. Battarbee, R. Kikau, I. Larocque, and F. Oldfield, "Human-Environment Interactions: Learning from the Past," *Regional Environmental Change* 6, no. 1 (2006): 1–16, https://doi.org/10.1007/s10113-005-0011-8; Ray Ison, Niels Röling, and Drennan Watson, "Challenges to Science and Society in the

Sustainable Management and Use of Water: Investigating the Role of Social Learning," *Environmental Science & Policy* 10, no. 6 (2007): 499–511, https://doi.org/10.1016/j.envsci .2007.02.008; Claudia Pahl-Wostl, "Towards Sustainability in the Water Sector—The Importance of Human Actors and Processes of Social Learning," *Aquatic Sciences* 64, no. 4 (2002): 394–411, https://doi.org/10.1007/PL00012594.

30. Keith Basso, *Wisdom Sits in Places: Landscape and Language among the Western Apache* (Albuquerque: University of New Mexico Press, 1996); Allan Pred, *Making Histories and Constructing Human Geographies: The Local Transformation of Practice, Power Relations, and Consciousness* (New York: Routledge, 2019).

31. Keith W Kintigh, Jeffrey H. Altschul, Mary C. Beaudry, Robert D. Drennan, Ann P. Kinzig, Timothy A. Kohler, W. Fredrick Limp, Herbert D. G. Maschner, William K. Michener, Timothy R. Pauketat, Peter Peregrine, Jeremy A. Sabloff, Tony J. Wilkinson, Henry T. Wright, and Melinda A. Zeder, "Grand Challenges for Archaeology," *American Antiquity* 79, no. 1 (2014): 20; Patricia A. McAnany and Sarah M. Rowe, "Re-visiting the Field: Collaborative Archaeology as Paradigm Shift," *Journal of Field Archaeology* 40, no. 5 (2015): 499–507, https://doi.org/10.1179/2042458215Y.0000000007; Torben C. Rick and Daniel H. Sandweiss, "Archaeology, Climate, and Global Change in the Age of Humans," *Proceedings of the National Academy of Sciences* 117, no. 15 (2020): 8250–53, https://doi .org/10.1073/pnas.2003612117.

32. Raymond De Young, "Changing Behavior and Making It Stick: The Conceptualization and Management of Conservation Behavior," *Environment and Behavior* 25, no. 3 (1993): 485–505, https://doi.org/10.1177/0013916593253003; Linda Steg and Charles Vlek, "Encouraging Pro-Environmental Behaviour: An Integrative Review and Research Agenda," *Journal of Environmental Psychology* 29, no. 3 (2009): 309–17, https:// doi.org/10.1016/j.jenvp.2008.10.004; Paul C. Stern, Thomas Dietz, Troy Abel, Gregory A. Guagnano, and Linda Kalof, "A Value-Belief-Norm Theory of Support for Social Movements: The Case of Environmentalism," *Human Ecology Review* 6, no. 2 (1999): 81–97.

12

An Asset of the People

A History of Urgency, Management, and Interpretation at the Tonto Upper Cliff Dwelling

MATTHEW C. GUEBARD, SHARLOT HART,
JADE ROBISON, AND IRAIDA RODRIGUEZ

> Ruins stabilization is most necessary now while we still have ruins to stabilize. Twenty or thirty years ago would have been the time to have done it. And twenty years from now will be too late. Ruins may well be likened to any depreciating assets. They are the assets of the American people.
> —*Southwestern Monuments Monthly Report*, March 1935

Beginning in the late nineteenth century, a collective sense of urgency for the protection of archaeological sites in the southwestern United States became apparent. This emergency resulted largely from increasing visitation and eventually led to the development of authoritative opinions that impacted the management of National Park Service (NPS) sites, including the Upper Cliff Dwelling (UCD) at Tonto National Monument. At the UCD and other well-preserved cliff dwellings on NPS land, management decisions intended to protect and preserve ancient architecture are inextricably connected with attempts to provide positive and educational visitor experiences. This connection results from the NPS's dual mission and illustrates the development of a unique form of public archaeology.

Many of the urgent issues affecting the UCD also drove widespread changes in how the NPS planned and implemented archaeological site preservation and public interpretation. This history profoundly affected how visitors learned about and experienced archaeological sites, thus creating a public archaeology that emphasized visitor connections to well-preserved architecture. Tonto National Monument's history not only illustrates the impact of these important changes but also shows how perceptions of public archaeology, site preservation, and public interpretation changed over time.

Created in 1907, Tonto National Monument sits in the Tonto Basin of central Arizona. The monument is located just south of Lake Roosevelt, the location of the once free-flowing Salt River and its surrounding floodplain. The Tonto Basin sits within the Upper Sonoran Desert ecoregion, an arid environment rich with plant and animal resources. The monument encompasses only 1,120 acres but contains nearly one

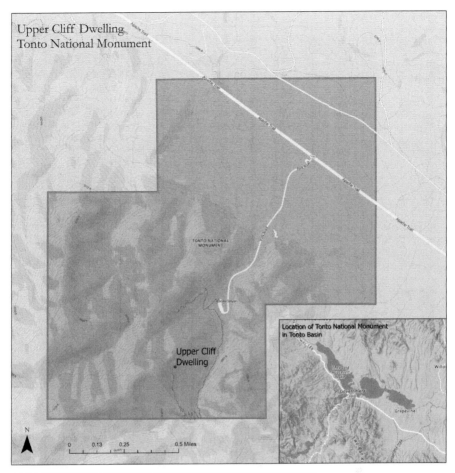

FIGURE 12.1. Map showing the location of the Upper Cliff Dwelling, Tonto National Monument. Courtesy of National Park Service.

hundred archaeological sites created by different groups over more than ten thousand years of human history.[1]

The UCD is the monument's largest site and was built and occupied by ancestral Native Americans during the interval between 1300 and 1375 CE. When occupied, it consisted of as many as thirty-three ground-level rooms, with several second- and third-story (parapet) levels. The UCD is associated with the Salado culture concept, which was developed by archaeologists in the 1930s to explain how patterns in the Tonto Basin's archaeological record represent ancestral Native American groups with shared beliefs and cultural practices.[2] Salado material culture is generally defined by polychrome ceramics with black, white, and red decorations, walled village compounds, and inhumation burials.[3]

The UCD was extensively modified in 1940 as part of a stabilization project that was developed out of an urgent need to protect and preserve the site following years of neglect and increasing public visitation. Preservation efforts were driven by the NPS's dual mission of preserving and protecting the site's integrity while allowing visitors to learn about, experience, and enjoy the cliff dwelling. Extensive reconstructions were undertaken to facilitate safe visitation and support archaeological narratives. The results of the 1940 stabilization profoundly affected the dwelling and continues to influence how the UCD is managed and interpreted today. This chapter focuses on extensive modifications to the Room 5/40(2) east wall, but many other modifications to architectural features were undertaken during this time. While the story presented in this chapter is unique to Tonto National Monument, it is also emblematic of preservation practices that are deeply rooted in NPS history, illustrating the evolution of ideas about the protection, preservation, and interpretation of the past.

The Antiquities Act, the Establishment of Tonto National Monument, and a Growing Sense of Urgency

Following the Mexican-American War, the federal government and private donors began funding explorations to record the geography, geology, and indigenous cultures of the U.S. Southwest.[4] Academics and explorers were especially intrigued by the newly acquired territory's cliff dwellings, which evoked romanticized notions of southwestern history and culture. Within the Tonto Basin, explorations funded by the Archaeological Institute of America and the Bureau of American Ethnology documented well-known archaeological sites.[5] By the 1890s, descriptions and illustrations of these well-preserved sites became a staple of scientific reports and popular periodicals that piqued interest in the Southwest and fueled visitation.

The expansion of rail lines into the Arizona Territory and the end of the prolonged Apache Wars allowed large numbers of curious visitors to experience the American Southwest. By the late nineteenth century, homesteaders, intellectuals, and casual visitors frequented the cliff dwellings. This interest and access also resulted in damage. Without a clear sense of archaeological etiquette, visitors often engaged in destructive practices such as artifact collection, digging, and vandalism. As accounts of damage spread, scholars and nonacademics alike became concerned about protecting these places and sought federal assistance.[6] These requests were framed as a time-sensitive matter requiring immediate attention to preserve ancient sites and the cultures they represent and to secure the future of archaeology as an academic discipline.[7]

Concern for the protection of cliff dwellings and archaeological sites culminated with passage of the American Antiquities Act on June 8, 1906. The act

FIGURE 12.2. Room 5/40(2) at the Upper Cliff Dwelling, ca. 1920s. Photo by Frank Zeile. Used with permission of J. Scott Wood.

identified archaeological site protection as a legal obligation of the U.S. government and implemented penalties for individuals who "appropriate[d], excavate[d], injure[d] or destroy[ed]" these locations without federal permits.[8] The law also introduced the notion that archaeological sites contained inherent educational and scientific value and should be preserved for future excavation and public education.[9]

The Antiquities Act also gave the U.S. president power to unilaterally "declare by public proclamation historic landmarks, historic and prehistoric structures, and other objects of historic or scientific interest that are situated upon the lands owned or controlled by the Government of the United States to be national monuments." Recognizing Tonto as a spectacular and endangered site, President Theodore Roosevelt established Tonto National Monument on December 19, 1907, to protect the "great ethnologic, scientific and educational interest" of the dwellings.[10] Tonto was the ninth national monument established under the Antiquities Act. Less than two years earlier, a congressional report written by archaeologist and anthropologist Edgar Lee Hewett had outlined the threats to well-known archaeological sites and proposed the creation of park districts dedicated to their protection.[11] This report did not specifically name the Tonto cliff dwellings but there is little doubt that the UCD was intended to be among those sites considered for protection.

Tourism, Depreciation, and Continued Urgency

Despite Tonto's early establishment as a national monument, the cliff dwellings remained in need of stabilization and repair as public visitation increased. Tonto National Monument's remote rural location and disorganized management as well as a lack of federal funds exacerbated the difficulty of protecting the site and magnified the sense of urgency.[12] For the first decade of its existence, Tonto fell under the jurisdiction of the newly created U.S. Forest Service. Because it lacked the workforce to appropriately manage and interpret the dwelling, the Forest Service struck an unofficial deal with the Southern Pacific Railroad to assume preservation and interpretive duties. The railroad promoted the Tonto Basin as part of a tourist package: visitors disembarked in Phoenix and traveled via automobile along the steep and winding Apache Trail to the newly constructed Roosevelt Dam. For four dollars, tourists could visit Tonto's cliff dwellings. The railroad frequently engaged in dubious interpretations of the dwellings, publishing sensationalized and inaccurate accounts in its promotional magazine. Furthermore, the company apparently made no repairs, suggesting a lack of interest in preserving the site.[13]

The Southern Pacific Railroad continued to exploit the tourist market until Tonto National Monument was absorbed into the NPS in the spring of 1934.[14] Charlie Steen, an archaeologist trained at the University of Denver, was hired as the first NPS ranger in charge.[15] Steen and his NPS colleagues quickly recognized the shortcomings of the railroad's management of the site. Archaeologist Victor Stoner reported in April 1936 that since 1920, walls had fallen down and original wooden ceilings collapsed, and he predicted that "within a few years, several more walls will collapse unless something is done very soon to strengthen them."[16] Stoner's observations contributed to a growing sense of dread regarding the protection of national monuments.

After arriving in the Tonto Basin in the late summer of 1934, Steen was not only the sole NPS employee at the monument but often the only person around for many miles. Steen had many responsibilities, including giving tours of the UCD that featured lectures on local archaeology and highlighted unique architectural elements. Given his professional training, Steen relied heavily on information collected from previous archaeological expeditions and professional publications. This adherence to science-based interpretation was also a reaction to previous generations of tour guides, NPS rangers from other parks, and promotional magazines, many of which spun "far-fetched yarns" with no educational value.[17]

By 1937, Steen had been promoted to a job in the Branch of Education at the Southwestern Monuments office, where his work as the lone caretaker at Tonto National Monument provided him with valuable interpretive experience. In his new job, Steen focused on the development of museum exhibits, educational content and on stabilizing "ruins." These responsibilities highlight the ways in which the agency saw the connection between site preservation and public education and how the complex archaeological and architectural history of each site served an educational purpose. During this time, archaeologists and preservation experts often drove the development of interpretive information at small national monuments across the American Southwest. The focus on interpretation resulted in the development of preservation practices that encouraged the partial reconstruction of archaeological sites for public pedagogy.[18]

The Stabilization of the UCD and the Reconstruction of Room 5

The deplorable state of the UCD led Steen to propose undertaking extensive architectural stabilization as soon as possible. In January 1940, a crew consisting of Navajo workers employed through the Indian Division of the Civilian Conservation Corps began work at the site.[19] Throughout the UCD, Steen and the crew reconstructed architectural elements such as walls and doorways, a heavy-handed approach justified by the urgent need for repairs and the desire to keep the cliff dwelling in an "ideal state" of preservation and interpretation.[20] The number of reconstructed walls and other architectural features at the UCD was staggering, even for Steen. In a May 27, 1942, memorandum to the superintendent of the Southwestern Monuments, Steen wrote that "the same criticism . . . levied at Canyon De Chelly National Monument, too much wall, may also be applied to the work at Tonto. . . . At Tonto, however, the situation is different. . . . Many of these walls had little support and in order to strengthen them fallen walls were rebuilt to serve as buttresses."[21]

Steen's justification of his work at the UCD was typical of the era. In general, NPS archaeologists and preservationists did not support large-scale reconstructions, preferring to manage sites in as-is condition.[22] However, in numerous cases at the southwestern national monuments, rooms and features—walls, doorways, windows, and wooden ceilings—were reconstructed to facilitate safe and positive visitor experiences.[23] In the absence of definitive guidance on the subject, park custodians and archaeologists made varying decisions about the best way to balance aesthetics with the need to enhance the ancient architecture's ability to convey educational information.

During work at the UCD, Steen and the Civilian Conservation Corps workers filled and reconstructed original doorways, cleaned debris from inside rooms, and reconstructed or built new walls to direct visitor movement and/or highlight what they judged to be important aspects of the site's archaeological history. While many rooms at the UCD were repaired, Room 5/40(2) experienced the most work. According to Steen, a "huge V-shaped break running from the

FIGURE 12.3. The east wall of Room 5/40(2) before reconstruction, February 8, 1940. Photo by Charlie Steen. National Park Service Photograph Collection (Accession TONT-00040).

top of the fill to the top of the wall" was sealed with stone masonry.[24] In total, nearly 258 cubic feet—45 percent of the east wall—was reconstructed. Once the void was filled, original plaster chunks were pulverized, reconstituted, mixed, and applied over the new wall surface, making it nearly indistinguishable from its initial construction. While excavating a trench to place a footing for the wall, Steen had noted archaeological evidence of a large fire that had caused the collapse of the room's original ceilings and likely the east wall itself. To inform future visitors about the fire, the crew collected "short stubs" of wood from nearby Rye Creek, charred the ends, and placed them within the wall so that they appeared to have been burned in the fire.[25]

The work on Room 5/40(2) illustrates the challenges of determining how much reconstruction and stabilization were appropriate. The installation of concrete footers, for example, was intended to support and stabilize the existing walls and was a common practice that had no visual impact on the room. Conversely, the full-height reconstruction of the east wall with the fake burned stubs seems to have served no demonstrable stabilization purpose but merely enhanced the wall's appearance and interpretive potential. But the work was justified not only by the urgency that had driven large-scale stabilization projects for decades but also by the NPS's dual mission. In Room 5/40(2) and throughout the UCD, reconstruction, stabilization, and interpretation combined to result in a treatment approach that was intended to serve multiple purposes but that actually created a false sense of the dwelling's history, with visitors exposed to features that had been rebuilt by the NPS but were interpreted as or presumed to be original and well preserved.

Similar occurrences took place at national monuments throughout the American Southwest. Less than six months after the completion of the UCD work, the NPS Director's Committee on Ruins Stabilization was considering definitions and standard practices.[26] The committee specifically addressed the issue of "restorations", discouraging large-scale reconstructions for purely interpretive reasons. Committee member Dale King, one of Steen's colleagues at the Branch of Education, was familiar with work in the Southwest, including the UCD, and no doubt contributed to the development of the committee's guidelines.

By 1949, the NPS published a comprehensive manual to guide the planning and implementation of stabilization projects.[27] The manual was based on the committee report and was the outgrowth of continued concerns about inconsistent historic preservation practices. The manual touted methods, like the installation of concrete wall footings, to stabilize original walls. Steen, a contributing author to the manual, used his experience at the UCD and other sites to develop the guidance, which marked the beginning of a new era in NPS preservation.

The Post–World War II and Vanishing Treasures Eras

In the American Southwest, the years after World War II saw increased funding for stabilization and park development. These funds eased the sense of urgency that had driven previous preservation efforts and inspired the development of new approaches. Standardized stabilization methods also resulted in the use of modern building practices and materials, including chemical additives and spray applications. This era also brought unprecedented numbers of visitors to national monuments, and by 1954, the fragile architecture at Tonto National Monument had suffered significant damage, causing officials to consider closing both cliff dwellings to visitors. The UCD required emergency stabilization in 1945, 1957, 1965, 1973, 1978, and 1991, though professional approaches to stabilization changed significantly over this time. For example, steel pipes, channel iron braces, and turnbuckles replaced masonry buttresses and wall reconstructions.[28] These new materials not only were stronger but also distinguished new work from ancient architecture. NPS archaeologists working in the field contributed to an evolution in the thinking about the treatment of historic places, and these changes resulted in updates to the stabilization manual in 1962 and 1974.[29]

During this period, the NPS workforce became more professionally diversified. Rangers rarely were tasked with both interpreting and managing park resources, and archaeology and interpretation became separate divisions with differing missions. Interpretation as a distinct field originated with Freeman Tilden's 1957 book, *Interpreting Our Heritage: Principles and Practices for Visitor Services in Parks, Museums, and Historic Places*.[30] This foundational work taught NPS rangers that interpretation involves not just information but revelation and provocation. Visitors were invited to forge their own connections with NPS sites, thereby promoting public support for preservation. The physical landscape and architecture where historical events occurred remained important, but the NPS gradually moved away from the "sage on the stage" brand of interpretation and began asking visitors to imagine the lives and experiences of past people. As a result, simply reporting on archaeological materials and archaeological interpretations of the past began to fall out of favor.

Throughout the last half of the twentieth century, the NPS also began to focus more on protecting and preserving the inherent research value and character-defining features of archaeological sites. Consequently, interpretations began to focus on a site's current appearance, a stark change from past efforts to keep walls standing at any cost. The use of heavy-handed techniques became less apparent, and the NPS began using traditional materials like unamended mortars. By the late 1990s, the NPS was on the cusp of another era. Managers began to recognize damage caused by incompatible stabilization materials, especially Portland cement. Ironically, much of this deterioration resulted from materials and methods endorsed in the 1949 stabilization manual, but the lessons learned became an important part of the visitor experience, with interpreters discussing the extent and negative consequences of past treatments.

Concerns for the protection of important southwestern sites resulted in the development of the Vanishing Treasures (VT) initiative, which originally sought to place professionals and craft specialists in parks to improve documentation and preservation and stabilization methods. As the initiative's name implies, it was inspired by a new but familiar sense of urgency. Like the Director's Committee on Ruins Stabilization nearly fifty years earlier, VT sought to improve the NPS management of these important places, and in 1998 it became a funded NPS program. Preservation experts became mandatory at many NPS units throughout the West, and Tonto National Monument received funding for one of these positions in 2000.[31]

VT advocated the use of new technologies such as lidar scanning and photogrammetry to document and interpret archaeological sites.[32] In addition, the program promoted research-based preservation approaches using traditional building practices and following the secretary of the interior's standards and guidelines for the treatment of historic properties.[33] In 1997 and again in 2009, VT published preservation guidelines.[34] While these guidelines included contemporary best practices, their origin can be traced directly to earlier efforts to standardize historic preservation practices.

Tonto National Monument took full advantage of the VT program, conducting site documentation and emergency stabilization between 2005 and 2010. The park also developed a detailed 2012 preservation plan that anticipated future needs and instituted standardized procedures for documenting and managing ancient architecture.[35] Similarly, park managers placed the UCD on a cyclic preservation schedule that included annual condition assessments of each wall surface to document and prioritize areas requiring treatment. Work at the UCD was so successful that no emergency stabilization work was required for more than a decade. During this period, the passage of the Federal Lands Recreation Enhancement Act and other measures began to shed light on the problem of deferred maintenance at NPS units throughout the country.[36] The NPS formalized the treatment of historic properties as assets by calculating metrics representing their value, depreciation, and cost of maintenance.

Just as park resource management programs have experienced waves of professionalization and standardization, so too has interpretation. The NPS's Interpretive Development Program published *Foundational Competencies for All Interpreters* in 2007 and released an updated version in 2016. In 2017, the document was rebranded as *Competencies for the 21st Century.*[37] Like the VT guidelines, these documents can be traced to the important work started by Tilden in 1957. Today, Tonto National Monument uses the foundational competencies to interpret not only the history of the dwellings but also past management practices. The separation of professional duties has also allowed preservation treatments at the UCD to serve fewer purposes. While the NPS will always have a dual mandate to "provide for the enjoyment of [monuments] by such means as will leave them unimpaired for the enjoyment of future generations," resource managers can focus on preservation while interpretive staff can prompt discussions.[38] But members of these staffs work in concert: interpretation relies on the information and actions of resource managers. Indeed, Tonto staff collaborate to ensure the appropriate enjoyment and interpretation of the UCD. For example, the public can access the UCD only on guided hikes in groups of six or fewer people. Interpretation is audience based and explores questions and answers beyond a simple retelling of the site's archaeological history. This approach can ultimately lead to genuine connections between the public and the cliff dwelling and its former

The UCD since 2018

During the summer of 2018, park staff noticed a large and widening crack in the northeast corner of Room 5/40(2) and determined that the east wall was destabilizing. Historic photographs showed that the crack was forming along the interface of the original wall and the 1940 reconstruction, indicating the potential for a catastrophic collapse and seriously endangering the east wall and other walls. The situation also threatened public safety, forcing the room and adjacent area to be closed to visitors. Park interpreters adjusted the physical boundaries of their tours and encouraged dialogue about site stabilization and resource protection.

By November 2018, park staff began consulting with archaeologists, engineers, and specialists from the Arizona State Historic Preservation Office; Native American tribal governments; local universities; and private consulting firms, and by February 2019, a plan was in place to document the wall's existing condition and appearance, monitor its movement over time, and determine the cause of its destabilization. The plan followed VT guidelines and included scanning with lidar, sampling original and modern plasters, and conducting ground-penetrating radar surveys and archaeological testing to investigate the condition of buried wall foundations. The lidar scanning took place the following month, and a temporary wooden brace was built to support the failing wall.

In May 2019, plaster was carefully removed from the 1940 repair, a difficult task because of the similarity between the ancient plaster and material added in 1940. The underlying masonry showed that the reconstruction was not tied to the original wall and thus moved independently of the surrounding walls, resulting in the formation of large structural cracks. The extant documentation does not indicate why Steen and his crew failed to tie the reconstruction to the ancient walls.

In November 2019, ground-penetrating radar was used to investigate the depth of bedrock beneath the room but generated inconclusive results. One month later, archaeologists began conducting test excavations to investigate the placement and condition of wall foundations as well as determine why they were moving. However, test units in areas thought to have been previously disturbed revealed sensitive archaeological deposits, and the test excavations could not be completed.

Despite the failed efforts to learn more about the wall's foundation and the mechanism of its deterioration, the park completed a partial deconstruction of the 1940 repair in April 2022. A team of historic preservation masons from

FIGURE 12.4.
A brace installed to stabilize the Room 5/40(2) east wall, January 2020. Courtesy of National Park Service.

FIGURE 12.5.
Iraida Rodriguez conducts a ground-penetrating radar survey of Room 5/40(2), November 2019. Courtesy of National Park Service.

FIGURE 12.6.
The east wall of Room 5/40(2) following deconstruction, April 26, 2022. Exposed masonry is visible at left; the white spheres atop the wall are used for lidar scanning. Courtesy of National Park Service.

Tuzigoot and Montezuma Castle National Monuments removed several tons of masonry, alleviating pressure on the original wall. A section of the 1940 reconstruction was left in place but with exposed and unplastered masonry that creates a visual marker of the complicated and intricate coalescence of public interpretation and preservation that has characterized the Tonto cliff dwellings since the 1940s. Interpreters use this section to prompt visitors to discuss the history of preservation and protection at the UCD rather than presenting them with what is purported to be a full and complete knowledge of preservation. Tonto National Monument is currently working with structural engineers and architectural conservators to design a more effective bracing system for the room that will tell a more comprehensive story of the site's recent management.

Conclusion

The sense of urgency that originally drove the creation of federal laws and standardized practices still exists, and substantial changes in preservation and interpretive methods often appear to coincide with periods of perceived threats to NPS resources. Across the Southwest, preservation methods are constantly evolving, often through important lessons learned while working in the field. At the UCD and many other important NPS archaeological sites, preservation experts are learning from the mistakes of their predecessors and adapting accordingly. At Tonto National Monument, the deconstruction of the east wall of Room 5/40(2) not only exemplifies this process but provides a metaphor for the way in which preservation and interpretation practices must periodically be reassessed, taken apart, and rebuilt and for how those practices themselves become part of a site's history.

Like preservation practices, interpretive methods and curricula must change. At the UCD and similar NPS sites throughout the Southwest, interpretation and management are nearly inseparable, highlighting the complex way in which politics, federal funding, the recent history of interpretation and management, and other factors can influence how the public experiences and learns about the past. At Tonto National Monument, these factors contributed to the development of a form of public archaeology that uses standing architecture to interpret the past. While early interpretive strategies focused solely on the opinions of professional archaeologists, new approaches foreground the sites' broader and more complex histories, allowing visitors to form educated opinions regarding their significance. As visitation continues to increase and new challenges such as climate change threaten park resources, the NPS will need to adapt in ways that will undoubtedly lead to further changes in how the public perceives and values the past.

Notes

1. Several Native American groups trace their ancestry to people who once lived in or traveled through the Tonto Basin. These groups curate information that includes place-names and oral histories. The NPS works closely with numerous tribal governments in managing the Tonto cliff dwellings: the Ak-Chin Indian Community, Fort McDowell Yavapai Nation; the Gila River Indian Community of the Gila River Indian Reservation; the Hopi Tribe of Arizona; the Salt River Pima–Maricopa Indian Community of the Salt River Reservation; the Tohono O'odham Nation of Arizona; the White Mountain Apache Tribe; the Yavapai-Prescott Indian Tribe, the Yavapai-Apache Nation; and the Zuni Tribe of the Zuni Reservation.

2. Winifred Gladwin and Harold S. Gladwin, *Some Southwestern Pottery Types: Series 1* (Globe, Ariz.: Gila Pueblo, 1930).

3. Jeffrey S. Dean, "Introduction: The Salado Phenomenon," in *Salado*, ed. Jeffrey S. Dean (Albuquerque: University of New Mexico Press, 2000), 3–17.

4. Ronald F. Lee, "The Origins of the Antiquities Act," in *The Antiquities Act: A Century of American Archaeology, Historic Preservation, and Nature Conservation*, ed. David Harmon, Francis P. McManamon, and Dwight T. Pitcaithley (Tucson: University of Arizona Press, 2006), 15–34.

5. Adolph Bandelier, *Final Report of Investigations among the Indians of the Southwestern United States Carried on Mainly in the Years 1880 to 1885, Part II* (Cambridge, Mass.: J. Wilson and Son, 1892); Walter Hough, *Antiquities of the Upper Gila and Salt River Valleys in Arizona and New Mexico* (Washington, D.C.: U.S. Government Printing Office, 1907).

6. Raymond Harris Thompson, "Edgar Lee Hewett and the Politics of Archaeology," in *Antiquities Act*, ed. Harmon, McManamon, and Pitcaithley, 35–48.

7. Robert W. Righter, "National Monuments to National Parks: The Use of the Antiquities Act of 1906," *Western Historical Quarterly* 20, no. 3 (1989): 281–301; David Harmon, Francis P. McManamon, and Dwight T. Pitcaithley, "The Antiquities Act: The First Hundred Years of a Landmark Law," *George Wright Forum* 23, no. 1 (2006): 5–27.

8. American Antiquities Act, 16 U.S.C. § 421 (1906).

9. Richard West Sellars, "A Very Large Array: Early Federal Historic Preservation—The Antiquities Act, Mesa Verde, and the National Park Service Act," *Natural Resources Journal* 47, no. 2 (2007): 267–328.

10. American Antiquities Act, 16 U.S.C. § 421 (1906); Tonto National Monument, Presidential Proclamation 787, December 19, 1907.

11. Edgar Lee Hewett, "Memorandum Concerning the Historic and Prehistoric Ruins of Arizona, New Mexico, Colorado and Utah, and Their Preservation," in *Circular Relating to Historic and Prehistoric Ruins of the Southwest and Their Preservation* (Washington, D.C.: U.S. Government Printing Office, 1904).

12. Righter, "National Monuments to National Parks"; Harmon, McManamon, and Pitcaithley, "Antiquities Act"; Hal Rothman, "Second Class Sites: National Monuments and the Growth of the National Park System," *Environmental Review* 10, no. 1 (1986): 44–56.

13. Nancy L. Dallett, *At the Confluence of Change: A History of Tonto National Monument* (Tucson, Ariz.: Western National Parks Association, 2008), 70–78.

14. NPS, *Southwestern Monuments Monthly Report*, April 1934, 30.

15. Will Moore, "Park Ranger Charlie Steen and the Southwestern National Monuments through the Depression and War," *Journal of Arizona History* 62, no. 1 (2021): 46; NPS, *Southwestern Monuments Monthly Report*, July 1934, 2.

16. NPS, *Southwestern Monuments Monthly Report*, April 1936, 304.

17. Dorr G. Yeager, "The Educational Program of the National Park Service," *Southwestern Monuments Monthly Report*, January 1940, 60–62.

18. In general, early NPS archaeologists and historic preservationists did not support large-scale reconstructions of cliff dwellings and other archaeological sites. However, rebuilding doorways, walls, and other features to improve safety and create positive visitor experiences was a common practice. Reconstructions at nearly every early NPS national monument were justified by the urgent need to protect or interpret important sites. See Todd R. Metzger, "Ruins Stabilization Report Technical Series No. 53," in *Ruins Stabilization: A Handbook* (Denver: Nickens and Associates, 1988), 3–4.

19. Charlie R. Steen, "Ruins Stabilization Report for the Tonto Upper Ruin," unpublished report, NPS, 1942.

20. Charlie R. Steen, "The Tonto Upper Ruins," *The Kiva* 6, no. 5 (February 1941): 17–20.

21. Charlie R. Steen to superintendent of the southwestern monuments, May 27, 1942, in Steen, "Ruins Stabilization Report for the Tonto Upper Ruin."

22. Roland Von S. Richert and R. Gordon Vivian, *Ruins Stabilization in the Southwestern United States* (Washington, D.C.: U.S. Department of Interior, 1974).

23. Todd R. Metzger, "Current Issues in Ruins Stabilization in the Southwestern United States," *Southwestern Lore* 55, no. 3 (1989): 2.

24. Steen, "Ruins Stabilization Report for the Tonto Upper Ruin," 16.

25. NPS, *Southwestern Monuments Monthly Report*, February 1940, 106.

26. NPS, *Report of the Director's Committee on Ruins Stabilization: September 27–October 2, 1940, Santa Fe, New Mexico* (Santa Fe, N.M.: U.S. Government Printing Office, 1940).

27. Gordon R. Vivian, Charlie R. Steen, and Erik K. Reed, *Ruins Stabilization* (Santa Fe, N.M.: U.S. Government Printing Office, 1949).

28. Louis R. Caywood, "Ruins Stabilization at Tonto National Monument, 1945," (document on file at the Tonto National Monument, 1945); Roland Richert, "Stabilization Report, Upper and Lower Ruins, Tonto National Monument, 1957" (document on file at the Tonto National Monument, 1957).

29. Richert and Vivian, *Ruins Stabilization*.

30. Freeman Tilden, *Interpreting Our Heritage: Principles and Practices for Visitor Services in Parks, Museums, and Historic Places* (Chapel Hill: University of North Carolina Press, 1957).

31. *Vanishing Treasures Year End Report: Fiscal Year 2005 and Proposed Activities for 2006* (Santa Fe, N.M.: NPS, 2006), 16.

32. Lidar (light detection and ranging) utilizes laser scanning equipment to accurately measure architecture and archaeological features. The data produced by lidar scanning can be used to produce maps and three-dimensional models.

33. Anne E. Grimmer, *The Secretary of the Interior's Standards for the Treatment of Historic Properties with Guidelines for Preserving, Rehabilitating, Restoring & Reconstructing Historic Buildings*, rev. ed. (Washington, D.C.: U.S. Department of Interior, NPS, Technical Preservation Services, 2017).

34. NPS, "Vanishing Treasures: A Legacy in Ruins," draft, September 1997; John M. Barrow, *Preservation and Management Guidelines for Vanishing Treasures Resources* (Washington, D.C.: NPS, 2009).

35. Theodore P. Tsouras, "Archeological Site Preservation Plan and Implementation Guidelines, Tonto National Monument, Arizona," 2012 (document on File at Tonto National Monument).

36. See, for example, U.S. Department of Interior, *Implementation of the Federal Lands Recreation Enhancement Act, Triennial Report to Congress*, 2015, https://www.doi.gov/sites/doi.gov/files/uploads/2015%20FLREA%20Triennial%20Report%20-%20Web%20Version.pdf.

37. NPS, *Foundations of Interpretation: Competencies for the 21st Century*, November 2017, https://nairegion8.weebly.com/uploads/1/6/6/4/16641970/foundations_of_interp_2018_508.pdf.

38. NPS, *About the National Park Service*, accessed July 27, 2024, https://www.nps.gov/aboutus/aboutus.htm.

Epilogue

Why Words, Shared Authority, and Seeking Community Benefit Matter in Public and Collaborative Archaeology

JEREMY M. MOSS

Many of the chapters in this book recognize one of my favorite aspects and emerging concepts of archaeology in the twenty-first century: archaeology can allow historically minimalized groups to speak across space and time. These groups are one segment of the public(s) often left out of archaeological inquiry, even when the subject matter is their ancestors. The plurality of the term *publics* includes many groups that over the past several hundred years have suffered oppression through mechanisms of "westward expansion," colonialism, racism, slavery and associated policies, nationalism, and socioeconomic hierarchies. Some of these inequalities and colonial structures are reflected not only in knowledge and education but especially in the terminology concerning archaeological sites, Indigenous cultures, and heritage management. Public archaeology can address these social and economic inequalities and provide openings through which historically oppressed groups can speak to us from the past and in the present, thus allowing for multivocality.[1]

During my quarter century as a cultural heritage manager with the National Park Service (NPS), I have had the honor to work with several Indigenous groups in the American Southwest. Some have been dispossessed of their original land bases and seen aspects of their culture minimized (or seen attempts to do so) through concentrated efforts such as boarding schools to "take the Indian out of the man." When given the opportunity, I work to tip the balance of the scales of history and decision making back toward these groups. Doing so requires humility and understanding not only their interests and concerns but also how we can conduct archaeology and anthropological inquiry in a way that benefits these communities.

My experiences can provide some important lessons about how to learn from and advocate on behalf of those traditionally associated with the parks. Archaeologists have sometimes contributed to racism, colonialism, academic subjugation, and generally disrespectful attitudes toward Indigenous peoples, and we now bear a responsibility to work to benefit these communities.[2] I am not suggesting that Indigenous peoples need archaeologists or non-Indigenous people to develop their histories or that Indigenous cultural leaders, scholars, heritage managers, and others are not capable of doing so on their own volition: in fact, they are engaging in this work across the United States.[3] Yet all archaeologists and heritage resource managers have an obligation to understand and consider the feelings of descendant communities related to the many pasts we study and to develop projects that serve communities beyond other archaeologists. Examples of this ethos are offered throughout this book, including Tori Mason's efforts at the Nashville Zoo to highlight enslaved African Americans and collaborate with descendant communities (chapter 4), Stephanie T. Sperling and Kristin M. Montaperto's work showing how public archaeology can help promote awareness and stimulate healing conversations about slavery and colonization (chapter 5), and Koji Lau-Osawa's Gila River project to engage the many publics in shared authority and to increase awareness and healing associated with Japanese American incarceration camps and their associated communities (chapter 9).

Why Words Matter

The terminology and classification systems used for ease of communication in archaeology and in Western culture more broadly often harbor hidden meanings that contribute to and bring forth past injustices, inequalities, and latent racism.[4] The federal government is working to be more conscious of how words matter and can reflect colonial structures that hold people down. For example, some Indigenous groups, especially those in the U.S. Southwest, have identified *ruins* as a loaded term with many negative connotations. What exactly is ruined? Since Indigenous groups view ancestral sites in the Southwest as alive, spiritually and culturally rich, and still inhabited by their ancestors, nothing about them is "ruined" and the connections are alive and strong.[5] Yet this and other terms persist and are hard to change quickly: the public generally sees only mounds that are difficult to visualize as communities.

Abandoned is another term that sometimes brings forth memories of forced exodus from homelands and implies that no one recalls or cares about ancestral places. Again, there is often nothing abandoned about these places, and they are remembered and referred to in songs and prayers. Indigenous people also visit these sites and conduct ceremonies and prayers, often without heritage managers' knowledge, showing that these sites remain an active part of peoples' lives and culture.

Issues of terminology intertwine with some of the general public's struggles to engage with historical and archaeological content and to understand past cultures and archaeological sites. At sites with rubble mounds that constitute the remains of above-ground architecture, the public often has difficulty understanding how these places looked when they were intact. Many of these sites were until recently—and often still are—called *ruins*. One of the goals of archaeological education and exhibits at village sites that once had standing architecture is to help the public envision an alive place where individuals, families, and groups lived and faced many of the same decisions we do. Such endeavors are ultimately humanizing since the frozen Stone Age Other pervades the public consciousness. We must strive to help the public see these places as still inhabited by the ancestors and sacred. Archaeologists are also increasingly recognizing that rubble mounds serve as important traditional mnemonic devices or cultural landscape features, helping members of a community remember and teach about the past.[6] Embracing these ideas will help visitors respect and protect sites and move us closer to Indigenous perspectives on archaeology and cultural landscapes. Working with descendant communities to help the public understand these places serves to better educate visitors and more democratically share authority.

Words matter even more when we refer to the ancestors of living peoples. I learned this important lesson during my first real experience with consultation under the Native American Graves Protection and Repatriation Act (NAGPRA) in the early 2000s, when I was at Tumacácori National Historical Park in southern Arizona.[7] Working with curators at the Western Archaeological and Conservation Center in Tucson, where many southwestern NPS archaeological collections are stored, we had set up a viewing of the human remains and associated funerary objects removed from Tumacácori. Representatives of some of the traditionally associated tribal nations informed us with tears in their eyes and passion in their voices that the terms we used showed that we lacked the respect needed to appropriately assist with repatriation. *Remains* and *viewing* reflect a focus on seeing their ancestors as objects to be studied and stored in museums and not as living individuals.

In the absence of these kinds of learning opportunities, many archaeologists adhere to this perspective because of our science-based material culture focus. Many Western archaeologists are not culturally conditioned to see time as circular and tend to emphasize recent linear or progressive history. How many of us think much about our ancestors who lived a thousand years ago? Is there a difference between a grandfather who recently passed away and a more distant relative who lived a millennium ago? Most Indigenous groups would say no.

The tribal representatives requested that we substitute *viewing* for *visitation*, since the spirits of their ancestors are still there and retain individuality. They are not just objects. I now use this experience to educate park staff about discussing burials as individuals removed from archaeological sites or ancestral places, often without consulting with descendants. I also now recognize that dealing with the bureaucratic red tape associated with NAGPRA can cause descendants pain and can tap into historical wounds and traumas that span generations. Moreover, we need to continue consulting with our tribal collaborators on these issues. Asking our collaborators which words are most appropriate for use in meetings and with the public often proves educational and is needed to ensure that we are not perpetuating injustices or opening wounds. Meanings are always changing, as many of the chapters in this book show.

Public Archaeology at Pecos National Historical Park

I currently work at Pecos National Historical Park in northern New Mexico, where park staff are striving to develop new exhibits and do archaeological research and education that can benefit the tribal communities traditionally associated with the site. Between the sixteenth and eighteenth centuries, when Pecos Pueblo was at its height, it consisted of two large

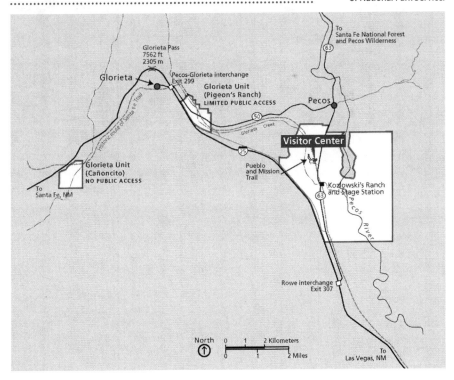

FIGURE 13.1.
Map of Pecos National Historical Park. Courtesy of National Park Service.

FIGURE 13.2. Pecos Pueblo as it might have looked in the early 1700s. Drawing by S. P. Moorehead.

FIGURE 13.3. Tribal members from Jemez Pueblo gather in front of the remains of the eighteenth-century Spanish colonial adobe church and convento in preparation for traditional dances during the annual Pecos Feast Day, which commemorates the connections between Pecos and Jemez. Photo by Stan Ford.

four- to five-story structures on which construction had started in the 1300s and that housed as many as two thousand people.[8] In the 1600s, Franciscan missionaries established a church and convento at Pecos. European-introduced diseases quickly reduced the population until the last of the Pecos people joined Jemez Pueblo in 1838, bringing along their traditions and memories of Pecos, which live on in prayers, songs, and other ceremonies.

Pecos is located on the eastern frontier of the Pueblo world, near a natural pass, where the western plains meet the

Rocky Mountains and the Rio Grande Valley. The Pecos people were often linked with Plains groups through trade, warfare, captive exchange, and intermarriage. The Pecos Pueblo and Spanish colonial complex archaeological site cover fifty-five acres.[9] The pueblo structural remains consist of prominent mounds and one excavated area left open for interpretation. To avoid using *ruins*, we now refer to the main path that takes visitors through the pueblo as the Ancestral Sites Trail and use the terms *remnants*, *remains*, *rooms*, *dwellings*, and *villages*. We call those who live there the Pecos people, but we do not know what they called themselves.

Pecos is well known in southwestern archaeology as a result of excavations led by Alfred V. Kidder from 1915 to 1929 and for his development of a cultural chronology for the region. Kidder documented a rather linear progression of culture change, the Pecos Classification, but it does not work well at Pecos.[10] In 1924, Kidder published one of the first textbooks on southwestern archaeology, and it remained in use in many classrooms through the 1960s.[11] The Pecos site is also an ancestral community for those from Jemez Pueblo, located northwest

FIGURE 13.4. Trail wayside exhibit at Pecos National Historical Park, with Pecos Pueblo (rubble mounds) on the mesa in the background. Photo by Jeremy Moss, National Park Service.

FIGURE 13.5. The remains of Pecos Pueblo looking south at the North Pueblo rubble mounds, 2023. Photo by Jeremy Moss, National Park Service.

FIGURE 13.6.
The tactile model at the Pecos Pueblo museum. Photo by Jeremy Moss, National Park Service.

FIGURE 13.7.
The re-created Pueblo room at Pecos National Historical Park. Photo by Jeremy Moss, National Park Service.

of Albuquerque, New Mexico. In the Jemez (Hemish) migration tradition, two groups diverged, and one (the Pʼǽkish) came to Pecos, while the other stopped at what is now Walatowa (Jemez Pueblo), which means "This is the place" or Heavenly Village (Wáanà Túuwa) in the Towa language.[12] The present Jemez (Towa) name for Pecos Pueblo is Pʼǽkilâ (the place above the water), which perfectly describes its location on the landscape as well as its centrality in the cultural and sacred geography of the Upper Pecos Valley.

To help visitors better understand the ancestral Pueblo habitation of the site and area, we have redesigned the 1980s museum, which was more like a history book than an experience. Many people have trouble envisioning the mounds along the trail as a village, so a new tactile model based on archaeological evidence and architectural interpretation shows the village at its height in the early 1700s. Future wayside development along the Ancestral Sites Trail will focus on new digital technologies to help people understand an intact pueblo village.

Working with our associated tribal communities we have developed a more immersive and interactive experience to help people see Pecos Pueblo as an active village rather than a static textbook archaeological example. In collaboration with tribal members from Jemez Pueblo we designed a replica Pueblo room with traditional handcrafted items made by Pueblo artisans. Since Pecos Pueblo is at a crucial node in a large matrix of trade routes, we devised an interactive exhibit designed to highlight intertribal trade routes for exotic items, showing geographic connections across western North America. The new exhibit also focuses on the links between the Jemez Pueblo and the last residents of Pecos—the twenty-one people who moved to join their brethren at Jemez. Listening stations allow visitors to hear statements from Pecos descendants in both English and Towa, demonstrating the continuing presence of these people. All of these exhibits remind visitors that Pecos Pueblo is not dead, ruined, or abandoned.

Finally, the new exhibit highlights an important event in southwestern archaeology and tribal relations: repatriations completed under NAGPRA during the 1990s. Kidder's excavations had removed almost two thousand individuals from burial contexts, where they had been laid on or covered with reed mats or cotton or turkey-feather blankets. These people had also been buried with about one thousand funerary objects, among them pottery vessels, exotic shell-and-turquoise necklaces, arrowheads, and medicine bundles.

In 1999, the individuals and associated funerary objects removed from Pecos were returned to the seventeen tribal nations affiliated with the park, one of the largest repatriations completed under NAGPRA. As a consequence of the well-documented connection between Jemez Pueblo and the Pecos people, the other tribes decided that Jemez should take the lead in the repatriation efforts. To allow their ancestors' spirits to rest, those involved agreed to return the individuals as closely as possible to where most of them had been disturbed—that is, near Pecos Pueblo.

This decision was not an easy one, however. Some of those involved argued that individuals who might be of Plains descent should be buried closer to those communities. Representatives of Jemez Pueblo argued that anyone who had come from Pecos should be returned to Pecos, regardless of descent, and this position won out: "The repatriation would respectfully be performed in the name of all ancestors, regardless of which Nation to which they were born." In the words of Pecos war captain and religious leader Pete Toya, "Never to discriminate anyone. They came out of Pecos, we want all of them back to Pecos."[13]

Using remote sensing and test excavations, archaeologists located an area free of buried cultural resources that could be protected by NPS staff. Led by Jemez Pueblo, the tribes allowed osteologists and physical anthropologists to study the individuals before their reinterment.[14] Such examinations are unusual in reburials today and demonstrate the tribal nations' recognition of scientific inquiry as well as their openness to this way of knowing as long as it complements rather than replaces traditional knowledge. In keeping with the statement by one tribal representative that anthropologists should be denied "the opportunity to use further skeletal analysis to determine who was Puebloan and who was Plains," the tribes prohibited DNA analysis that might specify biological affiliation.[15] Representatives of Jemez Pueblo also objected to DNA analysis because it is considered disrespectful to both living and ancestral people as well as invasive (destructive). But the most important objection was that DNA does not equal culture.[16] NAGPRA requires a determination of cultural affiliation, which is at times conflated with biological affinity, a process that can stimulate antagonisms between groups.[17] Many of the individuals were so fragmentary that no scientific determination could be made without DNA analysis, and the 1995 inventory includes many people labeled "biological affiliation indeterminate."[18] Nevertheless, the studies that were completed provide substantial knowledge regarding the Pecos people's health, diet, conflicts, and lifeways.[19]

NAGPRA labels items found with buried individuals *associated funerary objects*, a term that does not adequately capture their meaning to Pueblo peoples. During consultation for the repatriation, tribal representatives explained that "anything with living forms (anthropomorphic figures, corn, feathered or horned serpents, etc.), items of ceremonial use, (e.g. stepped rim bowl, very large ollas, burials, miniature canteens, cloud blower pipes) are considered [to be] tribal members... that are currently 'lost.'"[20] As Tara Beresh notes in chapter 8 of this volume, many Indigenous societies believe that objects used in everyday life and/or in ceremonies and traditional practices have a spirit and are alive. Objects' lives are spiritually connected to users and their ancestors.[21] If archaeologists rely on purely functionalist interpretations of materials in certain contexts, we may fail to understand their full meaning in either the past or the present.

Beneficial Ethnography at Pecos

Ethnographic work can empower historically marginalized groups but only when done in collaboration. While combining ethnography with archaeological analyses is not new, only in the modern era have informed prior consent and the development of Indigenous-led resource management divisions incorporated Indigenous perspectives on the past that blend oral history and archaeology to understand cultural ethnogenesis and change. In New Mexico, this phenomenon has been most evident in work in the Tewa Basin (near Espanola) and the Galisteo Basin since the late twentieth century and more recently at Jemez Pueblo and Picuris Pueblo.[22] A similar focus has now developed at Pecos, where ethnographers are working with the descendants of Pecos Pueblo now living at Jemez.

The most prominent holders of Pecos knowledge and memory in Jemez are the members of the Eagle Society (also called the Eagle Catchers Society), a religious sodality that retains cultural knowledge of Pecos and has worked with the NPS to define the full extent of the Pecos and ancestral Jemez cultural landscape both within and outside of Pecos National Historical Park. Recent ethnographic projects seek to develop a more Indigenous-focused history of Pecos Pueblo and the larger Upper Pecos Valley.

Cultivating an Indigenous perspective on Pecos requires extensive sharing of information and will succeed only in an atmosphere of mutual respect and trust. One way to build this trust is to find projects that offer benefits to communities— for example, by healing and preserving threatened cultural traditions. Current ethnographic projects related to Pecos focus on sacred sites and petroglyphs, cultural landscapes, and traditional uses. Members of Jemez Pueblo believed that the most benefits could be obtained from intergenerational and place-based interviews, which would teach members of the younger generation about the traditional aspects and place-based meanings of locations at and around Pecos Pueblo. The Pecos representatives also sought to document traditional cultural properties, since such documentation helps strengthen claims to ancestral lands. The specific types of knowledge shared remain the purview of Jemez Pueblo.[23] We are working with concepts of shared authority and moving away from the idea that there is only one way of knowing Pecos.

One of the most interesting concepts discussed during our ethnographic work concerns initiation into religious societies and their connections with the landscape. The word *initiation* is often synonymous with *emergence*. Emergence places are not only important cultural landscape features or locations for particular religious societies but also places where individuals begin new life paths. After an initiation ceremony, an individual is recognized as a new person who walks a path focused on the community and healing. Emergence is not specific to one story or event, such as a creation story, but a concept that permeates many different cultural traditions and sacred places. It is a personal rite of passage that reflects the many worlds Pueblo peoples have traversed in their migrations and histories.

Emergence may be an essential concept in understanding cultural landscapes and traditional cultural properties in the Pueblo region. The cultural landscapes associated with the Pecos people extend far behind the Upper Pecos Valley. Mountains to the north of the park play a vital role in initiation/emergence ceremonies associated with Pecos/Jemez religious societies and are a part of the area's sacred geography. The concept also relates to ethnogenesis and the process of becoming Pecos, and developing a better understanding of this process may enable us to move closer to Indigenous perspectives on Pecos.

The park has recently developed a podcast focused on the NAGPRA repatriation at Pecos, providing another example of a project that benefits the public as well as our traditionally associated communities. Based on two years of consultation and recorded interviews using questions vetted by Jemez tribal leaders, the podcast documents the repatriation event and highlights tribal perspectives on Pecos and Kidder's work there, archaeology in general, and NAGPRA. Many interviewees were directly involved in the repatriation, including archaeologists, park managers, and tribal leaders.[24]

Conclusion

The chapters in this volume offer hope that we can do archaeology for, by, and with many different publics. Archaeology provides a tool for positive change through collaboration and education and by seeking outcomes that benefit associated communities. Despite the challenges involved, archaeologists need to embrace the idea of collaborating with and considering the perspectives and wishes of descendants. Doing so not only is respectful of their connections to the places we study but also allows the development of more meaningful interpretations of the many pasts represented by material culture, architecture, and landscapes. Active collaboration during all project phases is a more democratic process that shares authority, equalizes inequities, and results in archaeology that recovers a usable past for historically marginalized groups.

Notes

1. Sonya Atalay, "Multivocality and Indigenous Archaeologies," in *Evaluating Multiple Narratives: Beyond Nationalist, Colonalist, and Imperialist Archaeologies*, ed. Junko Habu, Claire Fawcett, and John M. Matsunaga (New York: Springer, 2008), 29–44.

2. For a discussion of many of these topics, see Claire Smith and H. Martin Wobst, eds., *Indigenous Archaeologies: Decolonizing Theory and Practice* (London: Routledge, 2008).

3. The NPS-funded Tribal Historic Preservation Officer program, started in 1992 under the amended National Historic Preservation Act of 1966, has helped support tribal and heritage managers in federally recognized tribes. Since the 1970s, Indigenous tribes, First Nations, and other Indigenous communities have operated heritage-management programs. See Roger Anyon, T. J. Ferguson, and John R. Welch, "Heritage Management by American Indian Tribes in the Southwestern United States," in *Cultural Resource Management in Contemporary Society: Perspectives on Managing and Presenting the Past*, ed. Francis P. McManamon and Alf Hatton (London: Routledge, 2000), 120–41.

4. Some of these cultural classification systems, regional histories, and terms relate to essentialist ideas that have been part of the field of archaeology and have contributed to stereotyping that limited inclusiveness. These phenomena often create the false impression that identities in the past and the present are static when in fact they have always been fluid. See Mathew Liebmann, "Postcolonial Cultural Affiliation: Essentialism, Hybridity and NAGPRA," in *Archaeology and the Postcolonial Critique*, ed. Mathew Leibmann and Uzma R. Rizvi (Lanham, Md.: AltaMira Press, 2008), 73–90.

5. See Gaston R. Gordillo, *Rubble: The Afterlife of Destruction* (Durham: Duke University Press, 2014).

6. Bruce Bernstein and Scott Ortman, "From Collaboration to Partnership at Pojaque, New Mexico," *Advances in Archaeological Practice* 8, no. 2(2020): 95–110, doi:10.1017/aap.2020.3.

7. See the introduction to this volume.

8. *Pueblo* is a Spanish word for town or group of people that anthropologists have used to define various semisedentary agricultural groups in the U.S. Southwest. Each community has its own name for itself. The Spanish estimated that two thousand people lived at Pecos in the 1500s, but archaeologists believe that the number was actually between one thousand and fifteen hundred (Genevieve Head, "The Upper Pecos Valley: A Good Place to Live," *Archaeology Southwest Magazine* 33, no. 3 [2019]: 10–11).

9. For more about the archaeology of Pecos, see the Pecos National Historical Park web page at the Archaeology Southwest website, accessed August 8, 2024, https://www.archaeologysouthwest.org/explore/pecos-national-historic-park, and he official National Park Service website, accessed August 8, 2024, https://www.nps.gov/peco/index.htm.

10. Alfred Vincent Kidder, *Pecos, New Mexico: Archaeological Notes* (Andover, Mass.: Phillips Andover Academy, 1958).

11. Alfred Vincent Kidder, *An Introduction to the Study of Southwestern Archaeology* (1924; New Haven: Yale University Press, 2000).

12. Chris Toya, "P`ǽkilâ," *Archaeology Southwest Magazine* 33, no. 3, (2019): 7–9; Jo-

seph S. Sando, *Nee Hemish: A History of Jemez Pueblo* (Albuquerque: University of New Mexico Press, 1982). See also Samuel Duwe and Robert W. Preucel, eds., *The Continuous Path: Pueblo Movement and the Archaeology of Becoming* (Tucson: University of Arizona Press, 2019).

13. Vincent Toya and Benny Shendo Jr. to Gary McAdams, June 1, 1998 (document on file at Pecos National Historical Park), 2 (quoted in Heather Young, "Pecos NHP NAGPRA Reburial Event, May 22, 1999 description" [document on file at Pecos National Historical Park, New Mexico, April 2013]); Heather Young, "Scope of Work: Reburial of NAGPRA Inventory of CUI Human Remains, Pecos National Historical Park" (document on file at Pecos National Historical Park, New Mexico, 2010); [Heather Young?], "Notes: NAGPRA Consultation Meeting at Pecos NHP," August 28, 2008 (document on file at Pecos National Historical Park, New Mexico), 3.

14. See Michèle E. Morgan, ed., *Pecos Pueblo Revisited: The Biological and Social Context* (Cambridge, Mass.: Peabody Museum of Archaeology and Ethnology, 2010).

15. Toya and Shendo to McAdams, June 1, 1998.

16. "Casual Notes from 18 June 1998 NAGPRA Consultation Held at Pecos NHP," NAGPRA Consultation 1994–98 folder, Pecos National Historical Park.

17. For more on cultural affiliation, see NPS, *Native American Graves Protection and Repatriation Act: Identifying Cultural Affiliation*, accessed September 6, 2024, https://www.nps.gov/subjects/nagpra/identifying-cultural-affiliation.htm.

18. "Pecos NAGPRA Inventory Report," November 11, 1995 (document on file at Pecos National Historical Park, New Mexico). The notice of inventory completions for the 1999 repatriation were published in *Federal Register*, vols. 63–64 (1998–99).

19. Morgan, *Pecos Pueblo Revisited.*

20. "Casual Notes from 14 May 1998 NAGPRA Consultation Held at PSPM—Phillips Academy," NAGPRA Consultation 1994–98 folder, Pecos National Historical Park.

21. See *Grounded in Clay: The Spirit of Pueblo Pottery* (exhibit at the Museum of New Mexico, Santa Fe), accessed July 27, 2024, https://www.museumfoundation.org/exhibitions/grounded-in-clay-the-spirit-of-pueblo-pottery/.

22. Bernstein and Ortman, "From Collaboration to Partnership"; Samuel Duwe, *Tewa Worlds: An Archaeological History of Being and Becoming in the Pueblo Southwest* (Tucson: University of Arizona Press, 2020); Alfonzo Ortiz, *The Tewa World: Space, Time, Being and Becoming in a Pueblo Society* (Chicago: University of Chicago Press, 1969); James E. Snead, *Ancestral Landscapes of the Pueblo World* (Tucson: University of Arizona Press, 2008); Paul Tosa, Mathew J. Liebmann, T. J. Ferguson, and John R. Welch, "Movement Encased in Tradition and Stone: Hemish Migration, Land Use, and Identity," in *Continuous Path*, ed. Duwe and Preucel, 60–77; Severin M. Fowles, *An Archaeology of Doings: Secularism and the Study of Pueblo Religion* (Santa Fe: School of Advanced Research, 2013).

23. For example, representatives of Jemez Pueblo involved in the ethnographic work reviewed this epilogue prior to publication.

24. *Hollowed to Hallowed Ground: The 1999 Pecos Repatriation*, NPS podcast, accessed July 27, 2024, https://www.nps.gov/podcasts/pecos-podcast-hollowed-to-hallowed-ground-the-1999-pecos-repatriation.htm.

Contributors

TARA BERESH is a registered professional archaeologist and the curator and collections manager for the Moab Museum in Moab, Utah. She holds a master's degree in public archaeology from the University of New Mexico. She has previously worked on excavations at Chaco Culture National Historical Park as well as with the Chaco Collections at the Maxwell Museum of Anthropology in Albuquerque, New Mexico. She is a member of the Utah State Historic Preservation Board and the Grand County Historic Preservation Commission.

JAMES F. BROOKS is the Gable Distinguished Chair in Early American History at the University of Georgia. He holds a doctorate in history from the University of California, Davis. An interdisciplinary scholar of the Indigenous and colonial past, he has held professorial appointments at the University of Maryland; the University of California, Santa Barbara; and the University of California, Berkeley. He has received fellowships at the Institute for Advanced Study in Princeton; the School for Advanced Research in Santa Fe, where he also served as president from 2005 to 2013; and Vanderbilt University's Robert Penn Warren Center for the Humanities. He has served on boards of directors for the Western National Parks Association and the Santa Barbara Mission Archive/Library and as an advisory scholar to the Gilder Lehrman Institute for American History. He is senior consulting editor of *The Public Historian*.

DAVID BROWN is codirector of the Fairfield Foundation and co-owner of DATA Investigations. He holds a doctorate in U.S. history from the College of William and Mary. A founding member of the Werowocomoco Research Group, his research interests include the development of plantation slavery in Tidewater Virginia, historic preservation and adaptive reuse, public archaeology, and working with descendant communities.

MOLLY BOEKA CANNON is an assistant professor of anthropology and director of the Museum of Anthropology at Utah State University, where she specializes in community-engaged museum practice and training the next generation of students in museology. She holds a doctorate from the University of Nebraska and has received support from the National Endowment for the Humanities, the Institute of Museum and Library Services, and the National Park Service. Her work has been published in *American Antiquity*, the *Journal of Archaeological Science*, and *Advances in Archaeological Practice*.

CONTRIBUTORS

ANNA S. COHEN is an assistant professor of anthropology at Utah State University, where she researches and teaches about human-landscape relationships and scientific research ethics in the precontact Americas. Her publications cover topics such as comparative urbanism, archaeological lidar and ethics, ceramic archaeometry, and public archaeology in Latin America and the American West. She holds a doctorate in anthropology from the University of Washington and has conducted fieldwork throughout the Americas, Europe, and South Asia.

MEG GAILLARD is an archaeologist with the South Carolina Department of Natural Resources Heritage Trust Program, cofounder of the South Carolina Archaeology Public Outreach Division, and cofounder of the North American Heritage at Risk research collective. She earned a master's degree in visual anthropology from the University of Manchester, and her research focuses on archaeology, visual anthropology, public interpretation, disaster preparedness and recovery, and heritage at risk.

MATTHEW C. GUEBARD is integrated resource manager at the Southern Arizona Office of the National Park Service. As head of the office's resources team, he is responsible for assisting parks with historic preservation planning, cultural resource project management, and National Historic Preservation Act compliance.

KATHLYN GUTTMAN holds a master's degree in archaeology from the Cornell Institute for Archaeology and Material Studies at Cornell University. She has worked at museums, parks, and archaeological sites across the United States and has participated in public excavations at Fort Michilimackinac since 2015. She is currently employed by the National Park Service at Death Valley National Park, and her research interests include Indigenous-European interactions in the North American fur trade and the representation of minority communities in the archaeological record.

THANE HARPOLE is codirector of the Fairfield Foundation and co-owner of DATA Investigations. He holds a bachelor's degree in history and anthropology from the College of William and Mary. A founding member of the Werowocomoco Research Group, he runs multiple archaeology projects on Virginia's Middle Peninsula and Northern Neck and manages regular programming that engages community members in archaeological and historical research. He serves as the editor of the Archeological Society of Virginia's *Quarterly Bulletin*.

SHARLOT HART is an archaeologist with the Southern Arizona Office of the National Park Service, where she aids in cultural resource management and information management. She administers agreements, facilitates archaeological compliance projects, and produces educational material for the office's website, the public, and frontline interpreters.

KATHERINE HODGE holds a master's degree from Montana State University. After a stint as interim director at Project Archaeology, she currently serves as the youth and family program coordinator at the University of Chicago's Institute for the Study of Ancient Cultures. Her research focuses on scientific accessibility, the ethics of museums and their collections, and Inca architecture.

CONTRIBUTORS 197

KOJI LAU-OZAWA holds a doctorate in anthropology from Stanford University and is currently a postdoctoral fellow at the University of California, Los Angeles. His research centers on the archaeology of the Japanese diaspora and in particular on World War II Japanese American incarceration camps. He has also worked in archaeology at the Golden Gate National Recreation Area and for Stanford University Heritage Services.

PHILIP LEVY is a professor of history at the University of South Florida, where he also holds appointments in the department of anthropology and in the Patel College of Global Sustainability. He earned a doctorate from the College of William and Mary and is the author of numerous books, including *Where the Cherry Tree Grew: The Story of Ferry Farm, George Washington's Boyhood Home* and *George Washington Written upon the Land: Nature, Memory, Myth, and Landscape*. His work has been supported by the Virginia Foundation for the Humanities, the National Geographic Society, the Mount Vernon Ladies' Association, and the George Washington Foundation.

ERIKA MALO is a science communicator who currently serves as external relations and social media coordinator for the Montana State University Extension. She holds a master's degree in anthropology from the University of Alaska Anchorage and worked for more than a decade in public outreach for government agencies, private firms, and educational organizations.

TORI MASON is the historic site manager at the Nashville Zoo at Grassmere, where she created and curated the Morton Family Exhibit. She previously spent more than two decades as a zookeeper in Kansas and Tennessee and twelve years as manager of the Grassmere Historic Farm livestock barn.

ASHLEY MCCUISTION is a staff archaeologist at Colonial Williamsburg who specializes in public outreach and education. She holds a master's degree in archaeology from Indiana University of Pennsylvania. McCuistion previously worked for the Fairfield Foundation, where she designed and implemented educational programs that integrate archaeology into K–12 classrooms.

JEANNE M. MOE has worked in heritage education for more than thirty years, mostly while employed by the Bureau of Land Management. She helped launch the national Project Archaeology program in Utah in the early 1990s, coordinated efforts to bring the program to other states, and served as its national director from 2001 until her retirement in 2018. She remains active in heritage education and is a founding member and chair of the board of the Institute for Heritage Education. She serves as the editor of the *Journal of Archaeology and Education*.

KRISTIN M. MONTAPERTO is archaeology manager and chief archaeologist for the Natural and Historic Resources Division of the Maryland–National Capital Park and Planning Commission, Department of Parks and Recreation, Prince George's County, Maryland. She holds a doctorate in anthropology from American University.

JEREMY M. MOSS is the chief of resource stewardship and science, archaeologist, and tribal liaison at Pecos National Historical Park in New Mexico. He holds a master's degree in anthropology from the University of Wyoming. Jeremy has worked for the National Park Service for twenty-five years in archaeology, cultural and natural resource conservation, historic preservation, archaeological interpretation, and tribal relations. He is a member of the editorial board of *The Public Historian* and served as guest editor of the journal's November 2022 special issue on public archaeology.

DAVID MURACA is the director of archaeology for the George Washington Foundation in Fredericksburg, Virginia, where he oversees the excavations at Ferry Farm. He holds a master's degree in anthropology from the College of William and Mary and previously supervised excavations for the Colonial Williamsburg Foundation.

ELIZABETH C. REETZ serves as director of strategic initiatives for the University of Iowa Office of the State Archaeologist. She holds a master's degree in environmental education from the University of Minnesota Duluth. She is a member of Project Archaeology's national leadership team and recently completed two terms as chair of the Society for American Archaeology's Public Education Committee.

JADE ROBISON is an archaeologist at the National Park Service's Tonto National Monument in Arizona.

IRAIDA RODRIGUEZ is an archaeologist with the Southern Arizona Office of the National Park Service. She supports the office's Resources Division by assisting in GIS projects and 3D digital documentation of cultural resources as well as by helping with cultural compliance needs and on-site project direction.

STEPHANIE T. SPERLING is the senior archaeologist with the Maryland–National Capital Park and Planning Commission, Department of Parks and Recreation, Prince George's County, Maryland. She holds a master's degree in applied anthropology from the University of Maryland. She has directed excavations at a wide variety of sites and has worked in the public, private, and nonprofit sectors.

KATE SPROUL is a circulation assistant at the Nashville Public Library. She holds a master's degree in history from Middle Tennessee State University, where her thesis focused on the enslaved people buried at Grassmere on what is now the property of the Nashville Zoo.

JESSICA TAYLOR is an assistant professor of history at Virginia Tech. She holds a doctorate from the University of Florida. Her research interests include the seventeenth-century Chesapeake's Native people and nonelites, collaborative community projects, and oral history in the U.S. South.

VICTOR D. THOMPSON is Distinguished Research Professor of Anthropology and director of the Laboratory of Archaeology at the University of Georgia. He holds a doctorate in anthropology from the University of Kentucky and specializes in the application of archaeological science to the study of collective social formations and the historical ecology of wetland and coastal environments.

Index

Page numbers in italics indicate figures; those with a *t* indicate tables.

activity-differentiation framework, 39, 41–42, 47

Adventures in Preservation (organization), 81, 83

Akimel O'odham (Pima) people, 1–2, 7, 120

Amache Incarceration Camp (Colo.), 122

American Alliance of Museums, 111, 112

American Association of State and Local History, 113

Antiquities Act (1906), 114–15, 168–69

Apache people, 1, 168

aquaculture, 3, 17–18

Archaeological Conservancy, 19

Archaeological Institute of America, 168

artifacts, 20, 110; adornment, 44–47, 45t, 46t; definition of, 110; ethical concerns about, 112–18; funerary, 190–91

Asakura family, 124–26, *126*

Bandelier National Monument (N.Mex.), 2

Bangladesh, 157

Becker, Carl, 105

Begay, Richard M., 116

Bench, Raney, 115

Beresh, Tara, 6, 109–18, 190

Bernbeck, Reinhard, 132

Billingsley site (Md.), 67

Boito, Camillo, 93

Bosnia, 105

Botany Bay Plantation (S.C.), 25–35

Brooks, James F., 1–9, 10–24

Brown, David, 5–6, 76–89

Burwell family, 79

Butler, William, 94

Calusa people, 3–4, 10–24; chiefs of, 12, 16; languages of, 12–13; Pacific Northwest societies and, 12–13; tributary relationships with, 16–17

Camp, Stacey, 121

canals, 3, 19, 154–55, 157–58, *158*

Cannon, Molly Boeka, 7, 151–60

Canyon De Chelly National Monument, 171

Canyonlands National Park (Utah), 115–16

Carr, Lois Green, 97

catch-and-release analysis, 127

C'Bearing, Crystal, 138

Charles Town (Md.), 63

Cherry Hill Cemetery (Md.), 5, 62

citizen-science approach, 22, 23

Civilian Conservation Corps, 171–72

Clark, Bonnie, 127

climate change, 22, 105, 178; Ferry Farm and, 92; hurricanes and, 21–24; Mound Key and, 11, 15, 21; Pockoy Island and, 26–28, *27*; water resources and, 15, 152

Cohen, Anna S., 7, 151–60

Cole, Robert, 97

Colonial Revival style, 94–97, *95*

colonization, 38, 63; curricula on, 76; slavery and, 5, 62, 73, 183. *See also* decolonization

Colwell-Chanthaphoh, Chip, 132

community archaeology, 22, 25–35, 87–89, 154, 182–92. *See also* public archaeology

199

INDEX

Conkey, Margaret, 39, 42

COVID-19 pandemic, 7, 34, 140, 147; digital storytelling and, 155; place-based learning and, 87; public programming and, 69–72, *70–72*

Croft, Elise, 55–56

Croft, Margaret, 55–56

Cultural Heritage Trust Program (S.C.), 25, 32–34

curricula, 7, 87; collaborative, 76–82, 88; on migration, 137–49; on water heritage, 151–60, *153, 156*

Cushing, Frank Hamilton, 17

Dan O'Laurie Museum, 109–10

decolonization, 47, 119, 182–83. *See also* colonization

deep time perspective, 7

DeWitt, John L., 122

Didron, Adolphe Napoléon, 93, 96, 105

Diné (Navajo) people, 114, 116

Dinosaur Park (Md.), 62

DNA analysis, 190

Douglass, Frederick, 63, *64*

Dunn family, 4, 49, 50

Duvall, Gabriel, 71

Echoes of the Enslaved event, 70–72, *72*

Edisto Island (S.C.), 27

enslaved persons, 4, 41, 70–72; of Fairfield Plantation, 79–89; of Grassmere Farm, 4–5, 49–58, *51, 59*; of Mount Calvert, 70–71; of Northampton Plantation, 62, 63, 68–69; of Williamsburg, 98–99

Epperson, Terrence, 98

Estero Island (Fla.), 16

Eventbrite (event management app), 29–30

"eventscape," 121

Fairfield Foundation, 6, 76, 79–82, 87–88

Fairfield Plantation (Va.), 5–6, 9, 76–89, *77–79*

Fanning, Ralph S., 94

Federal Lands Recreation Enhancement Act, 175

Ferguson, T. J., 132

Ferry Farm (Va.), 6, 91–96, 101–5; map of, *9*; photographs of, *92, 101, 103, 104*

fishing societies, 17–18, 45

floating gardens, 157

Florida Public Archaeology Network (FPAN), 21–22

Fong, Barre, 132

Fort Loudoun (Tenn.), 22

Foucault, Michel, 98

Franklin, Maria, 98

French-Canadian fur traders, 37–47

Fukushima family, 124–25

fur trade, 37–47

Gable, Eric, 98

Gaillard, Meg, 4, 25–35, *33*

Gebhard, David, 94

gentrification, 85

George Washington Foundation, 91–92, 102

George Washington Memorial House (Va.), *95*, 95–96

Gila River Incarceration Camp (Ariz.), 7, 120–33, *130, 131*, 183; maps of, 128, *129*; population of, 123; research methodology of, 120–21, 127–28

Gila River Indian Community (Ariz.), *8*, 120–23, 127–33, 179

Godiah Spray Tobacco Plantation, 97, 101, 104

Gonzales, Sara, 127

Grassmere Farm, 4–5, 49–58, *51, 59*

Greer, Marvin-Alonzo, 71

Guebard, Matthew C., 7–8, 166–78

Guttman, Kathlyn, 4, 37–47

Halchin, Jill, 41

Handler, Richard, 98

Harpole, Thane, 5–6, 76–89

Hart, Sharlot, 7–8, 166–78

Hastings, DeCosta, 56

Hawai'i, 122, 124

Henry, Alexander, 44

Hewett, Edgar Lee, 169

Hillman, Joyce, 50, 55, 56

INDEX 201

historical silencing, 38–41, 47
Hodge, Katherine, 7, 137–49
Hodge, Shannon, 52, 54
Hopi people, 2, 6, 115–16, 117
Hoppin, Charles Arthur, 96
Hume, Ivor Noël, 95
hunter-gatherers, 12
hurricanes, 21–24. *See also* climate change

immigration, 7, 123–24, 137–49
Imwalle, Mike, 121
initiation ceremonies, 191–92
International Charter on the Conservation
   and Restoration of Monuments and Sites
   (1964), 93
Investigating Migration curriculum, 7,
   137–49; aims of, 137; evaluation of, 139–42,
   141t, *142*, 143t, 148

Jackson, Dondrick, 56
Japanese American internment camps, 7,
   119–33
Japanese Association of America, 123–24
Jefferson, Thomas, 99
Jemez Pueblo (N.Mex.), 8, *186*, 186–87,
   189–92 .
Jones, Alyssa, *29*
Jones, Scott, 33
Jug Bay Complex (Md.), 5, 63, 65, 67–68, 69

Kenmore Plantation (Md.), 102
Kidder, Alfred V., 187, 189
King, Dale, 173
Koji Lau-Ozawa, 7, 119–33, 183
Kowalczyk, Stefanie, 65

Lawson, Anna, 98
Levy, Gershon, 41–44
Levy, Philip, 6, 91–105
Lightfoot, Kent, 127
Lincoln, Abraham, 68
Linden Farm (Va.), 102
Logan (Utah), *8*
Lost Towns Project, 67
Loth, Calder, 93, 105

Madison, James, 99
Malis, Hideko Nishihara, 128
Malo, Erika, 7, 137–49
Marietta House Museum (Md.), 71–72
Marquardt, Bill, 10–11, 18
Mason, Tori, 4–5, 49–58, 183
Mattaponi people, 5, 67
Maxwell, Bruce, 53–54
McCuistion, Ashley, 5–6, 76–89
McGill, Joseph, 70, 71
McGimsey, Charles R., 25–26
McKee, Larry, 52
McTighe, Jay, 137–49
Menard, Russell R., 97
Menéndez de Avilés, Pedro, 14, 15
Menokin plantation house (Va.), 83
mentorship, 157–59, *158*
Michilimackinac (Mich.), 4, 37–47;
   adornment artifacts from, 44–47, 45t,
   46t; maps of, *9*, 42–43, *43*; Métis of, 38,
   44, 46, 47
migration curriculum, 7, 137–49
Moab Museum (Utah), 6, 8, 109–18, *114*, *117*
Moe, Jeanne M., 7, 137–49
Montaperto, Kristin M., 5, 61–73, 183
Montpelier House Museum (Md.), 71, *72*
Morton family, 50, 55–56, *57–59*
Moss, Jeremy M., 8–9, 182–92
Mound House (Fla.), 21, 24
Mound Key (Fla.), 3–4, 10–24; aquaculture
   at, 3, 17–18; construction of, 14; fresh
   water sources at, 14–15; maps of, *9*, *11*, *13*;
   population of, 18; preservation of, 19–23;
   size of, 15
Mount Calvert Museum (Md.), 62–67, *65*
Mount Vernon (Va.), 99–101, 103
Muraca, David, 6, 91–105
Muscogee Nation, 35
museums, 111, 112, 114, 115; partnerships with,
   155–57, *156*; small-town, 109–18, *114*, *117*.
   See also specific museums

Nashville Zoo (Tenn.), 4–5, *9*, 49–58, *51*, 183
National Historic Preservation Act (1966),
   193

202   INDEX

National Park Service (NPS), 73, 95–96, 120; mission of, 166, 168; museum collections and, 114, 115; reconstruction rules of, 93–94; Vanishing Treasures initiative of, 174–75
Native American Graves Protection and Repatriation Act (NAGPRA), 112, 184, 185, 189–91, 192
Navajo (Diné) people (Diné), 114, 116
Newman, Rico, 71
Nihonmachi (Japantown), 121, 123–27, 125, 126, 132
Nishihara family, 125
Northampton Plantation (Md.), 5, 62–63, 68–69

O'odham (O'otham). See Akimel O'odham people
Overland Trail, 7, 8, 137–39
Oxon Hill Manor (Md.), 68

Pacific Northwest peoples, 12–13
Paiute people, 114
Panis slaves, 4, 41
Parant family, 42
Patuxent people, 5, 67
Pecos National Historical Park (N.Mex.), 2, 8–9, 185–92; maps of, 8, 185; photographs of, 186–88
Peyton Randolph House (Va.), 99, 100
Pierce, Greg, 64–65
Pima (Akimel O'odham) people, 1–2, 7, 120
Pineland (Fla.), 10, 24
Pipaash (or Pee Posh) people, 7, 120
Piscataway-Conoy people, 71
place-based learning, 87. See also curricula
Pluckhahn, Tom, 17
Pockoy Island Shell Ring Complex (S.C.), 4, 9, 25–35, 31; climate change and, 26–28, 27; excavation trench at, 26; public tours of, 29, 29–30, 32–33, 33
Poston River Indian Community (Ariz.), 122
preservation projects, 114–15; reconstruction versus, 92–95, 105; of Tonto Cliff Dwellings, 166, 168, 171–73, 172, 177, 178

Prince George's County (Md.), 5, 9, 61–73
professionalization, 81–82, 112, 175
Project Archaeology (PA) curricula, 137–49
public archaeology, 3–4, 9, 166; collaboration in, 7, 77–82, 88, 116–17, 119–33; evaluation criteria for, 139, 145–46; impact of, 19–20, 61–73; interpretive strategies for, 178; long-term, 76–89; mentorship and, 157–59, 158; museum partnerships with, 155–57, 156; water heritage and, 153, 153–54. See also community archaeology
Public Historian (journal), 2–3, 9
Pueblo peoples, 8, 8–9, 116, 186–87, 189–92

questionnaire, 141

Randolph, Peyton, 99, 100
reconstruction. See preservation projects
Reetz, Elizabeth C., 7, 137–49
Rhodes, Anna, 86
Ridgely, Benjamin, 138
Riversdale House Museum (Md.), 68
Robinson, A. E., 123
Robison, Jade, 7–8, 166–78
Rodriguez, Iraida, 7–8, 166–78
Roosevelt, Franklin D., 122
Roosevelt, Theodore, 169
ruins stabilization projects, 166, 168, 183–84, 187; guidelines for, 173–74; photographs of, 169, 170, 172, 177; tourism and, 170, 173

Safety Harbor (Fla.), 17
Salado people, 167
Santa Barbara (Calif.), 7, 8; Nihonmachi of, 121, 123–27, 125, 126, 132
Santa Barbara Trust for Historic Preservation, 128, 131, 132
School for Advanced Research (Santa Fe, N.Mex.), 2
Scott, Elizabeth May, 41, 42
September 11 attacks (2001), 71–72
shell rings, 28. See also Pockoy Island Shell Ring Complex
Shoshone people, 154
sickle cell disease, 52

INDEX 203

silencing, historical, 38–41, 47
Silliman, Stephen, 39, 41
Slave Dwelling Project, 70
slavery, 76; colonization and, 5, 62, 73, 183.
 See also enslaved persons
Smith, Richard, Sr., 116
Snowden family, 71
Solomon, Ezekiel, 41–44
Southern Pacific Railroad, 170
Spector, Janet, 39, 42
Sperling, Stephanie T., 5, 61–73, 183
Sprigg family, 62–63
Sproul, Kate, 4–5, 49–58
Steen, Charlie, 170–73, 176
St. John's Site Museum (Md.), 97–98, 104
St. Mary's City (Md.), 6, 9, 97–98
Stoner, Victor, 170
StoryMaps, 147–48, 154, 155, 158
storytelling, 109, 110, 154–55
Summer Citizens Program, 158, 159
Surratt House Museum (Md.), 68

Taylor, Jessica, 5–6, 76–89
Thomas Stone House (Md.), 93
Thompson, Victor D., 3–4, 10–24
Tilden, Freeman, 174
Tobacco Plantation, 97, 101, 104
Tocobaga people, 16, 17
Tonto Cliff Dwellings (Ariz.), 7–8, 166–78;
 maps of, 8, 167; photographs of, 169, 172,
 177
tourism, 146; heritage, 4, 28; ruins
 stabilization projects and, 170, 173
Toya, Pete, 190
TRC Companies, 49–53, 51, 54

Trouillot, Michel-Rolph, 38–41, 47
Tumacácori National Monument (N.Mex.),
 1–2, 2, 184
Tung, Tiffiny, 53, 54

Ute people, 6, 114, 117

Valley Forge (Pa.), 93
Vanishing Treasures initiative, 174–75, 176
Van West, Carroll, 54
Venice Charter (1964), 93
vernacular buildings, 94
voyageurs, 37

Wakefield National Memorial Association
 (WNMA), 95, 95–97
Walsh, Lorena S., 97
War of 1812, 68
Washington, George: Memorial House of, 95,
 95–96; Mount Vernon of, 99–101, 103. *See
 also* Ferry Farm
Water Heritage Anthropological Project
 (WHAP), 7, 151–60, 153, 156
Webb, Henderson "Shorty," 55
Webb, Maude Morton, 58
Weems, Mason Locke, 96
white supremacists, 122, 124
Wiggins, Grant P., 137–49
Williams, Learotha, 54, 58
Williamsburg (Va.), 6, 98–99, 100

Yaqui people, 1
Young, Peter, 69

Zuni people, 17, 179

Printed in the United States
by Baker & Taylor Publisher Services